MW00980658

Where Is My *Happy Ending?*

A Journey of No Regrets

Karen Harmon

Thankyou so much
Earl for your
Kindness and
support! with loe
from Karen

Where Is My Happy Ending?
Copyright © 2020 by Karen Harmon

All rights reserved. No part of this publication may
be reproduced, distributed, or transmitted in any
form or by any means, including photocopying,
recording, or other electronic or mechanical
methods, without the prior written permission of
the author, except in the case of brief quotations
embodied in critical reviews and certain other non-
commercial uses permitted by copyright law.

Tellwell Talent
www.tellwell.ca

ISBN
978-0-2288-2948-5 (Hardcover)
978-0-2288-2949-2 (Paperback)
978-0-2288-2947-8 (eBook)

This book is dedicated to
the men
who have been
the most important
influencers in my life

~

To
Rob, Dale, Paul and Mackenzie.
Thank you for believing in me
and encouraging me to be
the best that I can be.
My life has been enriched
by your impact.

Special thanks to my dear friend and mentor,

Sharon Bodner

without her this book would not be possible

"Dear God," she prayed, "let me be something every minute of every hour of my life. Let me be gay; let me be sad. Let me be cold; let me be warm. Let me be hungry...have too much to eat. Let me be ragged or well-dressed. Let me be sincere — be deceitful. Let me be truthful; let me be a liar. Let me be honourable and let me sin. Only let me be something every blessed minute. And when I sleep, let me dream all the time so that not one little piece of living is ever lost."

—*Betty Smith*, A Tree Grows in Brooklyn

TABLE OF CONTENTS

CHAPTER 1

Starting Over

1992

I LOOKED AROUND THE CLUTTERED LIVING ROOM, ASSESSING THE damage, until I spotted the soft curls on my four-year-old daughter's head as she sat with her little sister in an empty packing box. Both were contentedly colouring: Jessica carefully trying to stay in the lines while Emma, sitting as close to her big sister as possible, was eagerly scribbling.

Pondering their sisterhood with a full heart, I gazed at my daughters as if I was a bystander, lingering and wondering what would happen next. I felt like I was a person not wanting to leave the movie theatre, hanging on until the closing credits had scrolled off the screen, eventually emerging from the darkened cinema to face brilliant sunlight or perhaps a dreary evening rain.

For the last thirty-two years, I had watched the movie of my life unfold, and it seemed as though I was unable to control the course or path. Before I had arrived, the script had been written and the actors cast. As the story took on twists and turns, plot changes, and various climaxes along the way, I sat idly by, watching the series of events unfold.

Thankfully alive and seemingly unscathed, I decided that nothing was regrettable, everything was memorable, and I could learn from it all. Like any other moviegoer, I had sat patiently, waiting for the plot to thicken or the knight in shining armour to arrive. Comedic interludes were just as prevalent as the nail-biting cliffhangers. Perhaps the happy ending was not meant to be, or maybe this, right here and now, was the happy ending, and I could not see it yet.

I was pleased with what a beautiful little girl my oldest daughter, Jessica, had become, not just outwardly but on the inside, too. Her spirit was soft and gentle, especially toward her two-year-old little sister. I realized now that she had become more of a mother to her younger sibling than I had been.

I looked deeper at Jessica's bowed head as she filled the pages of her Cinderella colouring book, and I felt her determination. I was filled with compassion and reminded of how she worried about me, silently asking if I was okay. It was evident and showed in her constantly furrowed brow and ever-present look of concern as she stared into my eyes and pleadingly searched my face for answers. I would do my best to respond, interjecting and interrupting her deep, brooding thoughts. My father always told me that laughter was the best medicine, so as often as I could, I would engage my girls in stories, jokes, and silliness, even if it was the furthest thing from my mind.

The first thing on my to-do list was to find some semblance of order amongst the stacked boxes, furniture, and garbage bags full of clothes. I was looking forward to my new beginning, our new beginning, and a fresh start in our unfamiliar home—subsidized housing for marginalized people.

Receiving a lucky break and chosen from a long list of applicants just as needy as I was, it had only been two weeks since

I had started praying, and now here we were in a two-bedroom, low-income townhouse unit, myself and two little girls. We were alone, the three musketeers, all for one and one for all.

Today I would finish unpacking, and tomorrow I would be applying for welfare. I was relieved to be free.

CHAPTER 2

"Gypsies, Tramps and Thieves"

1971–1978

IN 1971, I WAS ELEVEN YEARS OLD AND IN GRADE SIX. I WAS STILL playing with Barbie dolls and watching Saturday morning cartoons. At the same time, my entire class at Queensbury Elementary School in North Vancouver was getting together with the opposite sex, or so it seemed. Out of sheer peer pressure, I decided that I needed a boyfriend, as well.

I was reluctant to hang out with boys. I had nothing in common with them, and even by the age of eleven, I was still grossed out by them entirely. Boys were not interested in me, either, so when Russell, the only freckle-faced, red-haired boy in the whole school, asked me to the Sutherland High school carnival, I could not refuse.

I loved the underdog, and my empathetic nature was flourishing at a rapid pace. By sixth grade, I was a people-pleaser, and my inability to say "No, thank you" or a simple "No" was in full swing.

With little desire to go on a date, but pretending that I wanted to just the same, nerves and shyness consumed me. Quite frankly, I was mortified when the day arrived, and the inevitable knock came on our door.

My mother answered and enthusiastically let my date, Russell Rankin, into our modest 1970s living room, complete with green shag carpeting, La-Z-Boy recliner, and black velvet paintings. It was a late fall Saturday afternoon, the weekend before Halloween. The rest of my class, Russell included, was anticipating the haunted house exhibit that the high school students had been working on all month. Once looking forward to it, but now dreading it, I knew full well that Russell would want to hold my hand, and with my inability to say "No, thank you," the hand-holding would probably be the death of me!

When Russell first arrived to collect me, I was still in my bedroom, so as he pleasantly and politely greeted my mother, she told him that I would be out in just a moment. After removing his shoes, he walked over to the mantelpiece in our living room, where our family photo stood.

Admiring the picture, Russell stared mesmerized. Grabbing the side of his head and then sliding his fingers down his cheek, he said to my mother, "My, you have a lovely daughter." Flooring my mother with his courteous manner, instantaneously, *she* became utterly smitten with my new boyfriend. To make matters worse and to pull at my mother's heartstrings even more, Russell went on to apologize for a small tear in his jacket, explaining that it was a hand-me-down from his older brother Jeffery, and he would be getting it mended soon.

As I entered the living room, Russell "oohed and aahed" at the sight of me, making me feel incredibly awkward and self-conscious from the start. I was wearing striped bell-bottom pants and a brown sweater with my regular plain brown coat. I was neither smiling nor frowning at Russell's outlandish behaviour.

My mother, however, was pleased and grinning from ear to ear, happy to be a part of her youngest daughter's first date. She had many boyfriends as a young girl, not to be confused with the fact that they were only boys who were friends. Therefore, she was not able to fully understand the debacle that I had gotten myself into, specifically how the other grade-six girls and boys were making out in the forest behind our school, a thought that made my skin crawl. I could not bear to look at my mother, even to say goodbye. Be that as it may, Russell shook my mother's hand as we left on our date to the carnival.

We walked down my street and across Grand Boulevard to Sutherland High School and the imminent festival that awaited us. It was a short, tense walk, void of conversation, and filled with awkward silences.

Once arriving at the gymnasium of the school, we followed well-marked signs to the haunted house area, which was a classroom that had been converted into a makeshift ghostly mansion and adorned with creepy decorations.

Paying the cost of twenty-five cents to enter, we stepped into the pitch-black room, only to encounter strange, indecipherable objects hanging from the ceiling and ghoulish sounds coming from a tape recorder. The only thing visible was the glaring exit sign.

Making our way past a table, one of the teenage ghouls suggested we reach our hands into a bowl of cooked cold, slimy spaghetti that I assumed was to represent brain matter or someone's guts.

With all the lights turned out, witches, skeletons, ghouls, and goblins jumped out at innocent victims along the mapped-out route, trying to scare adults and children alike. Most of the patrons knew full well that the ensemble of spooky creatures were high school students dressed up in costumes, enjoying themselves immensely, proud of their antics and handiwork.

I was sure that much rehearsing had gone into the performances, and there would be a generous amount of back-slapping and merriment when the whole horror show and festive occasion was over. The older students would no doubt be sharing how they frightened and spoofed so many innocent victims. Later, the same students who had created the masquerade would be cleaning it all up while salvaging ideas, costumes, and decorations to be stored in dusty, dilapidated cardboard boxes in the bowels of the school until next Halloween.

The drama and blood-curdling screams only encouraged Russell to reach out and firmly grab my hand in his. Even though I had a foreboding that Russell might try something like this, it was far worse than I could have possibly imagined.

Feeling powerless, I was determined to make the best of the situation. I surrendered to Russell's display of affection, but I avoided eye contact at all costs. As he rambled on and on, I conversed as little as possible, answering his questions with small nods and hardly uttering a word. When I did, I could hear the awkward, incoherent sound of my own strained and monotone voice.

"Where did you get that sweater?" Russell queried me.

"I don't know," I replied.

"Are you scared?"

"No."

"We should come back tomorrow. Do you want to?"

I quashed that with a timid "No, thank you."

As we neared the end of the haunted tour, I became entirely preoccupied with my date's sweaty palms as he pulled me along to the lit exit. My mind wielded scenarios of how to free up my fingers from their unwanted entrapment. When we finally discovered the passage out of the spooky setup, I immediately took my hand back and wiped it clean and dry on the back of my jeans. I was sure my hand would never be held again for many years to follow!

The fortune teller was next, a palm reader who could predict my entire future in one fell swoop. I wondered what the mystery of my future would be. Would I die young and wealthy or live to be old and broke? Perhaps a parade of children would succeed me just like The Old Woman in the Shoe nursery rhyme. Maybe I would find out that my future held a lifetime of being childless as a successful businesswoman.

I took my place in a long line-up of bewildered victims, inching slowly forward. Soon it would be my turn to find out what lay in store for me. The makeshift booth beckoned me forward out of curiosity and peer pressure.

After paying five cents, a teenager dressed in a gypsy costume, with a scarf on her head, big hoop earrings, and wild eye makeup, gazed into my palm and forecast that I was at the fair with the love of my life and we would one day have four children together. I was to live a long, fruitful life, and I should try wearing the colour green more often. This forecast would stay etched in my mind forever, haunting me with its unwanted doomsday prediction.

Surprisingly, after hearing the gypsy's prophecy, I did not run for the hills and skedaddle home as fast as my legs could carry me. Instead, I smiled sweetly and nodded while my one-time boyfriend's face beamed, and his eyes twinkled in hopes that the prediction would come true. I knew with relief that this relationship would be ending almost before it had begun!

As we strolled away from the enchantress, looking for another exhibit, I warily kept my hands jammed deep into my pockets to avoid the entanglement of another sticky hand-holding situation.

One display that I was looking forward to was the cake walk, which was not in the big gymnasium, but a classroom somewhere else in the school. Beginning our search and on our way out of the gym, we passed the dunk tank, a contraption that I had never seen before. What I witnessed was intriguing and delightfully comical, seeing someone throw a baseball to try and knock a friend (or whomever) off a collapsible seat into an ice-cold tank of water below. "Three Tries For 25 Cents!" was scrawled on the sign. We stayed, watching for at least fifteen minutes, as students tried to get their teachers soaked or buddies taunted their friends. We even saw a young boy trying to send his father down into the frigid water.

The laughter around us was contagious. It made me think of my dad and how he would have thoroughly enjoyed the dunk tank and all the excitement of those involved with taking turns. I wished I was at the school carnival with my father instead of a classmate who had hopes of becoming my steady boyfriend.

Leaving thoughts of my father behind in the gymnasium with the dunk tank, we made our way out into the hallway. I was astonished by how enormous the school was and how scary but equally exciting it was to comprehend that one day, I would be attending such a place. Would I become a cheerleader or be on the debate team? Knowing that I would surely have a boyfriend by then, even envisioning how we would laugh, hold hands, and meet up for ice cream floats and study dates, I had no idea who the lucky boy would be. I only knew full well it would not be Russell!

We eventually found the cake walk, a game similar to musical chairs, but instead of chairs, there were coloured squares taped to the floor that one would walk on. As the music played, everyone walked around a mapped-out circle, stepping from one numbered, coloured square to another. As soon as the music stopped, the players each stood on the square he or she was closest to. Then out of a box, a number was drawn and read out loud. The person standing on the chosen number won the cake that matched their number.

Salivating customers would walk the route with trepidation and anticipation, passing cakes of every description. Chocolate

Devil's Food, Money, Angel Food, Smarties, and occasionally a Barbie Doll cake would be lined up in a desperate plea to be won.

The glamorous Barbie Doll cake, an out-of-this-world delicacy, was coveted by every young girl that ever lived. It was a unique cake in every way. A real Barbie doll was used, wearing a sparkly bathing suit top, while her naked lower half was shoved into the middle of a baked Bundt cake that enveloped her and became her fancy gown. Icing in pink and pastel blue colours made for a puffy, floor-length party dress. The best part of the game was having the Barbie doll after the cake had long since been devoured. Sometimes it was only a Kmart Barbie, not the real Mattel Barbie, but a new doll nonetheless.

Only one lucky person would win and take home the cake that represented the square they had landed on. Another five cents later, and in most cases, the cake walk was over as soon as it had begun. When not a winner, one could be hugely disappointed, slinking off to the next exhibit while still drooling over the hoped-for sweet treat that was never meant to be.

Not winning a cake and now penniless, Russell decided to bring me home. We walked even slower on the way back across the boulevard. I was relieved for the afternoon to be ending, while Russell wished that it would go on forever.

Soon I would be free from the whole boyfriend fiasco and carnival shenanigans to plop down in front of the television in the safety of my own home. It was Saturday, so I had *The Carol Burnett Show*, to look forward to. A predictable dinner would be on the table, and my life would go on, with me realizing that I was far too young to be dating anyway.

There were no other boys in my life until a moment, which seemed like a split second, in grade nine—an unexpected and random chance happening that was short and not so sweet and gladly over in an instant.

At the end of grade eight, I had moved away from North Vancouver, the town where I was born, to an acreage in Mission, BC, an area known as Stave Falls. It was a beautiful hobby farm community of log homes and a few dilapidated mobile trailers, complete with chicken coops, barns, and horses. The property was on a mountainside covered in old-growth forests. The hilly and windy country roads were rural routes for the mailman, and school students waited in bus shelters located here and there along the way.

I had a horse, which kept me busy when not at school, and making new friends was not difficult. I often chose shy girls like myself, or they chose me.

Alana Clark, one of my new school friends, lived next door to the school, and being the new girl in town, I was pleased to have been invited for a mid-week sleepover party at Alana's house.

Weeks before the party, there was a mantra going around the halls at school, stating "No boys allowed" to Alana's party. This did not affect me in the least because being new at school, I did not know any boys to speak of anyway and was still not very fond of them.

The party began directly after the 3:00 p.m. school bell, and once all the girls had arrived at Alana's house, we chatted, giggled, and gossiped about none other than . . . boys!

All was moving along fine and dandy until some vodka was pulled out of a cupboard. Each girl took a turn timidly sipping the bitter, sickening beverage. Burning down our throats, it caused grim facial expressions, which resulted in fits of laughter mixed with an alcohol-infused spray that came out of several mouths and noses.

During the merriment, a loud knock came on the door, and unexpectedly standing on the doorstep were three boys from school. Most of the girls were secretly happy to see the pimple-faced, toothy-grinned fourteen-year-olds there to crash the party.

In pure radical teenage girl form, there was a lot of curt yelling mixed with high-pitched screeches and loud chortling of "Get out of here," "No one invited you," "This is a hen party, can't you tell?!" The ranting girls and crimson faced boys battled it out, even though both groups were glad the other was there.

I had missed most of the hoopla because I was coming out of the washroom, the small bathroom in Alana's parents' bedroom. I had never seen a bathroom attached to a bedroom before. Alana called it an ensuite. *How convenient*, I thought. At the same time, the boys were pounding on the door and being let in.

With girls shrieking in the other room, I was anxious to see what was going on. I was still pondering the attached bathroom when I came face to face with one of the party crashers who had made his way into Alana's parents' bedroom, looking for me. A boy who will remain nameless came straight at me with a wide-open mouth full of braces trying to plant a kiss on my ever-so-shocked mouth.

Ironically, Alana came bounding into the bedroom at the same time, furiously snapping on the lights and angrily exclaiming, "There will be none of that in my parents' bedroom!" Meanwhile, I, the innocent bystander/victim, managed to sidestep the whole incident by pushing the pimple-faced intruder and unwanted kiss away.

The boys, including the kisser, were quickly escorted outside by two of the bossier, more dominant girls. The party crashers dutifully yet reluctantly obeyed and were only seen again in the confines of the classrooms back at school. The incident was never spoken of again (at least not by the culprits). I, on the other hand, was immensely flattered and could not help but wonder what would have happened had Alana not appeared in her parents' bedroom just when she did.

Afterward, we carried on having drinks, talking about the rude, indecent boys encroaching on our festive occasion, and how outrageous their antics were. The conversation eventually shifted to discussions about our least favourite, most horrible teachers, current makeup brands we preferred, the latest fashion trends, and how fun it was to drink alcohol and hang out together.

For once, we had a sense of being cool and rebellious teenagers like the ones we had learned about in health class, deciding that the dangers of alcohol did not seem as bad as our gym teacher had always professed.

The next day was a school day. With Alana living next door, it was easy to be up in time for the 8:30 a.m. bell. It was not until we made our way to our lockers and walked down the hall to our first class that the fogginess and queasiness set in, perhaps a consequence of still being a little bit drunk and tipsy. We, the girls who everyone thought were nerds, wallflowers, and painfully shy, all maintained a new-found secret—vodka and orange juice.

Feeling adventurous and naughty, we were happy to keep the party our little secret. There was just enough nausea left over for us to not try drinking again for quite some time.

On our property were old abandoned logging roads, which my father had manicured into trails on which we could ride our horses. The trails led up and around the fifty acres and came out to the opening of the power lines that were used by off-road four-wheel drivers and shared with horses and their Western-clad riders.

I was fascinated and interested in the history of the property, as my dad and brothers found some old abandoned cabins that still had china dishes, authentic Japanese soup spoons, and liquor bottles intact. Shredded curtains hung from the broken-paned windows, and on one of their treks exploring, they brought back for me a child's wooden folding chair that they speculated to be about one hundred years old. They explained some of the histories to me, and I was able to imagine how hard the lives of the settlers must have been, making my own life seem a breeze.

The Whonnock First Nations claimed land along the Fraser River between Stave River and Whonnock Creek as theirs, but this land was not included in the Whonnock Reserve and was released for settlement. Permanent settlers came to the Stave Falls and Ruskin area after the inauguration of the transcontinental railroad in 1885. Below Stave Falls was an area named Ruskin, located on the Fraser River.

After the First World War, Japanese immigrant workers started farming in Ruskin, mostly growing raspberries and strawberries. There were Japanese logging operations in the area and a couple of small Japanese sawmills. It all came to an end with the expulsion and internment of Japanese-Canadians in 1942. The Japanese were the ones who began any significant type of agriculture in the area.

After my brother showed me some of his findings, he placed them carefully and strategically into an empty horse stall in the barn. He built shelves in which to display his collection and would spend hours polishing and preserving them.

By grade ten, boyfriend number two was unavoidable and inevitable, as I was desperate for love and utterly smitten with the new boy in town. At fifteen, all my aspirations and longing for earth-shattering love and romance were to be initially fulfilled by this one boy: a mysterious, tall, dark and handsome stranger. Word was out in Stave Falls about a new resident by the name of Todd Barnes.

The stomping grounds that I called home, where the eyes had ears, and the ears had eyes, was a gossipy little community situated in what people called the "boondocks" in the middle of nowhere, east of Maple Ridge, northwest of Mission, and just above the Ruskin Dam. In 1975, when word got out and secrets were leaked, one could only blame the number one source for being something called a party line. A party line was a landline telephone system where families shared their telephone lines with various neighbours on the same street. Party lines provided no privacy in communication and were frequently used as a source of entertainment and gossip.

Often when one party was on the phone chatting, they could hear breathing coming from someone else. Another noticeable sign that one's privacy was being infringed upon was an almost undetectable click, as if someone was picking up or hanging up an extension phone at the same time you were on with someone else. The party line system in rural Stave Falls is how word spread like wildfire that a gorgeous new boy had moved into the neighbourhood, bringing with him mystery and romance. He was single and looking for things to do; he had a horse and wanted friends.

During my teenage years, my sister, who was thirteen years older than me and lived next door on the adjoining property in a mobile home, had created a horseback riding club. Almost every kid in the neighbourhood wanted to join. We called ourselves The Rolley Lake Trail Riders, named after a lake in the area. We had meetings two or three times a month to discuss our monthly mini-rodeos, rules and regulations, local parades, upcoming trail rides, and Friday night drives to the horse auction. Everyone who belonged to the group lived on an acreage and had a horse, and if not, we made a point of sharing.

With the buzz of conversation and curiosity about the handsome stranger in town, the local busybody, Margaret Dundle, elected herself to be the one to invite Todd to our next horse club meeting. Margaret did not have a horse, and she did not want to ride anyone else's. She was the secretary for the Rolley Lake Trail Riders, taking down the minutes and keeping tabs on everything and everyone because that is how busybodies operate; they somehow get their foot in the door and try to run the entire show.

On that occasion, I did not mind Margaret's overbearing nature because at our next horse group meeting, there he was, a combination of David Cassidy and John Travolta, all rolled into one human being—Todd Barnes! He was there because Margaret Dundle had invited him. "Bless you, Margaret," were my unspoken thoughts, sentiments, and nightly prayers of appreciation.

Todd had feathered brown hair, wide-set, almond-shaped green eyes, and an adorable space between his two front teeth. He was the most handsome boy I had ever laid eyes on. His attire was nothing if not hip, current, and fashionable. He wore high-waisted bell-bottom jeans, a short brown leather bomber jacket, and platform clogs on his feet.

The best part about meeting Todd and having him be a part of the Rolley Lake Trail Riders, was that from the beginning, it was apparent that it was me he wanted. Flattered and honoured, and desperately seeking a boyfriend, the riding group took on a whole new meaning for me. It was not just a horse club anymore, but a reason to get all dolled up to see the new boy of my dreams.

However, there was a snag in my plan when I found out that Margaret decided she wanted him, too. She even took it upon herself to drop in on him at his house one day and pretend to fall asleep on his couch. Rumour had it that Todd made her leave, and she stole one of his kitchen spoons as an excuse to have to return it, therefore getting another chance to get inside Todd's home when he asked her to bring it back.

My concern over Margaret and her obsession with Todd was all for naught, because it was me who Todd pursued. He had the habit of gazing at me from across the room during our horse club meetings. With Todd's eyes fixed on me, I pretended not to see him, overly laughing at others' jokes while on the inside, a turmoil of butterflies played havoc in my stomach. I was sure that everyone could hear and see the fluttering sensation that was going on inside of me.

Eventually, Todd managed to find a spot next to me, sometimes bumping someone out of the way or stealing their seat when they got up to refill their Hawaiian Punch drink. Anytime he was next to me, my heart sped up and skipped more than one beat. Despite my shyness, I was flattered and excited at the attention this older, wiser boy was giving me. Inevitably, we became an item: boyfriend and girlfriend.

Todd showered me with compliments and gifts, love notes, earrings for my birthday (not one but three pairs), and an occasional long-stemmed rose. He even dropped by my school once to visit me and waited at my locker. I never quite figured out how he knew where my locker was. I cared that out of hundreds of lockers in my high school, he had found mine. How romantic!

At fifteen, I was inexperienced at just about everything, especially relationships between opposite sexes. Todd told me that if I loved him, I would need to prove it, which I did, and found the whole lovemaking experience to be traumatic—not romantic in the least, but painful and definitely not fun. I was not ready. On the other hand, I was confident that there were dozens of other girls who were willing and would have fallen for Todd's advances in a heartbeat. My fifteen-year-old teenage wisdom gathered that he would leave me for another if I did not put out, and I could not bear the thought of losing Todd.

Initially, Todd said that he was nineteen. On finding out much later, after he had his way with me, that he was twenty-two, I was stunned and unprepared for a man to be showing an interest in me. Doing my math correctly for once in my life, I figured out that Todd was seven years older than me—an adult of legal age while I was still a minor. It took me a while longer to figure out that Todd was a full-fledged creep, and I was undiscerning.

One Sunday afternoon I got a phone call from Todd, saying that he would be by to pick me up. He was with his four buddies from Surrey, and they wanted to go to Rolley Lake, near my house, to smoke some pot. Shortly after that, a car honked outside, and when I told my mother what I was about to do, minus the pot-smoking part, she put her foot down and said that I could not go.

She was always very liberal and would often let me do anything I wanted to do, mostly because there was very little that I wanted to do. So, putting her foot down was unexpected. All I knew was that I wanted to be with Todd, while she saw something in him that I did not.

When I went out to the waiting car to say I could not go, smoke was wafting out of the windows, and the guys were already obviously stoned. I badly wanted to join them but made up a story of homework to stay within my mother's wishes. Once back inside the house, I fled to my bedroom in a fit of tears, rudely ignoring my mother for the rest of the day, and made a mental note not to ask for permission next time.

My friends had blatantly been telling me that Todd drank too much. I did not want to believe it. He seemed perfect in the "love is blind" sense, and it wasn't until I saw him pass out in a chair from too much alcohol, and wet his pants in the process, that I began to feel a sick dread about my steady boyfriend.

I found out through the grapevine—or the party line—that Todd had initially been sent out to his father's ranch in Stave Falls to look after his dad's two horses, for the sole purpose of getting straightened out. Excessive drinking, stealing, and getting fired from his job while living with his dad and stepmom in Surrey was more than any family could handle. Todd was an adult and needed to grow up and act the part, and this was his father's intention in relocating him.

On the other hand, Todd had his ideas apart from his father's. With love, or rather lust, on his mind, he ended up wooing a fifteen-year-old girl and setting off a chain of events that might have been averted if his presence had gone unnoticed. The straw that broke the camel's back was after a night of Todd begging and pleading with me to have sex with him, as if I owed it to him, I reluctantly gave in, and my mother caught us in the act.

As distant as I had become from my mother, I did not want to hurt her or disappoint her. Her reaction was that of outrage and fury, which brought forth screaming and yelling as she spat out the words, "I thought that you were going to be different from the others." I assumed she meant my older siblings, but I was never entirely sure as to what "others" she was referring to.

After nine months of dating, Todd vanished, never to be seen again. Even though common sense told me that Todd was bad news, my heart still broke into a million pieces every day, as I missed his smile and undying love and attention for me. I had mistaken his attraction for me as respect and romance instead of manipulation and abuse.

My mother was relieved that Todd had disappeared without a trace, my friends said, "We told you so," and my two older brothers said, "Good riddance." Having what I thought I wanted, I allowed Todd into my world, and it would take until my next boyfriend two years later for me to begin to get over the boy who was a man with no good intentions whatsoever.

My mother professed that nerdy guys, dorks, and the "brainiacs" were like ugly ducklings, awkward and shy, and it had been her experience that they would eventually blossom and grow out of it, becoming auspicious, handsome swans.

Trying to grasp her concept, I decided that perhaps it was their academic minds that got them through the murkiness of adolescence, therefore coming out the other side unscathed, victorious knights in shining armour. I concluded that their heads were so full of knowledge that their brains did not have any room left for nonsense or misbehaving. Being cool was the last thing from their thoughts, therefore summing up the unlikeliness of me ever being attracted to a boring nerd.

The ground rules had been set forth by Todd, and my image of a healthy girlfriend-boyfriend relationship had been tarnished.

My father, not being one to teach and talk about the dating scene, was supremely handsome, debonair, and fit, always displaying a witty and charismatic sense of humour. And yet my mother seemed to think a nerd was the best bet for her youngest daughter. Or so it appeared.

Despite my mother's irregular teachings, it was apparent that she loved Arthur Fonzarelli, aka "The Fonz," from the hit TV show *Happy Days*. We gathered around the television every Tuesday at 8:00 p.m. to laugh at Potsie's and Ralph's antics, Richie's common sense, and Mrs. Cunningham's motherly wisdom. But it was the leather jacket-clad, motorcycle-riding Arthur Fonzarelli with his slicked-back hair that my mother and I tuned in to watch. She had decided that he was the one exception of a bad boy making it good.

Enamoured with Arthur Fonzarelli, my fantasy of being Pinky Tuscadero is what kept me in perpetual wonderment as to why most of the rough-around-the-edges types were so attractive, asking myself the question and daydreaming as to whether I could snag a boyfriend like Fonzie.

My mother was absent most of my teenage years, not physically, but mentally, emotionally, and spiritually. She had bipolar disorder, a syndrome that was not talked about or readily diagnosed in those days. Her mother had been overbearing and manipulative, and also struggled with mental illness.

In addition to her unbalanced mother, her only sister had drug and alcohol problems, something else that was not a topic of conversation. Therefore, family history, learned patterns, and mental health issues were my mother's road map. It was the only life she knew until she met my father.

Teaching, guiding, and mentoring were not my mother's strong points, nor were they her mother's, and so on and so on, like the popular Breck Shampoo television commercial emulated. She was raised in a more innocent time, a generation that went to dances and movies, picnics, and church socials. They did not have the pressures of drugs, sex, and rock and roll, which unfortunately was the era that I was in whether I liked it or not.

My world kept me unaware of anything around me that did not involve myself, my social calendar, boys, school, and my future hopes and dreams. I missed signs that my mom was struggling in her world, not coping with her life, causing her to be inattentive, and many times unavailable.

Earlier on, when I was younger, before her mental health issues were in full swing, I enjoyed the stories she recounted and revealed about her youth and young adulthood, and suitors and beaus who took her to dances and the movie theatre. She recalled loving the theatre and sometimes sat through two or three different movies, all in one afternoon. She expressed that her favourite actor was Tab Hunter and that she and her best friend Ruth would swoon over the many Hollywood leading men.

Bad boys were indeed not anything new. My mother's era produced deep, dark, brooding characters played by Errol Flynn, Don Juan, Marlon Brando, James Dean, and Elvis Presley. Movie stars, but bad boys, just the same.

I concluded that my mother would not admit it, but she adored the rough-around-the-edges bad boys as much as I did.

We never spoke of Todd Barnes again. Her finding us intertwined in an awkward, embarrassing position was devastating. I often regretted not being able to confide in my mother and tell her about my dislike for the whole lovemaking act altogether.

By the summer of 1978, at seventeen years old, I was relieved and happy to have grade twelve over and done with. High school was under my belt, I was eager for life to begin, and I had the entire world ahead of me. I could hardly wait to get started.

My older sister had a summer job working the last two weeks of August every year at the Pacific National Exhibition in Vancouver, BC She worked in the accounting and payroll department during the famous, well-known fair.

Since the early 1900s, the PNE has operated a fair that has become a favourite destination for locals and tourists to enjoy. The festival is famous for its wooden roller coaster, helium balloons, show home prize draw, games on the midway, and the greasy, delicious food. Most notable are the mini donuts, known fondly as Tom Thumb Donuts, a traditional deep-fried sweet treat. Crowds gather to watch the miniature dough climb the tracks, much like the old wooden roller coaster, to free-fall into a vat of hot oil. Sizzling and popping up, they are then ready to be scooped up and tossed into a bed of sugar and cinnamon, a delightful sight for sore eyes and empty bellies.

The livestock buildings have always been informative and fun for city kids to see farm animals and the country kids to showcase their 4-H Club prized goats, pigs, cows, and bunny rabbits. The horse shows are crowd-pleasers, especially the Clydesdale horses, majestic and commanding in all their mammoth glory, as they prance and follow the orders of their keepers.

The food pavilion was where my father insisted on getting a Ukrainian sausage in a bun every year, and my mother gravitated to the British scone stand. The mini donuts and having my father win me prizes on the midway were my two most cherished traditions as a child.

I had often dreamed of one day working at the Pacific National Exhibition, which was a second choice to dressing up as Snow White and working at the Disneyland theme park—out of the question, with Disneyland being far off in California and what seemed like a million miles away. The next best thing would be a summer job at the PNE.

It has often been said that people get ahead in life based on their connections, not on their skills or knowledge. I first found this to be true when my sister got me a job as a cocktail waitress in a place called The Exhibitors' Lounge at the PNE.

My only other experience waitressing was a two-week stint in grade eleven at a Chinese restaurant called The Mandarin Palace in Mission. As a new server, I accidentally spilled piping hot sweet-and-sour sauce on a bald man's head. Mortified, I immediately quit due to the embarrassment of having to wipe down a stranger's scalp.

A year later, I was keen to try again. Serving drinks at the PNE sounded grown-up, and I had always heard that the tips waitresses made were astronomical, so I was eager to learn the ropes.

The purpose of the lounge was a place where people could come to relax, have a drink, listen to music, watch TV, and play Pac-Man, a popular video game back in the day. It was set up with couches, comfy chairs, dim lighting, a buffet food service, and cocktail waitresses to be at the customers' beck and call.

Mind you, the patrons of the Exhibitors' Lounge were not just any people; they were the vendors who sold their wares in booths at the Home Show Pavilion, from slicer-dicers, mixers and mashers, to knives, foot soakers and head massagers. You name it, and almost any gimmick or essential household item could be purchased at two for the price of one. If anything, it was fun to peruse and watch the demonstrations.

Other exhibitors tirelessly worked the midway and had snow cone stands, corn on the cob outlets, and burger counters. Some sold leather purses, fake tattoos, motorcycle vests, and belts. They were selling their products to the many customers who made it a yearly tradition to search for a deal, a chance to buy one and get the second at half price, ready, willing, and able to spend their money. Maybe they could even win the PNE Prize Home by entering the draw.

The exhibitors were my customers. Talking non-stop in their efforts to win a customer could be daunting and exhausting; therefore, a place of reprieve would be an advantage and a nice perk for the sellers who were renting space at the fair. Working in twos, my patrons would take turns coming into the lounge every other hour. While one worked the stand, the other would be slamming back drinks in the bar. When the hour was up, they would flip-flop and in would come the partner and so on for the entire twelve-hour day. With the fair open from 10:00 a.m. to 10:00 p.m., the day could be long and arduous for all the vendors, while also being incredibly profitable.

Vodka was the number one beverage ordered because the smell of this particular alcohol could not be detected on the breath, which was a definite advantage when talking to the public. The vendors could become quite animated and enthusiastic in their persuasive efforts to acquire a sale for their products that "no one could live without," and the aroma of liquor would be a hindrance to their success.

With the copious amounts of alcohol consumed, the Exhibitors' Lounge could get wild and harried. I learned the ropes quickly and found out that the more drunk people became, the larger the tip would be. A typical order would be a triple vodka and orange juice, costing $7.50. Each shot was $2.50 multiplied by three. Most times, I would be given a ten-dollar bill and told to keep the change. As the evening progressed, for the same order, I could be given $15 or $20 and still be told to keep the change.

With a receipt book in hand, a black apron around my waist, and a tray for beverages, matches, and a stack of ashtrays, it was not long before I was able to balance numerous drinks with one hand while doing mathematical calculations and holding a pen with the other.

Occasionally an extra drink was purchased for the server, which I would not consume. It was hard enough to do my calculations on my own without being inebriated as well. The other waitresses who did partake automatically joined in with their customers' camaraderie and were rewarded with more significant tips.

Most of the vendors had trailers and stayed on site at the fairgrounds. You could see them parked and set up down by the racetrack. So, at the end of the night, it would just be a bleary-eyed walk to a nearby bed. If they fell asleep on one of the many couches, the bouncers would be sure to come over and nudge them awake, sending them on their way.

The bouncers and waitresses became friends, and we girls revelled in the support of the doormen; they watched over us, stood behind us, and often walked us to our cars at the end of the night.

Because the PNE was only two weeks every summer, it was thought of as a perk to one's real career, merely an add-on for some extra money. Plus, it was loads of fun and a great way to meet people. It opened my eyes to how much fun the bar scene could be.

My mother had always wanted an adventurous life for herself. She often read two or three books a week and saved every newspaper she could get her hands on to read at a later date. In turn, she was well versed in current events, politics, and all the gossip and goings-on in Hollywood.

Unfortunately, her often crippling depression, combined with extreme highs, detracted from her parental duties of helping and guiding me to plan my future.

At times, my mother's behaviour could be tricky to understand or hilariously comical, if one could allow oneself the freedom to see things in a different light. In other words, life with my mother was often all over the map, and it took patience and tenacity to manoeuvre around her mood swings.

At specific points in my teenage years, developing a plan, instigating an idea, and following through rarely came to be. If my mother was entrenched in depression or having a manic spell, her thoughts and ideas could be fleeting or completely non-existent. Her plans of opening a bed and breakfast when she disliked cooking and entertaining, or writing a letter to the president of the United States complaining about the Vietnam War, ebbed and flowed with each passing day. I was often relieved that the FBI did not land on our doorstep to take my mother away in handcuffs. Or worse, a straightjacket.

Her overall desire for me to leave the nest directly following high school graduation was more for her own sake than mine. As per her wishes, I moved out and began the life of a grown-up with no safety net, advice, wisdom, or experience. As Cinderella once sang, "A dream is a wish your heart makes," and I, without a doubt, had many.

CHAPTER 3

"You're the One That I Want"

1978–1979

MY MOTHER HAD ONCE LIVED IN AMONGST THE HUSTLE AND
bustle of the city. She had many fond memories of working,
dating, friends, movies, and strolling through Stanley Park. It
was her idea that I should move to Vancouver, and so, Vancouver
was where I moved to.

In the grand scheme of things, she was bound and determined
that her youngest daughter would, could, and should live life to
the fullest, so she offered to help me in the only way she knew
how—setting me up in an apartment, paying my rent, buying me
a vehicle, and the gasoline that fuelled my car. At seventeen years
old, how could I refuse?

My car was a 1978 Chevy Chevette, brand-spanking-new,
bright yellow with an orange racing stripe down the side. The
seats were black-and-white plaid, and the whole interior was shiny
black vinyl. It smelled beautiful, fresh, and new.

The apartment she rented me came furnished and was located
on Cambie Street near King Edward in Vancouver, far from my

country bumpkin lifestyle in Stave Falls. It was a three-story brownstone for $380 a month, thanks to my mother. I was excited and ready to be a woman of the world.

My suite was on the ground floor, and when I opened the window, neighbouring cats would come in looking for action. They were attracted to the dim lighting, I assumed, and the odour was much like a root cellar filled with canned goods, old suitcases, and wool blankets. To keep things smelling fresh, I kept the windows perpetually open, giving the roaming cats free-range and a haven in all hours of the day or night.

The small sofa that came with the suite had seen better days and was lumpy like a sack of potatoes. The small single bed was not any better, but more like a flat slab of concrete. I was thankful that I had my flannelette sheets to offer some semblance of comfort. My new home was meagre, dark, and dumpy, but I loved it! I nicknamed my apartment the little Mole Hole.

Shortly after moving in, my high school friend Sarah came and visited me. She drove her Honda Civic from Mission to Vancouver to stay in the big city. She brought me a housewarming gift of six drinking glasses with three little owls painted on them, decorated with expressive little faces, hooting with open mouths and blinking eyes. I was surprised and felt grown up to be getting a housewarming gift, my very first one ever. Sarah was the kindest, most thoughtful person I had ever met.

The first time I had laid eyes on Sarah was on the school bus in grade nine. She had offered me a seat with her, and we hit it off immediately. She was pretty, with thick, naturally highlighted blond hair and a cute overbite that was in the midst of being corrected with braces. As a highly trained Scottish dancer who regularly took lessons, practised, and entered contests, she was fit and dedicated. I was in awe at how grown-up Sarah appeared to be because she had babysitting jobs and made dinner every night for her family. She also firmly believed that Todd was a creep and was instrumental in telling me that I could do much better.

Here we were all grown up, having a sleepover at my new-to-me, but dingy older apartment. The first night that she came to stay with me, not only did she give me a set of drinking glasses, but she took it upon herself to remove a stain from my kitchen counter. When I asked her how she had done it, her response was, "All you need is a little elbow grease, Karen." We both laughed at Sarah's diligence for hard work and how she turned my pocket-sized Mole Hole into a sparkling, livable residence, almost like *Bewitched* had twinkled her nose, or *Mary Poppins* had uttered "spit spot."

Having my apartment, I felt independent and modern, but after Sarah left, I was lonely. I missed my parents, my horse, and my bed back in Stave Falls. To get me out of the doldrums, I went home to Stave Falls every Sunday night to see my parents and to enjoy the comforts of home.

The closer my little car sped toward my past, the happier I would become. I often thought during the one-hour drive how I had forfeited our hobby farm with its pigs, chickens, burly old sheep, cats and dogs, trampoline, swimming pool, and a ride-on lawnmower for a Mole Hole in the city.

Propelling me forward was the fireplace stoked with wood and my mother's traditional roast beef dinner, with mashed potatoes, gravy, and broccoli with cheese sauce. All were waiting for me when I burst through the door.

As I drove through the city and on to smaller communities, the landscape changed from high-rise apartments to big homes, car dealerships, supermarkets, and finally stretches of deep, wooded forests.

It warmed and fed my soul, recalling my past, making the drive more enjoyable. I could envision my dad darning socks and pickling beets, puttering around on the property, tending to the garden, the animals, or helping a neighbour.

At the same time, my mother would be inside knitting. Projects were rarely completed: half-finished sweaters, blankets, and baby hats. Bags and bags of yarn, knitting needles of varying sizes, and patterns would be scattered on the floor or tucked away in cupboards and overflowing from baskets. The droning sound of soap operas and game shows blared, as the television was rarely turned off.

It all made me smile as I careened closer to home.

Fleeting images of Todd Barnes tried to invade my reminiscence, but I was determined to think only of happy times. Shaking my head to remove the creeping thoughts, I was able to return to memories of both my parents sitting in their chairs, watching TV while balancing mugs of instant coffee made with Coffee-Mate, and a store-bought cookie.

Game shows were watched every morning at 10:00 a.m. like clockwork, where another contestant would be asked to "Come on down," joining Bob Barker in hopes of being chosen for "Contestant's Row" on *The Price Is Right*. Together my mom and dad would estimate the prices of strawberry jam, dishwashers, and motorboats and marvel at how young Bob Barker looked.

Long before *The Price Is Right* rose in popularity, *Let's Make a Deal* was our number one game show choice. I adored Carol Merrill, the woman who allowed you to see behind door number one, door number two, or door number three. We would be sitting on the edge of our seats in anticipation of a speed boat, sewing machine, or a real live donkey to be won by some lucky or unlucky contestant.

Carol was stunningly beautiful in her cute little dresses as she gracefully extended her arm to display what the prize package was going to be. I hoped that one day I could have a job like hers.

There was a time when the filming of *Let's Make a Deal* moved from Las Angeles to Vancouver, up in a North Shore studio. My mother thought it would be great fun if she and I could try our luck at being contestants. The schtick with *Let's Make a Deal* was that one had to wear a costume and jump around, acting wild and crazy to get picked, in turn making the show hilarious for the TV viewers' entertainment.

My mother left it up to me to choose what our costumes would be, and then when we were ready, we would show up for a scheduled taping. I had never seen my mother play charades or act silly in any way, so the undertaking of dressing up was out of character for her. I had my work cut out for me to find what I could use from around the house. I eventually put together a mouse costume for myself, and knowing that my mother had a white tracksuit, I created a cardboard wedge and made her into a big piece of Swiss cheese. We hung mousetraps from her ears, and at five feet ten inches tall, she became a massive chunk of cheese with me as her little mouse sidekick.

Driving to the studio, we had no idea what to expect. We found the place way up on the mountainside in West Vancouver. After parking and finding out where to go, we waited in a huge outdoor covered area.

Not long after we assembled, the judges came through to pick people for the show. There were two groups chosen—Group A to be on the show as potential contestants, and Group B (the leftovers), who would sit at the back as the audience. The whole lot of us were told to act up, carry on, and do just about anything to get noticed by the judges. The more outlandish our antics, the better chance we had of being chosen for Group A.

Following directions, I squeaked and jumped up and down like a mouse, and my mother just stood there. Her excitement had diminished considerably, but cheese can be boring at the best of times, so there was not a whole lot she could do in the way of a performance for the judges. Unfortunately, we did not get picked to be contestants, but we did get to be in the studio audience, which turned out to be great fun nonetheless. We found out later the show had gone bankrupt, so nobody received their hard-earned prizes anyway.

My visits home could be unpredictable, depending on my mother's moods. Often she would be happy to see me, and then other times, she would be quiet, showing no emotion and offering no conversation. It was in those times that my father would pick up the slack and talk nonstop about the latest goings-on in the neighbourhood or funny stories that he recalled from his past. I would listen and chime in here and there when I saw fit, allowing my mother the opportunity not to engage, as it seemed she preferred it that way.

Slipping twenty dollars into the palm of my hand as I was leaving, my mother would tell me not to say anything to my father about it, and he would sneak a fifty-dollar bill into the console of my car. I never told either what the other was doing, and after dinner, off I would go to my little Mole Hole in Vancouver, a one-hour drive back, having just earned seventy dollars and a full belly.

Driving back to the city, I would feel a tightness in my throat that signalled the onset of tears. I was only seventeen years old going on eighteen and felt far too young to be out of the house on my own in the vast, big beautiful world that my mother professed to love.

One of my earlier teenage dreams was to become a flight attendant, formerly known in 1978, as an airline stewardess. When I found out that to become a stewardess in Canada, one needed to be able to speak two languages, this became an inescapable deterrent from the very start. A second language was something I had long since given up on after failing grade eight French class at North Van High School. In my mind, the next best thing to a stewardess was a model, so onward I would go; dreams were meant to be followed and next up, modelling school.

After my mother's diligent research proved that Blanche MacDonald's School of Modelling and Fashion Design was rated number one in the city, I was interviewed and accepted for enrolment.

My mother relished the career and independence that Blanche Brillon MacDonald (May 11, 1931 – June 8, 1985) displayed. She was only five years older than my mother and a Canadian Metis born in Faust, Alberta, of French and First Nations heritage.

She launched her career after winning the Miss English Bay contest in 1949. In 1952, Blanche was living in the West End of Vancouver and modelled for the Elizabeth Leslie Modelling School and Agency. In 1954, Blanche moved to Edmonton to open another branch of the school, where she met and married her husband, Jack MacDonald. In 1960, the MacDonalds moved from Edmonton to the British Properties in West Vancouver and opened the Blanche MacDonald Modelling Agency and School of Fashion, Ltd.

Blanche MacDonald's philosophy was to encourage people to reach their highest potential through personal development. Through the 1960s, her career consisted of fashion shows, lectures, and social events, working with designers, hair salons, airlines, and department stores, creating specialized courses, and running a tour across Canada to promote Canadian designers.

The influence of Blanche's Cree-speaking grandmother and witnessing traditional Aboriginal practices as a part of everyday life resulted in Blanche becoming a proud, influential leader of Aboriginal women throughout her life. In the '60s, she became involved in support of the rights and culture of Aboriginal peoples, as well as many women's organizations. Blanche worked with First Nations designers and promoted Indigenous models. She also ran self-appreciation classes in prisons (for men and women) at Oakalla, Matsqui, and Twin Maples Women's Prison.

My mother admired "women libbers," and Blanche Brillon MacDonald was at the forefront of Vancouver's emerging fashion scene and culture, becoming a businesswoman and trailblazer at a time and place in history when a woman in business was not common or favourable.

I did not know what the enrolment fee was, but my mother undoubtedly paid the price, and off I went, five days a week, 9:00 a.m. to 5:00 p.m.

My modelling teacher, Susan, was as stylish and fashionable as she was beautiful. She walked with poise, and all the girls in my class aspired to be just like her.

Going to modelling school was like being at Barbie doll summer camp, except I was the Midge doll, not quite pretty enough to be Barbie, but at least a part of her beautiful Barbie doll gang.

The program was two weeks in length and did not guarantee that everyone would become a model, although there was a possibility, or so we were told. The instructions were to work hard, follow the appropriate steps, and do the homework, consequently making a career as a model a reality.

We were told not to stop with Modelling Level 1 and encouraged to enroll in the Introduction to Modelling Level 2 even though Level 1 had barely begun. We would then have a much better chance to travel the world, with our face on *Flare* or *Seventeen* magazine.

I enjoyed every minute of the program.

We started with makeup application lessons, face cleansing lessons, and hairstyle lessons; fashion to suit your body type, the importance of accessories, diets to change your body type, self-esteem improvement coaching, and runway-walking techniques.

Part of the package was a photoshoot with a professional photographer for a modelling portfolio. Last but not least was a graduation ceremony, complete with a fashion show by us students, and cheese platters served by my fellow students and me. Invitations were sent to the parents so they could see how the money they spent was working out.

In conclusion, the lessons I learned were invaluable. I found out that I had an oval-shaped face, olive skin, pimples in the T-zone, looked better without a perm (which meant getting rid of the one I had), and required more self-confidence if I was ever going to land a job.

My insecurity waited in balance for someone to drop the bomb that I was overweight or too big in the hips. Inevitably, I was spared the mortification of such a critique.

After graduation, as advised, I diligently traipsed around to the fashion headquarters at The Bay and Woodward's department stores, taking with me my modelling portfolio and wearing my most stunning outfit and a look of confidence.

At five feet six inches tall, I was repeatedly told that I was too short and therefore was turned away. Followed by three more rejections from other businesses, I decided to give up my dream of being a model. I did not want my parents to spend money on the Introduction to Modelling Level 2, anyway. My modelling career was over, even before it had begun.

On the bright side, when all was said and done, I had enjoyed myself immensely, and I did feel more confident upon completion of Blanche MacDonald's Modelling Level 1. I concluded that I still had my backup plan of marriage, complete with a white picket fence, and was convinced that my Prince Charming would be around the next corner.

Both of my parents were supportive of anything I chose to do, and with university never mentioned, I entered the world of becoming an employee, a wage-earner and working stiff.

Following my stint at modelling school, I found a minimum wage job working in Gastown at a jean warehouse for the Bootlegger clothing store chain. Both of my parents were worried, because in their day, Gastown was an undesirable place to spend time.

Gastown is located at the northeast end of Downtown Vancouver and was the original settlement that became the core of the creation of Vancouver, British Columbia—named after "Gassy" Jack Deighton, a Yorkshire seaman, steamboat captain, and barkeeper who arrived in 1867 to open the area's first saloon.

In 1870, the borders of Gastown were the waterfront and the CPR tracks, Columbia Street, Hastings Street, and Cambie Street. The town quickly prospered and became a general centre of trade and commerce, as well as a place for out-of-work loggers and fishermen to hang out, therefore becoming a rough and rowdy place to be.

Many merchants established warehouses in Gastown, and up until the Great Depression in the 1930s, it was thriving as the centre of the city's wholesale produce distribution centre. Three hundred licensed drinking establishments covered a twelve-block radius. After the Depression Era, Gastown was largely forgotten. It fell into decline and disrepair as a continuation of the skid row area, with cheap beer parlours, flophouse hotels, and loggers' hiring halls.

In the 1960s, a campaign led by business people, property owners, and citizens of Vancouver was put in place to preserve Gastown's distinctive and historic architecture.

Henk F. Vanderhorst, a Dutch immigrant who had become a Canadian citizen, was one of the first to open an art gallery, the Exposition Gallery, on Water Street. His influence with the revitalization of Gastown was acknowledged in 1976 by being awarded The First Pioneer Citizen of Gastown, awarded by Mayor Art Phillips. A "key to the city" was presented to Vanderhorst for his dedication and hard work. Gastown was declared a historical site, protecting its heritage buildings to this day.

In 1971, a legendary riot took place between the police and the hippies, in the downtown near the waterfront, over marijuana. I am sure my older "hippie" brother must have attended, as he was as close to a hippie as I had ever seen.

By 1978, the popularity of Gastown was on the rise, and as more and more businesses were popping up, I felt grateful and excited to be working there. I prided myself at being only seventeen years old, living on my own, and getting a job as a salesgirl. The job itself certainly did not hold the same clout as a model or airline stewardess, so there was a happy indifference to my mood, but that changed once I met my new co-worker, John MacFarlane.

It was love at first sight, and my prince had arrived in a blue jean clothing store.

John had sparkling blue eyes, thick brown hair and a cute smile filled with straight white teeth. He stood five feet ten and, standing next to him, I felt petite—a feeling I rarely had. Before modelling school, I had always felt self-consciously too tall, but as it turned out, I had not been tall enough for walking the runway and making it big in Milan.

John and I had instant chemistry; we both liked to laugh, and we shared a good sense of humour. His was dry and sarcastic, and mine was cute and charming, or so I wanted to think. Thankfully, by no means did he appear to be another Todd Barnes, or rather, a wolf in sheep's clothing.

Our duties at the makeshift discount store were to help other teenagers find the right size or style of pant, and set them up in a changing room, calling to them while they changed behind a thin curtain, and running back and forth to find them another size, colour, or style if need be.

In the meantime, John and I would fold clothes side by side, tidy up, wait on customers, and spend the entire day laughing and having fun with each other. Sharing lunch breaks and walking the cobblestone streets of Gastown turned into hanging out after work, so when our summer jobs came to an end, we were officially a dating couple, and I could not have been happier.

Over the summer, John shared his hopes and dreams of becoming a PE teacher. He excelled in sports, and his parents were thrilled that he had chosen teaching as a profession. Come September, John started his teaching diploma at the University of British Columbia, and I found a job at another Bootlegger clothing store, this one at Arbutus Village Square in Vancouver, which was a short drive from my apartment on Cambie Street.

The sexual encounters I had before meeting John were with Todd. Every aspect felt wrong and unpleasant, therefore damaged. My first and only love interest was a man who preyed on teenage girls, and he had not respected my position of not being ready. I do recall saying no to Todd numerous times, but it did not seem to make any difference to him—he, or we, went ahead with the act anyway. I thought that I loved Todd with my whole heart and soul, and yet ironically, or rightly so, I hated every aspect of the lovemaking experience.

This time, I knew that things would be different. Two years had passed. I was more mature and worldly than I had been with Todd, and I was ready to try again.

A magazine named *Cosmopolitan* that guaranteed satisfying results in the bedroom became my number one reading material and go-to self-help romance guide.

In 1965, Helen Gurley Brown became editor-in-chief of the magazine. She transformed it into a racy, successful magazine for modern single career women. Her goal was to erase the stigma around unmarried women, not only engaging in sex but enjoying it. She also wrote a book entitled *Sex and the Single Girl*. Even my mother approved but downplayed her opinion of the feminist magazine significantly, to not appear too involved with her daughter's emergence into womanhood. Perhaps she was shy and embarrassed, but I did catch her on occasion reading it if I had left a copy lying around.

The bottom line—she and I both knew that I needed all the help I could get.

With that thought, I was reminded about the time in grade six health class when a permission form was sent home about a four-week health series on "a girl becoming a woman." My mother's response was in full support as she indicated in so many whispered words, "I am glad that someone is going to tell you about that stuff because when it happened to me, and I got my, you-know, time of the month, I thought that I was dying because of the blood. I screamed bloody murder, and then MY mother threw a rag at me and said 'Here, use this.'"

My sister bought a copy of *Cosmopolitan* magazine in 1972 because Burt Reynolds was in a centrefold. She removed the staples and mounted the full-page layout on the bedroom wall in her mobile home. My mother refused to look, shaking her head like an Etch-a-Sketch to remove the image from her mind. His private parts were covered up, but his hairy chest and full-length nude body blended in quite nicely with the bearskin rug he posed on while clenching a skinny cigar between his teeth. At that time, he was considered one of the sexiest men alive.

Every morning I would eat a breakfast of fried eggs, hash browns, crispy bacon, and toast with strawberry jam for $3.95 at the White Spot on the corner of King Edward and Cambie Street, which was next door to where I lived. I would sit up at the counter on a swivel stool to chow down before driving my little yellow car to work, which was less than a ten-minute drive away. Any concerns over caloric intake had not yet been ingrained in my head.

My mother was pleased with my career and lifestyle thus far, especially my educated and goal-oriented boyfriend, John. She wanted the best for me, and even though she never said as much, a girl knows when her mother approves or disapproves of her boyfriend. The subtle ways, the knowing glances, and the freshly applied lipstick whenever I brought John around were distinct.

Working at a trendy, modern clothing store, I often felt out of place. The insecure plain girl in my head whispered to my inner ear that I was not cut out to be a representative for the company, as I did not look like the girls on the posters or the skinny, faceless mannequins.

Catching glimpses of myself in the abundance of mirrors in the store, I could not help but notice that the signature blue jeans I had to wear did not fit me well. They were snug in the hips, with a gaping waistline in the back. To wear a belt only scrunched up the midsection noticeably, and to stitch in darts or pleats would have made the pants fit better but would have also turned them into an outdated, freakish embarrassment. The image I had of myself was not healthy, as I was always comparing myself to others, sure that I was overweight according to the beauty industry's standards.

There was nothing I could do about it. Employees were expected to wear the Bootlegger jeans like a uniform to advertise and promote the store, like a walking billboard.

I tried to keep the green-eyed monster at bay when the petite, Twiggy-like girls, came in and looked fabulous in everything they tried on. Girls my age and younger were the ones that I waited on hand and foot as their salesgirl, and I dutifully smiled and praised them for how wonderful the jeans fit and looked on them.

We sold all the well-known brands such as Seafarer, Big Blue, Howick Riders, Levi's, and Le Cloutier, along with overalls and painter pants that fit the customers like gloves but fit me either like a lumpy sack of potatoes or a sausage in a too-tight casing.

The tops were also fashionable and cute: hoodies with zippers up the front, striped T-shirts, turtlenecks, and cowl-neck sweaters pulled every outfit together.

Aside from being envious, I was still sincere in my compliments. It was noted by the manager that my enthusiasm had assisted in yet another sale as I moved up the ranks to a twenty-five-cents-an-hour raise.

Mostly, I continued to read fashion and relationship bibles such as *Seventeen*, *Glamour*, and *Cosmopolitan* magazines, gaining knowledge and confidence with every turn of the page. Even though the skinny blonde models set me back a notch with their sulky facial expressions as if to say, "At least I was not a beauty school dropout like you were."

As much as I tried to understand the advice and sex stories about how to please a man, all the adjoining escapades and life lessons made very little sense to me even if they sounded crucially important. I experimented with their suggestions about how to be sexy, whether I wanted to or not.

In pure form, I was often taken back to what Blanche MacDonald Level 1 Modelling School taught me—we must all face our fears and love ourselves to make it in the world. This statement always gave me pause because both were the last two things I wanted to do.

My duties were not rocket science and would involve folding jeans and corduroy pants, hanging up tops and hoodies, unpacking new shipments, putting them on the appropriate shelves, lining them up correctly, and waiting on customers. It was a full-time job making the standard minimum wage of $3.50 an hour (after my twenty-five-cent raise).

Saturdays were our busiest days, and we always had to be on the lookout for couples going into the changing rooms together. Apparently, having sex in clothing store change rooms was a thing and needed to be kiboshed immediately or before anything could get underway.

Policing and patrolling teenagers was not my strong point. I would much rather stick pins in my eyes or look the other way and pretend that I had not heard or seen anything, or at least use the rendezvous of others as an opportunity to take out the garbage or fold yet another pair of pants.

Addressing the indiscretion of others in the fitting rooms was the worst part of my job, causing me to wince, play dumb, or look the other way. With my weak voice and downcast glance, I just wanted to be left alone; being nonconfrontational was a strategy I learned from my mother when faced with an awkward moment. This reaction had worked during math class, as well, when asked a question I had no idea of how to answer. "Leave me alone" was my facial expression.

One afternoon, the head honcho from the Bootlegger head office came in and asked to speak with me. He ushered me into the small back room, which had a sink, boxes of new shipments, and two small stools. The closet-like storage room was where we took our breaks if we did not feel like traipsing around the mall or getting a hotdog and chocolate malt from Woodward's.

His line of questioning went as follows: "Was I ever in the store alone?" "Who closed up?" "Who locked the doors?" and "Did I ever use the cash register?"

All my answers were truthful. "I was never in the store alone." "The assistant manager let me go home early on most days." "She was the person who would close up at the end of the night," and "Yes, I used the cash register," I sweetly and self-assuredly responded.

I found out later that the reason for the boss's visit to the store that day was because the head office suspected me of stealing from the cash register. They were looking for clues, and since I was so truthful and appeared innocent, they summed up that it could not have been me, but rather the assistant manager Rachael who had been embezzling money from the till.

Rachael, from what I could tell, knew blue jeans like nobody's business. I learned a lot from her, except for the stealing part, and from that day forward, I would never see her again. No longer would I be sent home a half-hour early with pay. But in the grand scheme of things, I was utterly relieved that it was her and not me that got fired. Even though I had done nothing wrong, I felt like I had after the interrogation.

I carried on as was and came to like the new assistant manager, Sydney, who was moved from another Bootlegger store to replace Rachael, the thief.

I had not heard of the name Sydney before, only as a city in Australia. With her unique name came the perfect image of what a girl named Sydney should look like—wispy short blond hair and enormous blue eyes with eyelashes that met the lenses in her oversized talk show host glasses, which were red.

Not only did Sydney have a delicate persona that appealed to everyone, especially the guys, she was also willowy thin and every pair of jeans, no matter what style, fit her like the girls in the magazines.

Our existing manager, Andrea, whom I had worked with since day one, was a petite brunette with stunning wavy black hair. Even without a perm, her dark locks were curly (the style of Stevie Nicks) and framed her delicate facial features perfectly. She was about ten years my senior and was obsessed with the singers Billy Joel and Gino Vannelli.

It was a new trend for stores that appealed to young people to have music soundtracks playing with loud, hip tunes that could relate to the teenage mind, but also get one in the mood to shop and spend money. As a manager, Andrea insisted that we play both of her favourite singers. We never disagreed or got tired of Billy or Gino, getting to learn all the lyrics so well that we naturally sang along while selling, folding, and pricing pants.

There was one other employee at the Bootlegger store, whose name was Natalie. She was a university student who only worked Friday nights and all day Saturdays. Natalie always reminded me of the actress Natalie Wood, and I wondered if her parents had a premonition or willed her to look and be like the famous movie star from *West Side Story, Rebel Without a Cause,* and *Splendor in the Grass.* Bootlegger Natalie was just as pretty or prettier than Hollywood Natalie.

We, as co-workers, were quite disappointed when Natalie's boyfriend initially came into the store to visit her. He did not appear to be a perfect match, as we were expecting a James Dean type or Warren Beatty lookalike. Instead, we got Clive Hornby, an average guy with average looks and ordinary clothes.

He did not appreciate the silent treatment we all gave him and could never in a million years have understood that it was his lack of movie-star quality that rubbed us all the wrong way. Superficial on our part, yes, but it was how we rolled: catty, and hopelessly romantic. Clive began to make his visits fewer and farther between, and we all told Natalie that she could do way better.

On Friday nights after closing, Andrea, Sydney, Natalie, and I would head downtown to Pharaoh's Disco, located on the west side of Gastown at the point where Water Street and Cordova Street meet, in an old, narrow building that jutted out into a pointed entranceway.

Descending a steep red-carpeted staircase, we entered the small darkened nightclub. In 1978, Pharaoh's was well known and famous for its disc jockeys and disco dancing routines of the patrons.

We never gave it a second thought that we were underage and did not have proper ID. We waltzed right through the doors together as an entourage to our fearless twenty-seven-year-old leader Andrea, as if we owned the place. At no time were we stopped, questioned, or asked to show proof of our age.

Nestling in at a table, we ordered drinks and anticipated the playing of our most requested and sought-after song, "We Are

Family" by Sister Sledge. This famed disco number became our gal-pal anthem, along with every other female dancing queen in the club.

When the first few bars came on, every woman in the place would assemble on the dance floor to sway their hips and croon out the lyrics in unison. All four of us, my Bootlegger co-workers and I, dashed to the dance floor to unite in a circle, to bond and dance the night away, singing our mantra accompanied by Sister Sledge.

Some men tried to join in our circle dance time, but somebody would end up hip bumping them out of the way or turn their back on them in an obvious snub.

After meeting John in the summer of 1978 at the Bootlegger warehouse in Gastown, the memory of Todd Barnes began to fade. But not completely. As Rod Stewart once vocalized, "The First Cut is the Deepest," a song title that belonged to Todd and me. Whenever the ballad played on my car radio, it reminded me of Todd, once again feeling the sting of a wound that occasionally broke open. Knowing full well that he was a wrong choice for a boyfriend, it was my first cut, a scar that ran deep and one that I had a hard time forgetting, just the same.

I continually reminded myself that I was with John, a charismatic, handsome, and smart jock on the outside, but a nerd in a cute guy's wrapper just the same. He was the jackpot I had always hoped to cash in on. Eventually, Todd Barnes became a distant memory, or nightmare, depending on how I chose to remember him.

Adding a whole new element to our relationship was John joining a fraternity. I had never heard of a fraternity before, and it appeared to be an academic party house where guys could let loose, drink, and carry on like lunatics. Shortly after John joined his frat, the movie *Animal House* came out with John Belushi, and I felt like I was the only one in the movie theatre who was not laughing with side-splitting cackles. Of course, I faked my chuckles to fit in, and John thought that it was funny, so that was all that mattered.

Having grown up in Vancouver, John knew all the places to go and had a lot of friends ready to hang out with him.

He was always full of ideas, and every weekend there was a selection of parties and events to attend. Our weekends were filled with bike rides, walks along the sea wall at Stanley Park, and hiking in the North Shore Mountains. At night we ate at bistros, went to parties, lounges, and discotheques.

John was more of a rock and roll guy, so he eventually informed me that the disco scene was great for my friends and me, but he would opt out.

Age seventeen turned to eighteen in the blink of an eye. I busied myself during the week with work and television shows at night and drank excessively on the weekends, keeping in time with other young people enjoying the nightlife of Vancouver in 1978.

The Commodore Ball Room on Granville Street, Pharaoh's Disco in Gastown, The Sylvia Hotel at English Bay, and Chicago Tonight out in New Westminster were our go-to establishments. We danced and drank, drank and danced the night away, at least until closing.

When the bars closed, we made our way to one of the twenty-four-hour eateries: Bino's on West Broadway, The Knight and Day, or Fresgo's on Davie Street. Everyone would be hungry and ready to feast on copious amounts of greasy, cheap junk food available when the bars closed at 2:00 a.m.

It was good, clean fun, and nobody got hurt, at least not in our circle. Occasionally there would be a fistfight over a spilled drink or small brawl for no good reason, but in a nonconfrontational manner, we would all turn a blind eye.

Since John was busy with school and sometimes opted out of the disco scene, my girlfriends and I regularly attended a hotspot in New Westminster called Chicago Tonight. The decor was unique, with booths curved around tables and the seats covered in smooth white vinyl. Each booth was equipped with an in-house telephone so a person could call another booth and ask a girl or guy to dance. It added a less awkward element to asking someone to dance, and if one got turned down, nobody was the wiser.

In true discotheque fashion, flashing lights and a disco ball offered pastel pinks and swirling blue hues that seemingly flattered one's appearance. With the rest of the club in total darkness, the whole experience felt glamorous and elite. The music lifted us up and away, and the unique learned dance moves matched every song.

In 1979 and onward, whenever the song "Time Warp" from the movie *The Rocky Horror Picture Show* came on, all-nightclub-goers had another reason to flock to the dance floor. Following the instructions during the chorus, we the dancers followed in conjunction with the singer's request.

Another crowd-pleaser was "Rock Lobster" by the B52s. The theme for this song was twisting our bodies down as close to the dance floor as possible. Each time the singer crooned "Down, down, down," we wondered if our legs would hold us up long enough for the song to come to an end. Quite a quad workout and a little hard on the knees, but we managed.

The song "Y.M.C.A." by the Village People involved forming the letters of the acronym above one's head with the arms to spell out the four letters of the song's title. It was silly, but we all secretly anticipated the letter C so we could tip to the side with our arms overhead forming the big letter C. Little did we know that the letters stood for the Young Men's Christian Association.

Upon the song's release, the YMCA threatened to sue the band over trademark infringement. The organization ultimately settled with the composers out of court and later expressed pride regarding the song, which saluted the organization. Willis, the group's lead singer, wrote the song in Vancouver, BC, while he was staying at the YMCA and has often acknowledged his fondness for double entendre. The group initially targeted gay men, but eventually, they became more accessible to all genders and more mainstream over time.

"Rasputin," a 1978 Euro-disco hit single by the German-based pop group, Boney M, was a semi-biographical song about Grigori Rasputin, a friend and supposed advisor of Tsar Nicholas ll of Russia during the early 20th century. What made this song so fun and so funny was that only the boys on the dance floor would crouch down in unison and kick their legs out with folded arms, like an authentic Russian folk dancer—another real knee-breaker but a great workout, nonetheless.

Earth, Wind and Fire, KC and the Sunshine Band, Lady Marmalade, and The Pointer Sisters were just a few more of the highly acclaimed disco divas and disco stars whose music my friends and I enjoyed.

The glamour of every club could harshly diminish when the last call for liquor was announced, and the lights abruptly came on. At the end of the evening, a shocking brightness and glare from the fluorescent lights shone onto each of our faces, bringing into full view sweaty, pimply complexions, smeared lipstick, and mascara stuck in the corner of the eyes. Permed hair had become frizzy, and feathered bangs were limply flattened to our foreheads, revealing us as weary, bedraggled partygoers. The smell of sour alcohol and stale cigarettes was on the breath of most, and dirty drink-stained carpets shocked us. The walls and furniture all displayed a dingy grey and tobacco-stained yellow hue.

Leaving the club, before "not drinking and driving" was instilled by the law, I would make my way to my car on the deserted streets. Driving a friend or two home, we would relive the night and reminisce about all of our favourite songs, dances, and partners that went with them.

One evening at Pharaoh's, I was asked to dance by a blond, moustached guy in a full-on white three-piece suit, and since I had a difficult time saying no, I got up and joined him. My friends smirked at the sight of him and as he took my hand, we each brought our dance style to the floor, he with his *Saturday Night Fever* rendition of John Travolta's famous strut and me with my twirls and most impressive Bump move: hands in the air while my hips swayed in a bumping motion. The Bump was a reasonably easy dance that did not require a lot of complicated steps or moves. Partners stepped or swayed to the music—standing apart from one another—and came together to bump hips (or other body parts) about every second beat.

During one of my well-calculated disco dance twirls, the heel of my shoe broke off. These were not just any high heels. They were white, with three-inch heels, a peek-a-boo toe, and thin leather laces that wrapped around my ankle halfway up my calf. These shoes were showstoppers. Paired with a black, Lycra wrap-around dress, I looked and felt like one foxy lady. Coveting my high heels, I was deeply disappointed to be standing with one leg noticeably shorter than the other while I held the broken heel in my hand, pouting to my partner.

My nameless dance partner said in a confident all-knowing tone, "I know just how to fix your broken heel. Give it to me. I will repair it and then take you out for dinner to return your fixed heel." My response was, "Sure." We exchanged telephone numbers, and off I went with one shoe still on, limping through the cobblestoned streets of Gastown alone to the parkade and my car to drive home.

Within a few days, I received a phone call from my shoe-fixing dance partner to invite me for dinner in Chinatown and to retrieve my shoe. Nervous and cautious, I was a tad reluctant but accepted the invitation, mainly for the return of my shoe.

Arriving at the restaurant by myself, I found him with his friends, huddled together around a big round table. Half-eaten dishes of fried rice and Almond Gai Ding sat cold on the Lazy Susan. They were all drunk, so I offered a weak smile as if it did not matter, even though I was crushed and felt slightly derailed by the empty plates with only a few stray noodles left as a reminder.

Not only did I not get any dinner that night, but I also did not get my coveted shoe back. Leaving the restaurant, I heard the term "Catch you on the flip side" echoed in unison by my nameless dance partner and his friends. While fuming inside, I sweetly waved goodbye and returned to the parkade to drive myself home. Imagining that guy as my boyfriend instead of John made me realize how good I had it. Sighing and pleased with that realization, I turned 14 CFUN up on my car radio as loud as it could go, rolled the windows down, and drove away.

Aside from parties and dates with John, working at Bootlegger, and disco dancing with my work friends, Sarah, my best high school friend, still periodically came into Vancouver from Mission to visit me. Staying in my little apartment and cleaning until I returned from work, Sarah's knack for tidiness turned into a running joke, but neither of us minded just the same.

During one of Sarah's visits, John invited us over to his friend's house. His buddy Rod lived in Shaughnessy in a mansion, and his parents were going to be out of town.

Up until now, my dating life had been primarily about John. So, I was proud and excited for Sarah to join in the fun with my boyfriend. I shared with Sarah who all might be at the party. Most of John's friends were rich, or at least their parents were, and they had no problem flaunting it.

Sarah already had a secret crush on Rod, even though she had not met him yet. A skinny genius type with a wicked sense of humour, he wore his dark hair longer so it peeked out of his baseball cap and curled up on the ends. Wire-rimmed glasses only highlighted his deep-set brown eyes, and he never wore anything other than a baseball jersey, blue jeans, and brown loafers.

Just after seven on a Saturday night, Sarah and I drove over to John's place in my car to pick him up. Somehow John had a connection to get alcohol since we were all underage, and what's a party without getting smashed?

As we approached Rod's house, I was fascinated with the tree-lined streets, large homes, black steel gates, and towering hedges that made up the neighbourhood.

Rod's house was the most magnificent house that I had ever seen. Pulling up to the roundabout, we parked my Chevy Chevette in between a Bentley and a Rolls Royce.

I eventually had to close my mouth to gain control over my spellbound expression, glancing sideways at Sarah to see if she was experiencing the same thing. Catching her eye, we both lifted our eyebrows in disbelief as we approached the front entranceway with big white pillars that held up the porch.

Once inside, the usual gang that made up John's core group of friends was all there hanging out in Rod's kitchen, sitting on countertops, perched backward on chairs, and drooping over stools. Most of them were already three sheets to the wind, and then someone brought out a marijuana cigarette.

Sarah and I were both highly against drugs of any kind even though pot smoking was "what people did" at parties. The last thing we wanted was to look like country bumpkins, so we slipped out of the way just before the joint was passed in our direction. Making ourselves an extra-strong Rum and Coke, we left the confines of the kitchen to look around the rest of the house.

Next to the kitchen was an archway into the living room. Hardwood floors and white Persian rugs invited us over to an extensive hi-fi stereo system and an abundance of record albums just waiting to be played and listened to.

As everyone became more out of it, Sarah and I took it upon ourselves to man the record player and acted as the party's DJs. We chose our favourite albums from groups such as the Doors, the Beatles, and the Rolling Stones. We danced and talked and laughed.

At midnight, whoever was left at the party and still coherent was rallied into the master bedroom to flop down on the bed and watch a new show called *Saturday Night Live*. It was a hilariously funny late-night American TV variety show, not at all like *Carol Burnett* or *Ed Sullivan*, but rather comedy sketches which often parodied contemporary culture and politics. It reminded me of *Laugh-In*, but more astute and less campy.

A different celebrity guest hosted each weekly episode, delivering the opening monologue. The introduction always ended with someone breaking character and proclaiming, "Live from New York—it's Saturday Night!" properly beginning the show.

Saturday Night Live was new to me, and I enjoyed it, but on this particular night, I could not help being distracted from the TV by the enormous bed we were all loitering on. John said that it was called a king size, and I could see why because it took up the entire bedroom. I thought it fascinating that a person could lie in pretty much any direction, and they would still get a good night's sleep. An entire family of five could have slept without infringing on the others.

I marvelled at the wall-to-wall white shag carpeting and how the velvet wallpaper had a pattern of flowers; if you ran your fingers across the surface, it felt like you were reading Braille.

Closing my eyes and opening them quickly, I imagined I could just as well have been at the Bayshore Hotel in an executive suite on the top floor. The decor throughout the room was just as impressive as the massive bed, consisting of ornate picture frames, crystal vases, and lush green ferns.

I was a hick from the country who spent her teenage years growing up in a log cabin, with wagon-wheel upholstery on the furniture, a La-Z-Boy recliner that we took turns sitting on, and a pink ballerina bedspread on my single bed. Wondering how on earth Rod's parents could afford a home like this and if they were looking for a boarder, I smiled at the thought of it.

Lost in my daydreams and called back to reality by loud, disorderly drunken cackles, I remembered the show at hand. I marvelled at the sketches and female characters played by Jane Curtin, Laraine Newman, and Gilda Radner. Dan Aykroyd, John Belushi, and Bill Murray were also comical. Still, it was the women who delivered the humorous and sometimes raunchy bits that gave me pride in being a girl, and the go-ahead to be entertaining and comical myself. It brought forth a coolness to being a woman and permission to be smart, witty, and funny. My first examples of television humour were *Lucy* and *Carol Burnett*, and now it was the women from *SNL*.

As the night ended, we all parted ways to drive home. Sarah and I dropped John off before going to my Mole Hole, never once thinking or worrying about what drunken state we were in.

I had begun to grow tired and unimpressed with folding Bootlegger jeans for a living. Feeling restless and wanting a new job, I started to have increased fantasies about a different life, daydreaming about an alternative reality to working in a clothing store selling pants.

Even though my eventual goal was marriage, a house, babies, dinner parties, patio furniture, and a gorgeous husband mowing the lawn surrounded by a white picket fence, I knew I was still too young, and it was far too soon. I had decided that John was the man for me, and with him still having four more years of university to get through, I decided I would wait and find a new career in the meantime.

After meeting John's friends and fraternity brothers at UBC, the outward image of myself started to change—or at least how my boyfriend's academic friends saw me.

Whenever we were at a party, and someone asked me what my major was, I had to explain that I was not a student, and I worked in a clothing store. I often felt judged and humiliated when the person immediately lost interest in me and caught someone else's eye from across the room, leaving me to stand alone, glancing from side to side, looking for John.

As a relatively quick thinker, I soon learned how to make my meagre little job sound worldly and exciting by accessing my storytelling ability. When John's friends asked me what classes I was taking, I told them about my job at Bootlegger. Before they could lose interest, I enthusiastically brought up the sexcapades in the changing rooms, my boss stealing from the cash register, and staying up all night at the discotheques with my pretty co-workers. How living in an apartment gave me the independence to be footloose and fancy-free!

Although this made me feel better, deep down inside, I knew that working for minimum wage was not the be-all and end-all when speaking with law students, guys in the engineering program, and pre-med undergraduates.

As I grew more self-conscious and restless about my job, I thought about my older sister and her career.

My sister worked for the Bank of Commerce in Mission. The manager for her branch lived across the street from us in Stave Falls. He was an odd duck, with twenty cats who ruled the roost inside his magnificent log home. Decked out with perches, frayed scratch posts, cat ladders that went up the walls high into the rafters, and gangplanks leading out open windows so his feline friends could have twenty-four-hour access to the outdoors, this also meant the outdoors could have twenty-four-hour access to the log home.

The cats would drag in every varmint known to man as endless love offerings—mice, snakes, birds, and the occasional squirrel or rat. Each cat had its personalized dish, and the vet made house calls. Sprinkles, Chester, Spice, Blackie, and Whitey were names of just a few of the menagerie of felines.

The odour in the home was unlike any other. It would attach to your clothes just like the stench of cigarette smoke, yet it was more like a combination of cat spray, urine, dusty hairballs, and critters from the forested outdoors. One knew full well that after leaving the cat-infested home, a clothing change was in order, and scented laundry detergent and Bounce dryer sheets were a must.

The neighbour/bank manager/cat enthusiast was a kind and gentle man, nonetheless, and my parents were friends with him and his very gracious wife, who was not quite as enthused by his favoured four-footed friends. Over Sunday dinner one weekend at my folks' house, I shared with them my desire to up the ante from selling pants and try to get another, more career-oriented job.

In a short period and a few phone calls, my sister's bank manager who doubled as my parents' friend got me a job in the personal loans department at the Bank of Commerce in downtown Vancouver on Pender Street. No experience required.

My mother upgraded me to a new apartment on Sixth and Fraser Street, just east of Main Street in Vancouver. It was a three-block walk to the corner of Broadway and Fraser Street, where I took the bus directly to my new job.

Having the belief and feeling that everything in my life was aligned and going as planned, I had the world at my fingertips, and I was beginning to think that I could conquer anything. Therefore my self-esteem had a brief moment of increase.

I had always hated math, numbers, and calculations of any kind, which made me fearful and wondering what my new job requirements would be. Banks conjured up the thought of money and computations. I was relieved to find out my duties included only answering the phone, taking calls from various loan officers at different Banks of Commerce from all over British Columbia, and giving the caller loan information and status on their clients' loans.

I worked in a room with eight other girls. We each sat at a desk, had a telephone, swivel chair, notepad, and pencils. There was a woman who watched over us who was pretty, with bleached blond hair and an orange suntan. Her name was Kelly, and it was apparent that she was not there to make friends. She rarely smiled and rarely spoke to us.

It reminded me of high school, except we did the same subject all day long. Our coffee break was fifteen minutes in length, comparable to recess, and our lunch was thirty minutes. We were not allowed to talk, and if we did, if something slipped out, Kelly would give us a stern look as if to say, "We are here for a long time, not a good time."

The air was stuffy and hot and smelled like erasers.

When things were slow, I was sent into the basement to file, file, file small little recipe-like cards into a big filing cabinet in a cold, dank vault until all my nails broke, and my fingers bled. Alone in a crypt-like setting, while doing a monotonous job, it was easy for my mind to wander and deviate from the task at hand.

Thinking about my past, present, and future, I still sometimes thought about and remembered how Todd Barnes had run out on me, never saying goodbye or breaking up or leaving a trace as to where he had gone. Reasoning with myself that it was all for the best, I still periodically wondered what had happened to him. My thoughts would then move forward to John and all the fun I was having. Traversing back and forth in my mind, I would soon find myself fantasizing about my eventual wedding day and how it would look, decorating the hall in my daydreams, and shortly after that, picking out names for my children.

Whiling away the hours and flipping through personal loan cards, I accidentally came across the name Todd Barnes. I caught my breath, and I had to sit down on a little stepping stool for a moment. The small filing drawers went from floor to ceiling, A to Z, and there were thousands of personal loan cards on thousands of clients for the bank, so how odd to me that his name came up. The information was vague but told me that Todd Barnes was living in Creston, BC, with an outstanding loan of $3,700. My findings made me reluctantly ponder my first love yet again.

But once I put the card with Todd's name on it back in the filing cabinet, it felt final, like I was tucking him away in a sealed tomb, lock, stock, and barrel, never to be thought of again.

John was not Todd, of that I was sure.

Every day at 10:15 in the morning, most of the staff took a fifteen-minute coffee break. Eight to ten girls and I would make our way to a small local café for a donut, called a Cindy, consisting of dough, sugar, and cinnamon, deep-fried to a crispy sweet sugary mass.

Due to my ever-increasing dilemma about my weight and width of my hips, mixed with earlier teachings from the Blanche MacDonald Modelling School, I knew that fat and sugar could add to the acne on my face and the cellulite on my thighs. Therefore, I decided that I best not indulge in the delectable treat. I nevertheless watched in envy while the other girls of all shapes and sizes gobbled up the greasy, calorie-laden delicacy. I proudly abstained as I sipped my sugary sweet Orange Crush soda pop instead.

Only a few days into my banking career, my colleagues, who were young women mostly the same age as I was, became my new companions. Having moved on to a more well-to-do job for the Bank of Commerce, my Bootlegger friends and co-workers had quickly become a thing of the past. I was reassigned to planning nights at the disco with my bank friends, which included late nights and lots to talk about at the water cooler the next day.

Not yet a year into our dating, John was well into his studies at UBC and finding less and less time for cruising around town with me. Warding off the pangs in my heart of missing him, I managed to keep busy, always looking forward to our nightly telephone call before bed, me at my apartment, and John living at home with his parents. Since he did not have a lot of time for me, he encouraged me to go out, have fun, and live life to the fullest, which in turn reminded me that it was also my mother's wish for me.

My recent change of job and apartment had given me a fresh start and a different attitude. The modern apartment felt much more beautiful than my Mole Hole, a definite step up, and now on the third floor with a view of Grouse Mountain and the entire North Shore, it was a great place to start entertaining my boyfriend.

The only catch was that John did not want to stay the night.

Even though his reasoning would have made any parent thrilled, I was not. *Cosmopolitan* magazine professed that couples benefitted from cuddling through the night, and there was something called "spooning" that I was desperate to try.

With John's parents paying for his education, he was reluctant to be disrespectful, and as disappointed as I was, I also understood. Besides, we were both only eighteen years old and had a whole lifetime ahead of us for canoodling and carrying on behind closed doors, which made my daydreams about John and the eventual happy ending even more worthwhile.

When not out with my friends at the disco, I enjoyed catching up on my television shows, especially relatable programs such as *Mary Tyler Moore*, with her boss and workmates, Lou Grant, Ted the anchorman, Sue Ann Nivens, Murray Slaughter, Rhoda Morgenstern, Phyllis Lindstrom, and Georgette Franklin. In addition, the program called *That Girl* with Marlo Thomas, who played another modern working woman named Ann, who had a boyfriend named Donald Hollinger, was also a favourite. Both women fell in and out of precarious situations while fashionably dressed, living in super cool apartments like mine, doing quite fine on their own, especially knowing that they would one day marry and settle down.

No longer feeling like a teenager, even though I still was one, I had moved on and evolved from dreaming about *Brady Bunch* siblings, a *Partridge Family* mom, or living out my life with John Boy from *The Waltons*.

Between my boyfriend, mother, father, and Mary Tyler Moore, everyone was pushing me to have a great big remarkable life, just like a swinging single, but not really, because I had John waiting in the wings. Or perhaps it was I that was doing all the waiting.

Shortly after signing the one-year lease for my apartment, my mother and I drove to a local furniture store on Kingsway and Fraser called Wosk's. We decided on a sofa bed so my parents could sleep over occasionally (this justified them paying my rent) and a black-and-brown kitchen table and chair set, made from fake wood with black vinyl covering the chair seats. The silver legs on the table extended at just the right angle, which I found out later was perfect for banging toes on whenever I walked by.

Into the mix was a matching coffee table with elaborate carvings in fake wood, including an Italian motif carved into the little swinging door. Accompanying it were matching side tables of the same, two cream-coloured lamps and a brand-new television with its stand, all at my parents' expense.

I felt like a princess or a spoiled little rich girl, stylish and happy, with the utmost appreciation for everything my parents did for me. I was their youngest daughter, and my mother often joked that she was more of a grandmother to me than a mother because she had me so much later in life.

Around the same time as my move to Fraser Street and my job at the downtown Bank of Commerce, a place called Granville Island Market was in the developmental stages. It was located down by the water in between the Granville Street Bridge and the Cambie Street Bridge. John and I would occasionally ride our bikes through the construction zones to get a look at the new development and the remarkable setup.

It was fun and romantic as I trailed after John on my bicycle through the flag girls, jackhammers, cement trucks, and welders, him in the lead guiding my way.

John was fascinated with the development, growth, and changes to Vancouver, and I could listen to him for hours explaining the history of the city. I learned that Vancouver was initially called Granville until it was renamed Vancouver in 1886, while the former name was given to Granville Street, which spanned the small inlet known as False Creek.

The Granville Island Market was planning for fresh fruit and vegetable vendors, artisans and crafts, unique food, homemade pasta, butchers, fresh fish, and bakeries. In and around the shops were to be restaurants and a marketplace especially for children called The Kids Only Market.

Apartments, townhouses, and condominiums would be added, creating a community that was an appealing and unique place to live. On the water in a man-made inlet, with sailboats, seagulls, and the surrounding city, everything was designed to be aesthetically pleasing to all buyers, homeowners, and upwardly mobile people with a zest for life and success.

My mother and father suggested they purchase me a place to live at False Creek near the new Granville Island Farmers Market. Apartments and townhouses were pre-selling for sixty thousand dollars, and my parents thought of the potential purchase as an investment, in addition to a home for their youngest daughter.

Feeling like a burden to my parents, my response to their offer was, "No, it's okay. You have already done so much for me. I could not have you spend any more money on me than you already have, but thanks anyway."

Sarah and I often shared our hopes, dreams, and goals, just as best friends do. I was eighteen, and she was nineteen, and both of us wanted to travel before we got serious about furthering our education or working our way up the corporate ladder. Or better yet, becoming housewives and mothers. The question was, how could we make our dream a reality, and where would we go if we could?

Sarah suggested that if we saved our money, then quit our jobs, Palm Springs was a secure bet because Sarah's grandparents had a mobile home in a seniors' trailer park. All we would have to do is save enough money for living expenses since we could probably get free rent. I think it was my idea to quit our jobs, but regardless, we both dreamed of travel, primarily before we settled down.

Our discussion and plan evolved around us taking short trips here and there throughout California with our home base being the old folks' trailer park in Desert Hotsprings, just outside of Palm Springs.

Taking it one step further, we thought that we could get "under the table" jobs while there. Young people everywhere were doing it. It had become a common practice in the '60s and '70s for college students, hippies, and drifters to make money while being a non-resident in a different country. The idea was to do odd jobs and get paid in cash, with no "paper trail," the terminology one used when scamming the government.

We both put our nose to the grindstone to work and save money, and precisely a year later, we each managed to put away

$1,000. After handing in a two-week resignation, we quit our jobs. I had concluded that answering phones and filing would not a career make, and therefore my departure from banking would not be missed by the bank or me.

Leading up to my trip, John and I talked about my travel plans. He was supportive and encouraged me to go. He had some friends who had taken a year off after high school to travel before university to "find themselves," so we both thought that perhaps my need for travel and adventure was along the same lines.

John and I considered ourselves to be hip and modern, so we agreed that we would stay together as boyfriend and girlfriend and correspond through letter writing. However, we made the stipulation that if we were to meet anyone else, we could go on dates without any hanky-panky. It all sounded quite mature, light, and breezy, especially since I had just read in *Cosmopolitan* magazine about what an open relationship was, a popular term in 1979. We concluded that the only difference was that we would not, under any circumstance, put our car keys in a large bowl to go home with a different partner at the end of the evening.

Another aspect of going to California was the anticipation of the glorious sunshine. Therefore, our time away would be a time of beautification. We were planning to eat healthily, exercise a lot, shop for stylish fashions for our figure types, and get copper-brown cover girl suntans!

Weeks before leaving, my weight had crept up to an all-time high, not to mention that I was exhausted from my bank job. Unexpectedly promoted, my new position required me to do some calculations, which I referred to as number crunching. I could not quite get it. Therefore I was making some mathematical errors, causing me high stress and worry. I shared none of my angst with Sarah, John, or my parents.

Consequently, my complexion had gotten exceptionally bad from all the White Spot meals, and no amount of Clearasil could fix that. Late nights at the disco, drinking, and not sticking to a healthy face-cleansing regimen joined in as culprits. All my tried-and-true lessons from beauty school had somehow gone out of the window, and it was apparent that my lifestyle was taking a toll on my health.

At eighteen, I saw the contrast between my current life and my life of two years prior, when I was taking the bus to school, riding my horse, and being in bed by 10:00 p.m. I was burning the candle at both ends and needed to stop.

Sarah and I made lists, schemed, and planned our upcoming trip. We spent hours going over our schedule—tanning by the pool, swimming, bike riding, dieting, and finding any adventure we could. Subsequently, our zest for life was increasing with each new activity we added to our lists, an immediate cure to the doldrums we thought was due to our arduous and tedious jobs.

We handed in our resignations, bought plane tickets, packed, and made tearful yet secretly ecstatic goodbyes.

Dropped off at the airport by our boyfriends, we checked in and proceeded to our gate.

Filled with giggles and excitement, we made our way toward an older-looking uniformed official. A stout, no-nonsense man with a furrowed brow, downturned mouth and expressionless eyes, he reminded me of a badger, and not a happy one. His secure necktie forced his chin to spill out over the top of his white crisp shirt collar as his belly spilled out over his trousers, contained by a thin black leather belt.

Our first mistake was not getting our stories straight. As the temperature began to rise into our crimson faces, nerves started to get the better of us. We felt like we were under interrogation.

The customs agent spoke gruffly as he asked, "Where are you going, and what is the length of your stay?"

We answered in unison with different answers.

Sarah replied, "Palm Springs, and we will be staying three months."

I said, "Palm Springs, and we will be staying for two weeks."

Sarah appeared to be a tad more honest than me. She had a *Rebecca of Sunny Brook Farm* appeal, and I did not. Someone once told me that I reminded them of Demi Moore from the movie *Saint Elmo's Fire*. Even though Demi's character was a reckless partier, I took the comparison as the utmost compliment.

Perhaps the customs agent sensed our naivety and apprehension. Maybe our eyes blinked too much or didn't blink enough, or we were scratching or rubbing our skin, biting our lips, and stumbling over our words. There must have been signs. Airport officials always know how to spot suspicious, deviant behaviour.

While being scrutinized, we were causing a stir. We must have both looked dishonest, like a pair of criminals—perhaps the next Bonnie and Clyde, or Lizzy Borden and her sister. We could not be trusted, or so the US customs agents were beginning to make us believe.

Envisioning the headline in the *Vancouver Sun* newspaper—"Two Canadian Girls on the Lam to a Seniors' Trailer Park in Desert Hot Springs, California"—in seconds, our fear and imaginations had run wild; we wondered if our trip had come to a grinding halt. Or in the worst-case scenario, would we be taken off in handcuffs, never to embark on our well-planned vacation?

The customs officials went through our purses and confiscated Sarah's little Bayer Aspirin tin, questioning us to the point of tears. We missed our flight and from the nearest pay phone, called my parents.

Fortunately, my mom and dad were close friends with a man who was also a customs agent at the airport—another reminder that it's not what you know, but who you know. After a few calls, we were somehow cleared to catch another flight but had to pay an additional fifty dollars, which dropped our hard-earned living expenses money down to $950. Regardless, we were relieved and once again back on track, ready to take life by the coattails and hang on for dear life while anticipating three to six months of hot, sunny, adventurous fun, still unsure of exactly how long we would be staying.

Touching down on the black tarmac and first laying eyes on the desert, I was taken aback at how dry, brown, and dismal the terrain was. I then noticed the cherished local bird, the roadrunner, that colourful bird from the *Bugs Bunny/ Road Runner* cartoon I had grown up with on television. He always had bright blue tail feathers and a brilliant yellow beak with a perpetual mischievous grin. We enjoyed the speedy little bird's antics of outwitting the Wile E. Coyote. Here in Palm Springs, the real bird was dusty brown, plain and ordinary, and considerably smaller than the fictitious television personality viewers everywhere had come to love.

Even the cactus was unexpected, covered in desert dust, greenish-grey in colour and not the radiant, flourishing green shades as depicted in the magazines and postcards I had seen.

Once over the initial disappointment of my surroundings, the only thing that mattered was that we had arrived. "Let the festivities begin!" Sarah and I blurted out in unison. Our collective energy, with heightened senses and a loss of inhibitions, meant we were off to a great start. We carried with us not an ounce of fear but only high hopes.

Sarah's grandparents met us at the airport and were thrilled to see us. Sarah's granny was a fantastic cook and had prepared for us a down-home country meal. Everything was fresh and homemade. I liked her immediately. She was petite and wore her hair short and curly. When I first met her, she was wearing white sneakers and a cute yellow shorts ensemble, and she had the most adorable laugh. Sarah's grandpa was fit and played tennis daily.

He was comical, with a calm grandfatherly demeanour, and very interested in getting to know me.

They were both genuinely happy about our upcoming adventures, and both were young at heart.

All of my grandparents had died years prior, except for my mother's mother, who I was informed had lost her marbles long ago, which was another reason for me to embrace Sarah's grandparents.

Once settled, the first thing we noticed was that one hundred per cent of the trailer park residents were old—ancient but always busy, energetic, and kind. They liked to talk in hushed tones about other residents' soap opera lifestyle, but managed to sort out their differences during golf games or daily happy hour at the swimming pool. We learned that cocktails were an excellent remedy, if not a Band-Aid for anything that ailed you, and helped you besides.

Within three weeks, the grandparents would be finishing their winter stay in the desert and heading back to Canada for the summer. They referred to themselves as "Snow Birds," which I found out was a North American term for a person who migrates from the higher latitudes and colder climates of the Northern United States and Canada in winter to warmer locales of the south, such as Florida, California, Nevada, Arizona, or elsewhere along the sunbelt.

Their imminent departure meant that in three weeks, we would be on our own, with sixty senior citizens watching our every move. I had come to love Sarah's family, but we were undoubtedly counting the days and anticipating our freedom, especially getting underway with our plan and new health regime.

In no time flat, we became a novelty and the little darlings of the Desert Hot Springs Mobile Home Trailer Park. Knowing all eyes and ears were on us, we felt safe and did not mind the extra attention.

The seniors organized weekly poolside barbecues that we never missed. They rode their bicycles around and around, always available and ready to chat and schmooze at a moment's notice. Surprisingly, Sarah and I enjoyed every one of the aging retirees, even the nosy and bossy ones.

We eagerly implemented our daily health and beauty routine from our list:

- Early morning swim and water aerobics in the heated pool
- A small bowl of Special K cereal with skim milk for breakfast
- No lunch, instead, giant plastic jugs of water throughout the day
- Suntanning, hair treatments, bike riding, more swimming
- 3:00 p.m. Phil Donahue
- A small salad with diet salad dressing for dinner
- TREAT: a Tab diet soda with a lemon wedge

Daily episodes of *The Phil Donahue show* included one hour of leg raises and sit-ups, plus Phil's guests with their thoughts on current events, and dysfunctional lives, all wrapped up in a sixty-minute program, including commercials. Our many magazines kept us abreast of fashion trends, homespun beauty remedies, relationship advice, and how to be liberated women of the world both in and outside of the bedroom.

Our beauty regime was working, the pounds were melting away, and my curly permed hair was growing out. Our faces and bodies were becoming leaner and sun-drenched with each passing day. The acne on my T-zone had completely cleared up, and I could imagine how my boyfriend back home would love my transformation.

We would go to sleep with mayonnaise and plastic bags on our heads and then squeeze fresh lemons into our hair during the day. We ate salad after salad and often smelled like one from our nightly hair treatments.

On our bedside tables were running lists. Wish lists of what to shop for; clothing items that we could mix and match to wear back at home; clothes that were different and unique, preferably on sale as we never dared to pay full price. Sarah was the queen of keeping to a budget and shopping for the best deals. She taught me everything from how to find a bargain to getting a nasty stain out.

All in all, it was our time to shine, and I was aiming to follow John's instructions to go and have the time of my life.

Perhaps the upcoming events and what transpired were up for interpretation, but we found out how to take the city by storm and were proud of it.

Still, after two weeks of being on our own, diligently following our regime, we started to become restless and ready for some action. Having been to Palm Canyon Drive scouting out stores and deals, we also kept in mind where the local nightclubs and hot spots were.

Considerably moderate old-fashioned girls, but not quite as straight-laced and proper as our trailer park elderly counterparts assumed, we did not hesitate to try our luck at getting into our first disco.

We discovered that in 1979, the drinking age of twenty-one was not closely monitored and that two fresh-faced Canadian girls could cause quite a stir in this swanky upscale town.

After entering the nightclub on our first attempt, we cruised through unnoticed. Feeling empowered, we gave each other a half shrug and a knowing glance. Surprised but not showing it, we were thrilled to have gotten in past the tinted glass doors with just a coy smile directed toward the bouncers.

In very little time, we were hobnobbing with the wealthy and elite, getting to see firsthand their excessive and extravagant way of life long before the hit TV show *Lifestyles of the Rich and Famous* with Robin Leach made its debut in 1984.

The disco ball lit up the room with its small tiles of mirrored glass, an array of faces scanned the crowd looking for their next partner, and the dance floor wooed us to its mecca of pounding disco beats. We marvelled at the couples in their matching shiny gold lamé jumpsuits. Clad head to toe in designer fashions, jewellery of every description adorned necks, wrists, and fingers. Earrings dangled, and bracelets jangled. Baubles and gemstones shone and sparkled as strobe lights pulsed.

Sarah and I had carefully and strategically put together our outfits: high-waisted jeans and platform shoes were a must. Sarah matched her pants with a light pink, fluffy angora sweater and three or four gold chain necklaces. My jeans were paired with a white-and-red striped fitted T-shirt with dangly feather earrings.

Without hesitation, we mingled and worked the room. Men of every description were unfailingly at our beck and call, buying us drinks and asking us to dance. We could not help but soak up the attention. Even though we had no intention of jumping into bed with every Tom, Dick, or Harry, our Canadian accents and seemingly innocent nature only made us more intriguing.

Added to our daily schedule

· After dinner get ready for the disco

We soon learned that the place to be was a hot spot called the PS Connection on Palm Canyon Drive. It was there that we caught the eye of a tall, relaxed surfer dude. His long blond hair was perfectly coiffed, and his loose white dress shirt, baggy white trousers, and bare feet in sandals was as Californian as they come. A puka shell necklace and tanned skin magnified his pearly white smile, completing his most attractive look.

When his eyes met Sarah's, he nonchalantly strolled over to us and casually ordered us some rum and Cokes with a squeeze of lime, which we found out was called a Cuba Libre. He introduced himself as Michael and asked us a few questions about ourselves as we chatted lightly. We were fascinated by how smooth he was. He had an air of confidence that was mesmerizing and yet evoked a hint of danger.

As a result of having so much fun dancing at the club and meeting Michael, we had no reason to do anything else. Our exercise-filled days turned into our disco-infused nights. Doing "The Hustle" never felt so good. Besides, when we were with Michael, they rolled out the red carpet, which meant doormen, waitresses, and bartenders catered to our every whim.

Michael was rapidly becoming our best friend, tour guide, bodyguard, and chauffeur. We felt popular and invincible.

One afternoon, Michael asked Sarah and me if we would like to take a road trip to Orange County to attend a motocross competition with his friend Tim. We gladly accepted. What took place next not only opened our eyes to what Michael was all about, but our rose-coloured glasses momentarily became crystal clear, giving us a glimpse into Michael's world that revealed his true colours.

Piling into his black Mercedes, Sarah sat in the front seat next to Michael while I was in the back seat with Tim.

Tim was not as outwardly confident as Michael, but carried himself sweetly with his short, dark, slicked-back hair and clean-shaven looks. Somewhat of a uniform, he wore a button-up dress shirt tucked neatly into his blue jeans, Calvin Klein belt, and white Adidas running shoes—real "take home to meet the parents" sort of guy.

Happy to be doing something different, we enjoyed the scenery of the two-hour drive to Orange County from Desert Hot Springs, stopping for Mexican food along the way, with Michael picking up the tab, as he always did.

When we arrived at the outdoor arena and got out of the car, I noticed that Tim had gone into the trunk to grab a locked briefcase. I naively thought it was a backgammon game. Not realizing that I was standing behind him, Tim could not see that I was in a clear view of his case. Inside, displayed in neat sectioned off rows, were various coloured pills, small baggies, and perfectly rolled little joints. I could not help but think about how tidy and organized everything looked. I glanced over to Sarah, but she had already walked ahead. Freezing in mid-movement with my mouth agape, I was not sure what to do next. Tim slammed down the trunk of the car, and with the briefcase in hand, contraband and all, his smile broadened when he caught sight of me. Winking, he said, "Come on, let's catch up to the others."

Concluding that Tim did not know that I knew, and right there in the Orange County Motocross parking lot, I realized that Michael and Tim were drug dealers.

We never participated, bought, or sold anything that Michael peddled, and we figured that was why he liked us so much. We were not a threat or after him for his money, notoriety, or his drugs. Call us careless, ignorant, or foolish girls, either way, we never gave Michael's lifestyle much thought after that. We kept our noses clean and continued to reap the benefits of Michael's stature at the clubs and his kindness toward us.

Sarah and I continued to be regulars at the PS Connection. The bouncers knew our names or just referred to us as "The Canadian Girls." With or without Michael's arms linked in ours, everyone treated us like queens.

Another watering hole a few blocks down the street from the PS Connection was a place called Zelda's. The patronage was a slightly older crowd, and the facility was exceptionally classier than anywhere else we had ever been. The winding staircase ascended from the street sidewalk to tinted black double doors at the top, with a few pink neon lights along the hand railing to guide the way.

Once inside, the dance floor looked like glass, luminous, and incandescent. There were two bars, one at each end of the room, and several side doors that high-rolling dudes and classy ladies entered and exited from, noticeably at a rapid pace—places which Sarah and I stayed clear of.

We were becoming more and more comfortable with our nightly routine and the alcohol that accompanied it.

A popular drink was called a Kamikaze, with 1 oz. of Triple Sec, 1 oz. of lime juice, and 1 oz. of vodka served in a shot glass, meant to go down the hatch the second the server brought it to the table. One or two shots later, and there was no turning back. As others guzzled their Kamikaze with heads tilted back, I would discreetly pour my drink in a nearby potted plant or ashtray. I delighted myself with what a good actress I had become, smacking my lips and clearing my throat. I pretended that it had burned my throat all the way going down, and my companions were none the wiser. This trick kept me sober and more clear-headed than those around me. The taste was like kerosene, so I concluded that I was not missing out in the least.

Sarah and I never got tired. After exercising and lounging about all day, we were always willing to go out, stay up late, and party the night away. The best part of the evening was getting ready and the anticipation of the night ahead. With the radio blaring, the prelude to an evening out was almost as fun as the actual event.

My *Charlie's Angels* black spandex pants, red cowboy boots, and silky shirt with a map of Texas emblazoned on it was a treasured purchase made on one of our many shopping expeditions. A white denim jumpsuit with a gold zipper, cinched in waist, and white platform sandals made me feel like a star. Adding in a side ponytail, caked-on mascara, and hot pink lip gloss made me feel like a million bucks.

With the toot of a horn, we would be out the door to catch our ride in seconds.

I was often a sucker for a cute, charismatic guy that would show me an ounce of attention, which came to be my only explanation as to why I was infatuated with Tyler, the disc jockey at the PS Connection.

Looking larger than life sitting high atop the dance floor in his DJ box, he played records while performing a laser show in time to the disco beat. Not a laser show from the new movie *Star Wars*, but almost as impressive. Tyler would wave his lightsabre up and around his head in perfect swashbuckling fashion as he swayed his hips and made eye contact with various young women on the dance floor. There was always a group of females swarming around his booth, and I was one of them. Tyler drove a Porsche and looked like Luke Skywalker.

After the last call one night, Tyler invited me up to the confines of his DJ digs to sit alongside him. Flattered and feeling celebrated to have been one of the chosen few, I climbed the wobbly staircase and opened the gate that allowed access to the star of the show and the music we all loved. Climbing up on a stool next to Tyler, he let me flick the switch and put the arm down on Donna Summer's classic hit song, "Last Dance."

As I perched, swooning, I decided to play my "I'm from Canada" card, which was always a hit, and sure enough, Tyler took a deeper notice of me. Our idle chit-chat brought us to the end of the song, and as the bright lights came screaming on, Tyler offered to drive me home to the trailer park. Quickly calculating my safety, I figured it would be fine to accept a ride from the in-demand stud as I had two things in my favour. Michael, who had become our protector/big brother, was a safeguard, and the other known fact was that Tyler had to work the next night. Concluding that nothing could go wrong, and without giving it another thought, my inner lofty eighteen-year-old brain and outside voice both said, "Yes, I would love a ride home."

Stepping down from disc jockey heaven, I was taken aback at how, once standing next to Tyler, my five-foot six-inch frame towered over him. I estimated that he was barely five feet, if not four feet eleven inches tall, when only moments before he seemed six foot two or taller up in his tower of power cubicle. Slightly disappointed with my new findings, but deciding a crush was still a crush in my books, we proceeded out to his reserved parking spot. On our way past Michael, who was seated with Sarah and his entourage, he gave Tyler a knowing stare as if to say, "Watch it, buddy," and off we went, climbing into the compact seats of his Porsche.

I was amazed at how the seat cradled and encompassed my entire body and just how low to the ground I was sitting, practically on the road—a very heady experience, to say the least. Instantaneously, the dashboard lit up, Tyler hit the gas pedal, and we were off. "I Was Made for Lovin' You" by Kiss boomed from the stereo, and speeding down Palm Canyon Drive, Tyler hollered above Gene Simmons, "I just need to stop in at my place to change my shirt," to which I naively responded, "Sure, okay."

Once inside his one-room rancher apartment, he went into the bathroom and suggested I sit down on the bed. Still unaware of any possible advances, I was shocked and dismayed when Tyler came strutting out of the bathroom in his red bikini-style underwear. Feeling sick to my stomach while immediately judging him on his taste in briefs, I abruptly stood up and said, "Please take me home." Ignoring my request, Tyler shrugged, let out a sigh of annoyance, and proceeded to climb into his bed, pulling the covers up and over his head to fall asleep, I assumed.

Being bold was not one of my strong points, but by no means did I want to sleep on a chair in this little big man's bachelor pad. I approached his bed, flung off his covers, and demanded that he drive me home this instant, stating that boys back home in Canada would never treat a lady like this. At first, he was startled by my request and then, begrudgingly, he slowly stood up and threw on his pants.

Still shirtless, he went outside with me sheepishly trailing behind him. Getting into his luxurious car to make the fifteen-minute drive, the shifting of gears became awkwardly noticeable with the absence of rocking tunes as he chose not to turn on his tape deck this time.

Sarah and I only laughed at the whole debacle or misunderstanding, depending on how you looked at it, and from then on, I could never again look the popular disc jockey in the eye. We still frequented the nightclub but pretended that nothing had ever happened.

Aside from getting in over my head with Tyler, another boy that caught my eye was the nightclub's valet service attendant. He was tall and tanned, with blond curly hair, resembling the movie actor Christopher Atkins. David K. Allen was younger than me, but after talking further, we found out that our birthdays were on the same day. I thought that this coincidence was a good omen, thinking he might be the soul mate that I had been looking for all along.

Never once forgetting about John back at home, I was, however, young and starved for attention and perpetually testing the waters. Besides, John and I had agreed to assess everything about our relationship when I got home. Recalling our agreement always made me feel better when I occasionally glanced in the other direction.

Unfortunately, David became far more enamoured with me than I was of him.

We went on a few hikes together, but my thoughts kept going back to John. I was also a little unnerved when David shared with me about the many older gay men who were pursuing him and bestowing him with beautiful gifts in hopes that he would become their own "personal" driver, so to speak. David had confided that he did not have a father; he lived with his single mother, and he liked the attention and gifts from the older men, and in no uncertain terms was that going to change.

Sarah, too, was having her coming-of-age moments, venturing out without me, and hanging out more with Michael. It was at his mother's house that she discovered an unlikely occurrence. Sarah had been invited for dinner, thinking it was a family dinner and a tame event; she was therefore bewildered to find that in the bathroom of the Palm Springs mansion was a fish bowl–sized candy dish. When she investigated a little further, instead of sweet treats, there was a multitude of different coloured pills. How odd this seemed and quite a contrast to the bathrooms we had grown up with, containing Avon soaps and Calgon bath beads.

Our innocence was a mixed blessing. There was a lot that we did not see out of pure ignorance, and probably a lot we chose not to see because of our goody-two-shoes mentality.

Sarah was a hardworking and very giving person, extremely dependable, and always keeping herself busy. I, on the other hand, was a people-pleaser and enjoyed languishing about, working on my constant beauty regime and exercise applications, perhaps not as keen on getting an under-the-table job like we had spoken about before our trip began.

Sarah managed to obtain a nanny job, which made sense, as she had babysat back in Stave Falls and cooked nightly dinners for her family. Her new job proved to be a perfect fit. The family that hired her soon adored her.

With Sarah working, I found that I had more time on my hands, so independently, I decided that a shopping day by myself would kill some time and be great for me to do something on my own.

I often followed along with Sarah's trustworthy capabilities of masterminding bus routes and schedule times. Deciding to throw all caution to the wind, with shopping on my mind, I walked out the sliding glass door of our trailer one mid-morning to wait for a bus. Coincidently, one arrived within minutes, so I was quite proud of myself that without any prior research, I was now on a bus relaxing in the comforts of air conditioning and a fifteen-minute ride to my destination.

I told myself that after shopping, my reward would be a diet Tab soda pop with a lemon wedge.

Hours later, with some well sought-out purchases in hand, I sauntered down Palm Canyon Drive with an assortment of decorative bags containing my precious items. Calling it a day, I decided to make my way back to Desert Hot Springs. I was looking forward to getting home, showing Sarah all my bargains, and sharing our usual low-calorie salad.

Making my way to the bus stop, I noticed that it had become increasingly hotter, perhaps more noticeable after frigid, air-conditioned stores.

Thankfully, the bus shelter kept the direct sun off my skin, and since I had worn a cute sundress with spaghetti straps and a fitted waistline, I was grateful to be protected from the scorching rays. Even though sun tanning was the main priority for Sarah and me, there was a limit. One-hundred-and-ten degree weather was insufferable, oppressive, and merely unacceptable even to our standards. I had always been prone to sunstroke and heat exhaustion, which, just thinking about, brought forth anxiety.

After thirty minutes of waiting, I was beginning to worry. An hour of waiting, and I was irritable. I wondered if I was standing in the right spot and questioned myself if a bus was coming. Coupled with my anxiety over the heat, I was starting to panic. So, when a pickup truck pulled up, driven by an older man who offered me a ride, I was relieved and happy to accept his kind gesture. After hopping into the vehicle, something did not feel right, and an instant foreboding came over me.

The driver asked me where I was going, and I told him Desert Hot Springs. I could hear the sound of my faint voice coming out of my mouth, not as strong and confident as I had hoped. Sitting as close to my side of the cab as possible, I gripped the door handle and started to plan my escape. My gut instincts told me that I was not reading into things or over-analyzing. I strained a fake smile and decided to put up a false front.

Words of wisdom from my father came back to me, his voice speaking in my mind loud and clear, "No matter where you are, or what you are doing, always look for the exit signs so you can plan your escape." He meant this for every situation, mostly about buildings, stores, hotels, offices, or schools, and this time, it rang true for a truck with a creepy driver.

Throughout the drive, I glanced over at him periodically and noticed his faded baseball cap, clean-shaven face, and thought that he was not bad looking for a forty-something-year-old man. But it was what he said next that made my skin crawl, and even though it was poor judgment on my part to get into the truck, I had enough street smarts telling me that it was time to get out.

Looking over at me, he said, "You are such a pretty girl, prettier if you smiled more, but your dress sure is sexy. I have some film equipment in the back of my truck, and I would like to do a photoshoot with you."

I don't know if it was repeated episodes of *Perry Mason*, *Sixty Minutes*, or *The Phil Donahue show* whispering in my ear that helped me. I proceeded to create a story that would let the would-be rapist know that people were waiting for me, and I was not falling for his lame, possibly deadly offer.

I calmly told the best lie that I could come up with, stating, "No, thank you, I really do not have any time at all. I am visiting here from Canada, and my mother, a newspaper reporter, and my father, a policeman, are waiting for me back at the trailer park, and I am already late. If you could please let me out here that would be great, so pull over right now, here, please."

He told me that he loved Canada and Canadians, and he would be happy to drive me right into the park and to my doorstep. I said, "No, thank you, you can let me out right here on the side of the road," knowing full well that I had eluded him, and we had not arrived at my destination, as I was still at least a mile from where I was staying. The sound of gravel crunching, and the sight of halted landscape, indicated to my senses that it was time to flee. I flung open the door and ran across the highway to the unknown trailer park. Finding some shade to regain my thoughts and composure, I waited until I was sure he had sped off.

My next strategy would be to walk through trailer park after trailer park until I was safely at Sarah's grandparents' mobile home. Many of the trailer parks were close to each other, but some were not due to fencing and gates, so at times during my one-mile trek, I had to run along the road, feeling exposed and anxious until I could cut into the next gated residence. My gaze flitted out to the highway and then quickly back to where I needed to run, while every passing vehicle felt like the man in the truck was there stalking me. I knew that what I had done was foolish, and I concluded that I would never speak of it to anyone, especially Sarah, my parents, or John.

CHAPTER 4

"Keep It Comin' Love"

1979–1983

NEARING THE END OF OUR STAY IN PALM SPRINGS, SARAH AND I were hungry for many things, food first and foremost, but also getting back to reality. We had dieted, danced, swam, shopped, and tanned to our hearts' content. We were now both three sizes smaller and running out of money. We had done what we set out to do and managed to see the sights, spending time at Newport beach, Venus Beach, Santa Monica, LA, Disneyland, San Diego, Sea World, and local areas such as Joshua Tree and Shields where the date palms grow. Plus, we needed to start thinking about our futures.

Back home, John's friends were planning a surprise birthday party to celebrate John turning nineteen, a monumental time in a young person's life in British Columbia and other parts of Canada. Because when one turned nineteen, it marked adulthood. It also meant you became of legal drinking age. With all the underage drinking we had done, it would be nice to finally not be breaking the law anymore.

I was planning to return home anyway, but when a letter came in the mail from a few of John's buddies asking me if I could be a part of John's birthday party surprise, I was flattered and excited at the thought of reuniting with my boyfriend. It was also giving me a reason to leave Palm Springs: a purpose, and a pressing engagement that would join me with my one true love. At this point, all the boys and men I had met could not hold a candle to John.

Sarah and I took extra care in getting ready for our trip home as if we were presenting ourselves as new and improved versions of who we used to be. It was a beauty makeover debut, and we were intent on making a splash as young women ready to face their futures head-on.

On the day we were scheduled to leave, Michael picked us up in a white stretch limousine to take us to the airport. Using our Kodak cameras, we took lots of photos posing in and around the expansive car. David also met us at the airport in a brand-new pickup truck that one of his older male friends had bought him.

Saying goodbye to Palm Springs was different than saying hello. I had grown to love the scenery that I had once considered bland and boring. We had spent so much time enjoying the nightlife that the purple and blue hues of the mountains against the cobalt night sky became our usual backdrop, enhanced by the far-reaching galaxy of stars.

Memories of our trip to Joshua Tree National Park and the massive cactus and immense boulders, mixed with dusty beige sand, were embedded in my mind just like that of the dry heat of the sun. A warmth that once felt stifling now offered a sense of healing that sank deep into my bones, piercing my heart along the way, encouraging me to fall in love with what now felt like my second home.

Saying goodbye and leaving behind the carefree nights of disco dancing with my dearest friend Sarah and the relationships with the American young men that were not meant to go any further would now become cherished memories. We thought, "Look out, Vancouver, here we come!"

Touching down on the runway in Richmond, it felt strange getting off the plane with no boyfriend's arms to run into; although I knew that soon I would be seeing John, it would just not be on this day. As part of the surprise for John's 19th birthday, the plan was that his best friend would pick me up at the airport, unbeknownst to John, and drive me to my apartment. The next day was John's birthday, and then the surprise of my homecoming would be revealed.

I was picked up by John's best friend Cal, the same height as me, of Asian descent, but born in Vancouver. We hugged and laughed at the absurdity of him picking me up and not John. John and Cal were lifelong best friends. He was cute and funny, an impeccable dresser, and laughed at everything I said, which was not much because most of the events from my trip would remain a secret. However, I was thankful to be back with good old-fashioned Canadians and excited to start fresh.

Throughout the twenty-minute drive from the airport to my apartment, it felt like a million years since I had been on Canadian soil. I was feeling exhausted and hungry from months of food deprivation, but once my head hit my familiar pillow, I was out like a light.

The arrangement was for me to drive to the Plaza 500 Hotel on 12th Avenue and Cambie Street in Vancouver to meet up with the guys at 4:00 p.m. on the day of John's 19th birthday. John's friends had rented a room for pre-party drinks and for John and me to stay in after the birthday celebration in the hotel restaurant had ended. Meanwhile, John was expecting a bros-only dinner and was not aware of my arrival home and that I would be his special birthday present. After the celebratory drinks and meal, the plan was for me to make my entrance into the dining room while bringing in the birthday cake. A phone call to the room would be my cue to come downstairs.

I drove over to the hotel at 3:30 p.m. to meet the guys. They all greeted me with open arms, everyone talking at once, offering suggestions to ensure the event was successful and ran smoothly. We were planning and obsessing over every detail. Hurrying to the elevator and up to the previously booked room, it was like we were rushing to make things happen more quickly.

There were cold beers, or as John's friends called them, "brewskies," on ice in the mini-fridge. We toasted my arrival, the plan, John, friendship, and any other topic and reason to clink our bottles. There was all-around enjoyment of collective energy. Eventually, they all left. One of the guys left to go pick up John, and the others left to wait downstairs in the restaurant for the festivities to begin.

Once alone in the room, my heart raced as I paced back and forth, checking and rechecking my hair and makeup in the mirror. I could hardly contain myself, realizing that I was one hundred per cent ready to settle down and create a life with John in the city I had missed and almost forgotten. Abruptly, I had the realization that it was almost our first anniversary of having met at the Bootlegger warehouse sale the previous summer.

Finally, enough time had passed, and the shrilling telephone signalled me to go downstairs, snapping all thoughts of wedded bliss temporarily to the back of my mind. The elevator took an eternity, and when the doors finally opened, I hurriedly made my way to the restaurant kitchen. The staff gathered to light the candles while thrusting a birthday cake at me for my presentation to the birthday boy. With shaking hands, and as the boys chortled out their rendition of "Happy Birthday," I came nervously into the room.

Photos were snapped, capturing the surprised and elated John. We embraced and laughed while the whole dining room of strangers cheered and clapped. Then it was up to the hotel room for our long-awaited reunion. We were both happy and in love.

What came next was a romantic first few days, getting to know each other again and living in the moment. It was summer, so we rode our bikes touring the city, eating at new trendy bistros, walking and talking, combing the many Vancouver beaches, and thoroughly enjoying each other's company. Nothing was mentioned of my brief—insufficient to the moment—dalliances and near-death experiences while travelling. And nothing was said of John and me settling down together as husband and wife. Within months I would be turning nineteen.

Perpetually in a state of wonderment as to what my future held, longing for a wedding ring, I would keep my dreams and fantasies to myself for a while longer.

Come Monday morning, after a busy weekend reuniting with John, he went back to his summer job, and I needed to find one.

It was only the end of June, so we had the whole summer ahead of us to work and play. John still had three more years of intense schooling, which meant I had three more years of hoping and praying that we would be getting engaged during that time.

I had enough money to carry me through for a few weeks, but I started to make lists and assess what I wanted to do for a career. Trying to help and offer some guidance, John found a job in the want ads of *The Province* newspaper, cut it out, and brought it over to my place.

Exercise classes, known as Aerobics, were popping up at various gymnasiums and community centres in Vancouver and all over North America. So this particular add caught John's attention:

European Health Spa
Full and part-time positions available
Duties to include spa tours, program set-up, sales, and more.
No experience necessary.

Start your career today!

My first response was, "No way could I do that job! I'm not fit, athletic, or a jock in any way, shape, or form!"

"You've been taking classes at Bogie's Fitness on Burrard Street!" John responded. A fitness expert named David Bogoch taught exercise classes that I attended before and after my trip.

"You took Jazzercize classes in Palm Springs. You like dancing, swimming, bike riding, ice skating, and horseback riding. You're friendly and have a great sense of humour. I think you would be perfect for the job, and I think that you should apply." John was adamant that I could do this.

John's advice, words of wisdom, and encouragement were convincing and made me feel worthy and confident. His kindness and sincerity touched me, and without a rebuttal, I smiled and said, "Okay, I will give it a try."

If not for the indication of "No experience necessary," I never would have applied.

Throughout elementary and high school, I was the girl in gym class who was picked last for teams. If the ball came in my direction, I jumped out of the way. I still shuddered with the memory of the volleyball smacking down on the floor as I recoiled or stood there doing nothing, while disgruntled remarks rang in my ears, "You could have got that one!" or "At least make some effort to hit it back!" I recalled standing in the outfield playing softball, uttering my silent prayers, pleading with the universe not to let the ball appear in my direction. I could still imagine myself fumbling it and unable to throw it back. Flashbacks of running to the opposing team's goal in grass hockey always brought a rush of heat and crimson red to my face.

Fear was at the forefront and lack of skill the guilty party.

With my dreams of becoming an airline stewardess and then a top runway model having been dashed, I supposed a fitness instructor could be considered the next best thing. I would try again to step outside my comfort zone.

Off I went to the European Health Spa at West Broadway and Balsam in Vancouver. It was an open call-out for weight room attendants, and no set interview times or appointments were necessary. The applicants were mostly young men, significant bodybuilder types, all wanting a career in fitness, milling about in the entranceway of the spa.

Arriving and joining the other applicants, we sat or stood wedged together, waiting for our turn, all with grand hopes of being hired. One by one, each candidate was beckoned into an office, and one by one, they left, some seemingly happy while others were downtrodden, slamming the big glass door behind them on their way out.

As I nervously waited, I was taken down a peg at the thought of the massive cold sore on my mouth that had raised its ugly self overnight. Waking up that morning and seeing the giant blister on my lip (an affliction that I had been plagued with most of my life, seeming to appear at the most inconvenient times), I almost chickened out of the interview entirely. With negative thought patterns, nausea, fluttering in my stomach, and not wanting to disappoint John, I nevertheless pushed forward and continued to wait.

When it was finally my turn, I entered the small office to see a cute, petite, and very fit woman, not much older than myself, sitting behind a desk. What struck my attention was an opal gemstone pierced into her long claw-like pinky fingernail. Just when I was deciding if I liked it or not, she looked up from a stack of resumes, and there on her lip was a giant cold sore, identical to mine. We both laughed at the sight of each other and then exchanged our cold sore remedies and cures. I was hired right there on the spot.

The European Health Spa had been around for years and already had a lot of members. Men and women did not attend on the same days, which was considered taboo and inappropriate.

The facility had an Ancient Rome appeal with white statues and gold-leafed wallpaper, white columns, and a swirling hot tub with floor-to-ceiling blue tiles, so one felt like they were in a Roman bathhouse.

Celebrating the news of my hiring with John, we decided on a supper picnic at Jericho Beach, so we picked up sesame-baked chicken and pecan squares at the Lazy Gourmet on 4th Avenue. John brought the wine. He was happy for me; I was ecstatic.

During my first training session, a list of my attire and duties were as follows: I needed to purchase black tights, a black leotard, and a pair of black high heels for my uniform. My duties were to include greeting new members, taking their measurements, and setting them up on an exercise program.

The equipment was free weights and universal gym machines: Lat pull-down, bench press, pec deck, leg curl, and leg extension made up the apparatus, and it was my job to demonstrate and then watch my client execute three sets of ten.

Some machines did the work for you, old pieces of equipment that were operated by a simple on/off switch.

1) A person would lie down on a vinyl-covered bench, and after flicking a switch, the bottom part of the machine would lift up and around to swivel one's legs and hips in a circular motion, assuming that this would whittle away and redefine one's waistline.

2) Next was a lower-to-the-ground set of rolling pins (like my mother used to roll out dough) that were joined together and rotated perpendicularly. The user would turn the switch on and sit on the moving wooden rollers. The purpose of this exercise machine was to remove fat from the derrière, pounding it right off, taking cellulite and fat cells right along with it.

3) The most popular station was a device that wrapped a thick belt around the waist or hips attached to a machine. Once turned on, a belt would jiggle the entire body in hopes that in the process, the excess weight would fall right off the limbs. It was not recommended for use after a meal.

In addition to setting clients up on exercise programs, I would also be responsible for taking prospective members on a tour of the facility. I would then pass the prospective member off to a sales representative. When not showing people around and guiding them through routines, we were to polish the mirrors, the equipment, and anything else that required cleaning.

Before the early 1980s and, unfortunately, onward, high-pressure sales were the only way to seal a deal, this being what many fitness facilities demanded of their staff. The salespeople encouraged possible clients not to leave without signing a contract. There were scripts in place for us as employees for various excuses that potential patrons might use.

To the phrase, "Let me think about it," the comeback from sales staff was, "The deal ends at midnight." If they needed to speak to their husbands first, they were questioned, "Don't you think it's time that you decided for yourself?" If the buyer seemed nervous or anxious, it was remarked, "You lack self-confidence; exercise improves self-esteem and self-confidence." If it was affordability that was getting in the way, the response was to be, "The monthly fee breaks down to only X amount of dollars a day," "You cannot put a price tag on your health," and so on . . . There was an answer to everything.

The day following my orientation and training, I purchased my black leotard and wore my own Palm Springs black high-heeled dancing shoes.

I enjoyed my first two days of work just fine, but on my third day, I was informed that I would be teaching the next day's aerobics class. I felt panicked and unsure of how I was going to pull off an exercise class that I had no experience in teaching.

As I pondered my dilemma, out of the sales office bounded a tall brunette girl, about my age and dressed as I was in a black leotard and heels with a badge that read: Dawna – Head Girl. Her bouncy shoulder-length permed hair set off her dynamic personality. I was captivated by her enthusiastic voice and was all ears as she began to explain how easy it would be for me to teach a thirty-minute aerobics class.

"All you need to do is push some of the equipment out of the way, kick off your high heels, and pop in a Rod Stewart tape. Then jump around on the floor, instructing the ladies to hop, bounce, twist, and gyrate. They will copy everything that you do. After ten to fifteen minutes, tell everyone to get down on their hands and knees in the fire hydrant position (which was a simple leg movement of raising the knee up and out to the side like a dog peeing on a fire hydrant). Repeat these until you feel the muscle burn." Dawna finished up by stating, "Don't worry, you'll be fine. I'll be right here standing next to the stereo to help you if you need it, but you won't."

I was familiar with all of Dawna's suggestions because of the exercise routines I had created while reading *Cosmopolitan*, *Seventeen*, and *Glamour* magazine, which were all in on the fitness trend, and in conjunction, the mantra "Feel the Burn" by Jane Fonda was sweeping the nation. Besides, I had already been a participant in classes by David Bogoch, owner of Bogie's Fitness at a gym on 16th and Burrard Street.

From that moment on, Dawna and I would become lifelong friends. Her confidence and take-charge style were mesmerizing, combined with a relaxed, encouraging way of speaking, as if she knew that I would be great, as if there was no doubt in her mind that I could pull it off.

The next day, I went out and got a matching perm to Dawna's, and the following day I taught my first aerobics class without a hitch. Her help of pressing play on the tape deck and flipping the tape over when needed was gratefully appreciated.

Later I found out that she had an identical matching car to mine that her parents had also paid for, which meant that we had a lot in common. Within weeks I gave my notice at my apartment, and Dawna and I moved in together to a beautiful townhouse in North Vancouver—roommates and colleagues, working together and playing together.

Thus began a whirlwind friendship of impulsiveness and running headlong into what would become memorable and life-changing experiences.

As I continued to twirl around the dance floor with strangers and my new friend and roommate, Dawna, my mind, heart, soul, and body belonged to John. I guessed that if John knew how insecure I was about our relationship, he would have broken up with me long before we were to get hot and heavy and deeply in love. He had no way of knowing that my heart ached for his attention and presence in my life 24/7.

Terrible feelings of jealousy began to creep into my thoughts. *Cosmopolitan* magazine had an article stating that therapists often regard the demon of jealousy as a scar of childhood trauma or a symptom of a psychological problem.

The write-up made me ponder its content and my mental state as I silently lost myself in perpetual thoughts of John, while he was oblivious to the so-called demon that plagued me, busy with his academics, volunteer work, and a tight-knit boys' club of friends, long-lasting relationships that had been gathered and maintained long before our serendipitous meeting at the Bootlegger store in Gastown.

In the mix with John's buddies was one female friend whom he always reassured me was just like "one of the guys, a mate, a chum, and a peer." Her name was Robbie, and she was petite and much prettier than I was, or so I thought. The fashion magazines would call her a "natural beauty," which meant no makeup required; unlike me and my numerous applications of hot pink lipstick, continuous strokes of the mascara wand, and sparkly mauve eyeshadow.

Robbie could also drink most guys under the table, had a raspy voice, and looked adorable in her faded boot-cut jeans and scuffed-up cowboy boots. She preferred rock and roll to disco, so in other words, every girlfriend's worst nightmare.

Robbie accompanied the guys on a bar-hopping trip to New York City, which had been a pre-planned vacation way before I was in the picture. Reservations had been made, tickets were bought, and long story short, off they went without me, an outsider and not part of the gang.

Another occurrence for blood-curdling jealousy on my part was when John and his crew, including Robbie, went to see Bruce Springsteen at the Vancouver Coliseum at the PNE. In pure insecure girlfriend envy, I singly drove my car to the parking lot just outside of the Coliseum on the night of the show. With the windows rolled down, I could hear the deep-felt melodies and sexy crooning of the Boss as it seeped out of the stadium, knowing that John, Robbie, and his lifelong friends were inside gathering yet more memories of togetherness.

Even though, after the concert, John played for me his number one song, "Thunder Road," I never spoke to John about my overly dramatic venture of sitting outside the show that night. I never addressed my torment of being left out of his activities. I wanted him to believe that I was a girlfriend beyond compare: carefree, independent, and easygoing without a jealous bone in my body. His constant urging for me to have lots of friends and activities only magnified my hidden insecurities and longing to be the love of his life. I was slowly but surely becoming obsessed and losing a sense of myself.

Periodically, I had a small voice in my head that said, "Don't let fear or insecurity stop you from trying new things. Believe in yourself." I concluded that it was Susan, my Modelling Level I instructor.

The "fitness craze" was at first thought to be a fad, and skeptics everywhere said, "This new fitness trend will never last." The negative buzz often surprised me because, to me, aerobics classes were liberating, and finally, I had found a form of exercise that I could do. I revelled in the fact that there was no team depending on me to perform, no competition, and as the instructor, I could be creative and entertaining. All in all, fitness became therapeutic for me and a healthier alternative than starving myself to slim down. I thoroughly believed the new trend of aerobics classes was here to stay.

The method of group exercise classes began taking shape in 1968, Kenneth H. Cooper, an exercise physiologist and Col. Pauline Potts, a physical therapist, both United States Air Force, developed a term and a method of exercise called Aerobics. In 1968, they published a book titled *Aerobics*, which included running, walking, swimming, and bicycling. When the book was published, there had been a need for increased exercise due to widespread weakness and inactivity. In 1979, a mass-market version was released.

At the same time was the release of American actress Jane Fonda's records in the late '70s and her VHS videos in the '80s. Aerobics quickly gained worldwide popularity. Her workout book and exercise records that came with posters depicting various positions and movements were a sensation, and if one had a VCR, then they were able to stay fit in the comforts of their own home. She became famous for her high-intensity aerobics, leotards, and leg warmers. Having impeccable posture, svelte legs, strong arms, and beauty all rolled into one, Jane Fonda became a mentor to young women all over North America as the most excellent fitness guru that ever was.

Milton Teagle "Richard" Simmons, an American fitness instructor, actor, and video producer, became prominent in the '70s, '80s, and '90s. Richard Simmons promoted weight-loss programs, through his *Sweatin' to the Oldies* line of aerobic videos. He was known for his curly perm, red striped shorts, and eccentric, colourful, energetic personality. Friendly to all, encouraging and all-encompassing, Richard Simmons, having been obese for most of his childhood, had a knack for reaching those who would not typically go to a gym, health club, or fitness studio.

Aerobics meant part dance, part calisthenics, and a reason to get up off the couch. Aerobics inspired millions to focus on cardiovascular fitness, flexibility, and reducing body fat levels. Public gyms, referred to as Health Clubs, and even the trendy European Health Spa, were still awash with all sorts of contraptions, such as treadmills, Lifecycle exercise bicycles, and intricate weight machines. Nevertheless, soon they were jumping on the bandwagon to offer organized aerobic classes as well.

The 1980s saw a boom in the rise of aerobic-styled activewear. Big hair, tight spandex bodysuits of all colours; leotards and G-strings over top of leggings; headbands, wrist bands, and leg warmers matched the ensemble to pull the whole outfit together. New Balance and Nike running shoes were a must, and eventually, a high-top exercise shoe was the going rage. Television companies started airing half-hour workout shows that you could follow along at home. Some were sexualized, but no one seemed to notice, or perhaps they just liked what they saw.

The fitness juggernaut of Jane Fonda began to rise. Movies such as *Flashdance* and *Staying Alive* were the hip new films to see. Every young woman wanted to look like actress Jennifer Beals with her permed hair and off the shoulder, loose T-shirt. Olivia

Newton-John was another singer/actress/movie star that was getting in on the fitness bandwagon with her album *Let's Get Physical*.

Shortly after my first attempt at teaching fitness, Suzi, who was the wife of one of the owners of the European Health Spa, talked her husband, Chuck, the big head honcho, into allowing all the staff to wear running shoes instead of three-inch-high heels. Collectively, the female staff thought it was archaic and chauvinistic to work in the health and exercise industry wearing improper footwear. Suzi put forth her opinions to her mate, with the rest of us cheering her on.

Well-liked, Suzi was statuesque, tall, and slim, with bowling ball–shaped silicone breast implants. She had a thick flowing mane of auburn permed hair and a thin waistline. Her outfits were well matched and impeccably made. Her long manicured fingernails were almost as hypnotic as her breasts that she wore like a plate of armour. To most of us girls, Suzi was the end all and be all, someone to aspire to, and someone to be mentored by. Men and women alike had crushes on Suzi. When she walked into a room, one became dazzled by her sheer presence.

She taught us, her diminutive groupies, every aspect of the fitness business, from sales to the maintenance of the club; workout procedures in the weight room and intricate exercise routines on the aerobic floor; how to dress, how to carry ourselves, and how to each be a modern woman. She was our Canadian version of Jane Fonda.

As part of our training, we were also taught how to measure the clients and record their measurements. This was to motivate them and help them to achieve their goals of losing weight, and therefore inches. Every six weeks, gym members were to be measured, with the number jotted down for comparison and optimal success.

In learning how to take measurements correctly, I was to be measured first. This way, I would know exactly where and at what angle to hold the measuring tape. When my upper thigh was measured and recorded at 22.5 inches, Suzi told me that I needed to trim down in that area. I felt immediately put to shame.

At that time, body-shaming tactics could be a deliberate form of manipulation, a voluntary judgment, or just a thoughtless observation and needless comment. This marketing tactic for selling the idea of fitness was about appearance and not strength, a healthier lifestyle, or longevity of life. It was about how you looked and not how you felt.

My measurement experience brought to mind other comments that had been said to me over the years about my body. A child I had babysat years prior once stated that I had a big bum. Later on, a friend said that I was the perfect candidate for liposuction because my upper thighs were so chubby. I had the nickname bubble butt in high school—I had read it on a cubicle in the library that someone had scratched into the wood, in addition to "Karen Bonner is a motor mouth," which was in no means as hurtful as a bubble butt. My boyfriend John joined the ranks and said as a casual observation that he thought that I might be gaining weight in my hip area. The Bootlegger jeans that never fit correctly still plagued me and were a reminder to all of the above.

The voices in my head were indications that I was not picture perfect, and peoples' comments stung. I often felt overweight, and my poor body image was why exercise was becoming so important to me. My so-called beauty regime while I was away in Palm Springs, and the starvation dieting tactics had boosted my self-esteem. The beautification industry was in full swing, and women everywhere, including myself, were listening. Be sexy, wear this, do this, don't do that.

If one could have published a beauty book called "Life Lessons from Suzi," they would have instantly been put on the bestseller list and could have quickly become a millionaire in the 1980s. Suzi expressed that by standing tall, one could ooze success, command attention, and take off five pounds without really doing so. A woman should always apply lipstick, have a contagious smile, and teach her classes with a brightly coloured scrunchie in her hair. Be prepared to say an enthusiastic yes whenever possible and never take no for an answer. These attributes were encouraged, instructed, and listed as valuable, essential aspects of "playing the game."

KISS—Keep It Simple Stupid—was a repeatedly enforced acronym that I could never quite understand. Did it mean to deliver all information as simply as possible so even a stupid person could understand? Or perhaps the information was, in fact, stupid? It was best not to question any of Suzi's teachings. One learned early on to never cross a successful businesswoman/fitness guru as powerful and as beautiful as our adviser and highly acclaimed boss.

Her wrath was far worse than any displeasure or boiling point from anyone I had ever met before. Here today, gone tomorrow, hiring and firing were a common occurrence. It was always best to stay on Suzi's good side; "don't rock the boat, and you won't fall off" was a pivotal warning to live and work by.

Staff breakfast meetings at the Four Seasons Hotel in downtown Vancouver happened monthly: linen napkins, china place settings, five different types of silverware, champagne mixed with orange juice, and chocolate-covered strawberries. Impressive, to say the least.

We, the young, easily influenced staff, were all duly impressed, passionate, and on the verge of becoming a little bit brainwashed by the beauty, glamour, and glitz peppered with the wheeling and dealing of selling gym memberships by using the format of high-pressure sales—and don't forget the KISS rule!

Soon I was teaching three classes per week, and my outfit was just as important as my music selection. My most treasured and coveted workout wear was a mauve spandex bodysuit, mauve headband, and purple leg warmers all tied together with a thin, stretchy purple belt, topped off with New Balance running shoes that almost broke my bank account. My sweatband did its job of soaking up the sweat while my spandex leotard encased my body like a girdle. I looked the part but never divulged my secret of wearing pantyhose underneath it all to keep my low self-esteem at bay and to cover up unwanted cellulite, dimples, and jiggly parts. My gorgeous new running shoes allowed me the extra cushioning to kick high, twist, and bounce up and down without ceasing.

The first three months of my aerobics instructor career gave me shin splints, which felt like my legs were breaking off just below the knee. Without the use of my legs, I would forever be inactive, and my fitness teaching occupation would come to a grinding halt. Suzi's instruction and years of wisdom were to ice my shins. I eventually recovered and set out to become the best instructor that ever was, feverishly whittling away my rear end in the process.

Inspired by the movie *Flashdance*, Dawna and I enrolled in jazz dancing lessons at a dance studio called Terpsichore in downtown Vancouver. I thought that because I was an aerobics instructor, jazz would not be much different. Much to my dismay and embarrassment, I was wrong. While the class was sashaying in one direction, Dawna and I were struggling to keep up as we floundered in the opposite direction. After many attempts at pirouettes and the physically impossible arabesque, we felt like Lucille Ball and Ethel Mertz. Mortified, we left the dance studio with our tails between our legs, eventually finding humour in our lack of coordination and deciding that jazz dancers were far too snobby for the likes of us, anyway.

We may have failed at organized jazz dance routines, but nightclubs were our go-to form of entertainment.

For $150, Dawna purchased a VIP pass to the newly renovated hotspot called Richard's on Richards. "Dick's on Dick's" in the early '80s was a "beautiful people" bar with a large screen mounted above the dance floor, showcasing the latest MTV music videos. It was strictly a dance venue that was notoriously referred to as a meat market, the kind of place some people adored, and others despised.

The VIP pass allowed its users to skip the lineup, parading past all the poor schleps that waited in their stiletto heels, sequinned tops, spandex pants, and feathered dangly earrings; the bigger the hair, the better. Our clothes and hair made me think of peacocks and finely painted birds of every description.

Strutting up to the bouncers and doorman, flashing Dawna's authentic shiny black VIP card, we would be ushered inside with a knowing nod. Once inside, we immediately shimmied up to the bar to order a Harvey Wallbanger or Brown Cow cocktail.

The big screen and music videos were unmatched in any other nightclub. Stevie Nicks, Tom Petty, Devo, and Deborah Harry were enthralling and larger than life, towering over the dance floor. Richard's on Richards was the place to be any night of the week, especially on Halloween.

The first year John and I were going out, Halloween was only a few months into our dating. John had a colossal fraternity party that we were planning on attending, so our costumes had to be unique and not like any others.

We decided to rent our outfits from an actual costume store. While milling about looking at rows upon rows, we came across a variety of gypsy and pirate outfits, witches, and sexy doctor and nurse uniforms. But we were not satisfied, so we kept digging, eventually finding something so unique and different way in the back of the crowded shop that we just had to have.

That year, our first Halloween together, John and I dressed up in giant chicken suits. I was a big-breasted feathered chicken, and of course, John was the ever-so-macho rooster—simply a must. All night long, we pranced and bobbed around the dance floor, pecking at strangers and shuffling our big chicken feet to the music. The only drawback was that we had to abstain from drinking AND urinating due to the giant poultry headpiece and the cumbersome yellow-bellied body that disabled us from fitting into the bathroom stall.

The next year, I decided that I wanted to be less weighty and slightly more attractive. So, I went as Minnie Mouse, with mouse ears, painted mouse face, black leotard, red-and-white polka-dot skirt, and high-heeled shoes. John went as a Blues Brothers musician, aka Dan Aykroyd and John Belushi, from our then well-loved TV show, *Saturday Night Live*.

However, our third year together was at the height of my nightclubbing scene, so I suggested to John that we spend Halloween at Richard's on Richards with Dawna.

It was touch and go for the first part. John, not being a disco fan, was not too enthralled with the venue. But he did enjoy a good party and Dawna's suggestion for our costumes. With it being two against one (my roommate/workmate and myself), John agreed: Richard's on Richards it would be.

Since Dawna and I already owned head-to-toe spandex bodysuits, we decided to dress up as felines: cats with whiskers, ears, and tails. Our black fitted leotard made us svelte, long, and lean. Dawna's thespian flair with makeup gave us cat-like features and striking doe eyes, with extra layers of black L'Oréal mascara that coated our false eyelashes.

The only dilemma was a matching costume for John. It was entirely out of the question for John to wear spandex, too, being the jock that he was. So, when Dawna suggested that John dress up as a safari hunter and we as his feline jungle catch, he agreed with a smirk and off to the costume store we went. Moments later, we pulled together a costume consisting of khaki shorts, a safari helmet, and a fake rifle to strap on John's back. John was transformed into a handsome game hunter with us as his captured prey.

With VIP pass in hand, the three of us waltzed past the long line of Richard's on Richards patrons and through the open doors. Once inside, it was straight to the bar for B-52 shooters. After a few cheers and toasts, we were all set to boogie on down to the disco beat while music videos played on a giant screen, and loud chants filled the jam-packed dance floor.

One could call Dawna a social director of sorts, as she always had grand ideas up her sleeve for elaborate fun. Her attention to detail and organization skills could only be applauded. Yet her underlying business schemes were a benefit to us both. With my one hundred per cent emotional backing and matching enthusiastic personality, we made quite the team.

Dawna called me into her office one morning, as she had the *Vancouver Sun* newspaper spread out in all its entirety on her desk. She wanted to show me a two-page spread promoting a place known as Whistler. The headline read: "Can Whistler Be Known as Aspen of the North?"

She had me sit down and read the article.

In 1858, some Hudson's Bay explorers were looking for an alternative route into the Cariboo and farther north. They surveyed the valley area between Whistler and Blackcomb. The road would later become one of the many paths used during the Gold Rush at the turn of the century and became known as the Pemberton Trail.

Alex and Myrtle Philip purchased ten acres of land in 1913 on the northwest corner of Alta Lake for $700. Their dream was to open a fishing lodge, so they built the Rainbow Lodge Fishing Resort. The same year, the Pacific Great Eastern Railway reached the lake from Squamish. Shortly after that, groups of twenty-five came in batches from Vancouver, where they would stay for a week at a time for two dollars.

Soon they expanded the lodge and added cabins, tennis courts, a general store, and a post office. It became the most popular west coast resort for the next thirty years. Soon others arrived, and the Alta Lake Hotel was built. It burned down in 1930 and was replaced with Jordan's Lodge. The surrounding area continued to grow.

In 1962, four Vancouver businessmen began to explore the area, now known as Whistler, with the intent of building a ski resort as part of a bid to win the 1968 Winter Olympics. Even though the proposal failed, construction began anyway, and the resort opened for the first time in January 1966. Blackcomb Mountain, initially a separate enterprise, opened for business in December 1980. Previously, Whistler was called London Mountain, named after a mining claim in the area, but the name was changed to "Whistler" to represent the whistling calls of the marmots. Marmots are also known as "whistlers," and they live in the alpine areas of the mountain.

The newspaper story went on, inviting skiers from all over the world to try the mountain. I asked my parents about the history of Whistler, and with having grown up in what my dad called the godforsaken Prairies, neither had any interest whatsoever in snow. They recalled the story of the businessmen, but that was as far as it went.

Dawna, on the other hand, had a blueprint for a game plan, and the two-page layout was just what she needed to tweak her interest and get the ball rolling.

She had a male friend who lived up in Whistler, someone she had met years prior, and someone that she wanted me to meet. Merv was muscular, tall, blond, and handsome, a real Adonis. Not my type but a real sweetheart, nonetheless. He and his friends lived and worked for their love of skiing. They were honest to goodness ski bums or ski demons, for lack of any other description. Their adventurous spirit, finesse, and daredevil approach to careening down the mountainside at breakneck speeds were comparable to the talent of an Olympic ski team.

Living together and working together also meant that Dawna and I had the same days off, which made planning activities together convenient and easy. Concurrently, John was passionately engrossed in school during the week, and homework and sports with his buddies on the weekend, which enabled me to generate my time with Dawna to be footloose and fancy-free, to coexist and traipse around the lower mainland having fun.

Whistler was to be our next plan of action to meet up and hang out with Merv and his friends. It was a mere ninety-minute drive from our apartment in North Vancouver.

Preceding our first trip to Whistler, it was necessary to look the part. In true ski-bunny fashion, off to the ski shop we went. Dawna chose a one-piece purple ski suit that held her five-foot-seven-inch frame beautifully. I, on the other hand, went with black spandex, hip-hugging ski pants, and an emerald green puffy ski jacket. Once again, being self-conscious of my hips, thighs, and small waistline, I wore my usual tight-fitting pantyhose underneath the spandex ski pants, which gave me the feeling of being a plump butterball turkey, ready to be stuck with a fork. This was decidedly uncomfortable, but there were no jiggling body parts, so I thought that I looked like a million bucks, and in my mind, that was all that mattered.

After researching equipment, ski passes, and costs, Dawna found a remarkable deal. The Whistler Blackcomb Ski Resort in the early 1980s was looking to bring revenue into the newly renovated winter wonderland. So, they advertised and promoted a proposition to first-time skiers. It was called the "The Never Ever Before" Ski Pass, which consisted of equipment rentals, a one-hour beginner ski lesson, and an all-day ski pass to use both mountains from opening to closing. All this for the mere price of twenty dollars! The stipulation was that the package was for people who had never been on skis.

Which, in our case, for the most part, was accurate. My prior ski experience dated back to grade six. I had participated in school ski lessons at Seymour Mountain on the North Shore. It ended up raining most of the time, so slopping around in snowy sludge was not appealing or manageable.

My next experience on skis was in grade nine. I went skiing a second time with my dad at Hemlock Valley, near Harrison Hot Springs. Upon exiting the chairlift, we collided with each other. I gashed my chin on the icy snow and became tangled in a heap with my father. I was embarrassed and mortified.

So, aside from my first few attempts at skiing, I considered myself to be a novice and ready at the age of twenty for a proper ski lesson with Dawna.

Dawna and I, decked out in our newly purchased, most stylish outfits, did quite well careening down the slopes on Whistler Mountain, but we did even better afterward in the Long Horn Pub with Merv and his ski buddy friends.

Every weekend after that, it became our practice to ski at Whistler, where all the glamorous people congregated, and we stayed for free at Merv's house. It became inevitable that we would meet guys along the way. But I was not interested in romantic escapades or dalliances of any kind. Whether they were studs, jocks, or the nerds that my mother would have approved of, none of the other guys interested me. I found myself always wishing that they all could have been John.

In the interim, John was hard at work back in Vancouver at UBC while I was traversing all over the mountain with my ski bunny companion, Dawna.

With me acting as Dawna's assistant, we came up with a plan to arrange a work party up at Whistler with the "Never Ever Before" Ski Pass promotion for our co-workers. Putting on our business caps, we took it one step further and organized a weekend retreat by using a group rate at Whistler's Delta Mountain Inn.

Through Dawna's expertise and know-how of finagling a deal, Whistler's Delta Mountain Inn gave us a remarkable package. To the rest of the staff at the European Health Spa, we advertised a fast-paced weekend of camaraderie, exercise, and merriment, a package deal of "food, festivities, drinking, ski lessons, and accommodations."

After payment, ten of us embarked on an outrageous weekend of skiing, hot-tubbing, drinking, dining, and dancing. Dawna had number-crunched the total and divided it by eight, so everyone would pay just a little bit more to enable us—Dawna and myself, the party planners—to go for free.

The suite we stayed in was exquisite, with the main gathering area in the centre of the room, couches, a fireplace, and enormous windows that looked out onto the ski slopes, making for a cozy weekend getaway. Four deluxe bedrooms with queen-sized beds were situated pod-like just off of the living room. Dawna and I had prepared snacks for the group's arrival, which we incorporated into the fee. It was BYOB, so that took care of the liquid libations.

The schedule started with a meet and greet Friday night, ski Saturday, dinner out afterward, and then back to the hotel to get gussied up to hit the clubs, and then home on Sunday. Our co-workers were pleased and impressed. Thus, we began our party planning committee and a way to have extra fun at work with always something to look forward to.

Having set an example on group activities, one of our male co-workers at the spa had some ideas of his own. His handmade invitations were left in a neat pile at the front desk, inviting everyone to a party at his apartment on Beach Avenue for the upcoming Friday night. All it said was the time, location, BYOB, and wear a toga!

Toga, Toga, Toga!

The theme "Toga Party" conjures up images of drunken frat boys from the 1978 film *Animal House* and John Belushi chanting "Toga! Toga! Toga!" The movie propelled the ritual into widespread practices all over North America. The Toga Party is one of the oldest themed costume parties, where attendees wear a toga made from a simple household bedsheet, and sandals.

In preparation for the European Health Spa Staff Toga Party, Dawna and I each purchased brand-new bed sheets for the occasion. She settled on a 500 count, pale yellow queen size that draped perfectly over her slim frame, flattering her milky white complexion. She cinched in the waistline and wore a thin gold belt, forming pleats in just the right places, while strappy gold sandals pulled the whole look together. From her ears hung her dazzling gold hoop earrings.

I, on the other hand, chose a pink floral-print sheet, also with a belt—a thick, wide, pink stretchy belt that accentuated my small waistline and drew attention away from my hips. Pink high-top running shoes gave me the cute factor. I felt curvaceous and pleased with my creation.

Parking on a side street down by the beach, we approached the address and rang the buzzer.

As we entered, the first thing we saw was a punch bowl filled with cherries that had been marinating in vodka all day. Scooping out the drenched fruit and eating them out of little paper cups, was the fastest, most effective way to get drunk, encouraging everyone to eagerly chug the remains at the bottom of their Dixie cup.

Seemingly the theme, besides the togas, was to become utterly inebriated so the alcohol could act as a truth serum, giving one the ability for past hurts, thoughts, and emotions of any kind to spill out like the cat being let out of the bag. The little magic cherries acted to numb one's pain or magnified their sadness, turn shyness into boldness, and boldness into introversion. In other words, anything can happen when alcohol is consumed in its purest form, straight up, no mix, other than that of a little piece of produce—cherries, a delicacy that should have been baked into one of my mother's pies rather than soaked with poison.

One of our co-workers, whom Dawna and I thought to be off-putting, had been given the nickname "Malibu Barbie" because of her bleached-blond long hair and excessive use of tanning beds. She had arrived in a miniskirt toga, four-inch heels, and her much older boyfriend on her arm. At least thirty years her senior, he seemed like a grandpa to the likes of us twenty-year-olds. However, she appeared to be head over heels in love with her older man and he with her.

Three or four little tiny cups of vodka-infused cherries later, Malibu Barbie and I had become the best of friends. She confided in me that her boyfriend was married and she was his mistress. I told her that I hated my boyfriend's female friend Robbie. We then broke out in thundering fits of slurred laughter, both knowing that what we had said was not funny at all.

As the night progressed, so did my personality. I perceived myself to be comical, invincible, self-assured, and the cat's meow all rolled into one. Thinking at one point how amazing I felt and how alcohol was genuinely the best thing since sliced bread, I found myself wondering why I did not drink to excess more often—never realizing the misconception of excessive drinking, the phony-baloney part of the putrid truth serum and mind-altering substance. Nor, worst of all, how it changed one's behaviour, exaggerating everything.

On this particular night, I adored everything about it.

As a fitness instructor I knew full well what the term "hitting the wall" meant. It refers to the depletion of glycogen stores while performing endurance exercise. It is a feeling an athlete gets when they "run out of steam" or "bonk out." The runners' phrase "hitting the wall" or "bonking" refers to running out of glycogen, the body's storage form of carbohydrate. This usually happens after a person reaches their "crossover point," which is when the body switches from using carbohydrates for energy to using fat stores. This can sometimes happen in the middle of a race; it is when the body stops functioning properly. An athlete will feel extreme fatigue, disorientation, and weakness.

"Hitting the wall," we all knew as fitness experts, was a term relating to athletes, but on this night of overly induced, drunken camaraderie, it made sense that the condition could pertain to other things, too. In my case, at the Toga Party, it pertained to drinking too much. Everything was running along quite smoothly when suddenly, it was as if all the partygoers, particularly the heavy drinkers, hit the wall at the same time, an immediate turning point when the term "under the table" indeed came to light.

One minute I was hugging a co-worker with immense joy, and the next minute, everything had gone sideways. Malibu Barbie was throwing up in someone else's purse, the host of the party had passed out underneath his kitchen table, and Dawna was nowhere to be found. Others were crying, some were dancing on the couches, and a fistfight broke out between two of the male trainers.

I dared not blink or close my eyes in any way, shape, or form because the entire room began to spin. It felt like I was on a ship sailing on turbulent waters.

The sound of a lamp crashing to the floor got me thinking that I needed to get out of there ASAP. Looking to grab my coat off the stack from the bed, I then realized that I did not even wear a jacket and was thankful that at least I had left my shoes on. Dawna somehow turned up, and with knowing looks, we decided to leave, escaping the mayhem. We blasted out the door without even thanking the host or saying goodbye.

Once outside, we gulped fresh air like thirsty dogs lapping up water. We ran down Beach Avenue, clad in our bedsheets. Dawna was flapping along in her sandals and I, clomping along in my sporty high-tops. Without speaking to one another or looking back over our shoulders, eventually, we spotted what we were running toward, the beach at English Bay, hard-packed sand, crashing waves, a place to catch our breath and sober up.

Throwing ourselves onto the sand, we laughed, and then we cried, glad to be rid of the evolving antics from our co-workers' drunken behavior, not knowing where it could have led if we had stayed. The morning was breaking, so we mustered up as much sobriety as we could and made it home to get a couple of hours of shut-eye.

The next day was Saturday and our day off from the spa. I would have been happy lounging on the couch for the better part of it, but Dawna had other ideas. John had a soccer game and his volunteer job, so I was happy to be kept busy. Dawna's plan consisted of a walk through Stanley Park and then a drive up to Cypress Mountain on the North Shore.

Feeling queasy, I wondered if Dawna was feeling the same even though she never showed it, stating that "Life is too short to feel sick, and besides, the fresh air will be good for us!"

We always took turns driving, as it was only fair, and it just happened to be my turn. Leaving the North Shore and taking the first exit after coming over the Lions Gate Bridge toward downtown Vancouver, we manoeuvred past Prospect Point. We drove around Stanley Park until we reached Lumberman's Arch. Parking near the Aquarium, and with a blanket in hand, we found a sunny spot under some brilliant cascading trees.

Stanley Park is amid the urban landscape of Vancouver, like a lush green oasis. The 400-acre park offers scenic views of the water, mountains, and majestic trees along Stanley Park's famous seawall. The park was developed and built between 1911 and 1937, named after the British politician Lord Frederick Stanley, 16th Earl of Derby.

Aside from history, many visited Stanley Park to see the caged monkeys, molting penguins, and sad, lethargic polar bears at the Zoo. The Aquarium held the killer whales in small tanks, dutifully doing tricks for their reward of a smelt or two. School field trips and family outings assembled to see and learn about wildlife. As cruel as it seemed, very few batted an eye and could hardly wait to offer a popcorn kernel to a desperate monkey scratching its butt, or catch sight of a whale confined to the space of a fishbowl in hopes of getting splashed with the slap of its tail while sitting in the audience.

After a night of drunken camaraderie, we spread out our blanket on the grass at Lumberman's Arch and flopped down to rest and ponder the past evening. We speculated about who went home with whom and laughed horrified at the person who would have eventually found Malibu Barbie's vomit in their purse, also sharing our opinion as to whose fault it was when the fight broke out.

I confided in Dawna my concern at how friendly I had become after consuming four cups of the saturated cherries. She reminded me that everyone, not just me, had been rapidly gobbling up the fermented fruit concoction, so we were all in the same boat, and therefore no one would have noticed anyone's behaviour one way or another.

As we reminisced about the previous night, we were astounded at how much alcohol was brought to the party, realizing that everyone was probably feeling a little under the weather, and they probably would not even remember the goings-on. So goes a night of partying, we both concluded.

Exhausting the topic of the Toga Party, we sat silently for a while enjoying the simplicity of the day, in addition to all the sights and sounds of children playing, squirrels scampering, seagulls swooping, and the usual Vancouver goings-on that park life brings.

A group of people began gathering near us. They wore long robes with ropes tied around their waists like belts. Their heads were shaven, except for a little scruff like a small ponytail sticking out from the top of their head.

Before Dawna and I could grasp who this group was or what they were doing, a few of them came over to shake our hands and ask if we would like to share a meal with them. As I was about to refuse, Dawna leaped up from our sunny spot on the ground and exclaimed, "Absolutely." She went on to say how starving she was, famished, and I had to agree that I was, too. As we made our way over to their buffet of food that was set out on long tables, it dawned on me that these people were probably honest-to-goodness Hare Krishnas.

Just before I left for Palm Springs with Sarah, we saw a group of this same magnitude handing out flowers at the Vancouver Airport. I was also reminded of how the Beatles chanted about Hare Krishna in their song titled "My Sweet Lord." If the Beatles supported this organization, they must not be all bad, or so I thought.

While Sarah and I were away in Palm Springs, my mother was fearful that we might fall prey to another cult-like group called the Moonies. She passionately warned us to be on the lookout and not get tangled up with a bunch of religious fanatics. Sarah and I were always on guard for any shady hippie-like characters that could congregate at any moment, who may like to brainwash two possible recruits such as us.

I shared my thoughts with Dawna as we casually sauntered over to the table. Much to our disappointment, the food looked unappetizing. With the combination of being hungover, operating on little sleep, and merely craving good old-fashioned bacon and eggs smothered in ketchup, we rolled our eyes in unison and politely loaded up our plates just the same.

The various dishes laid out before us were indiscernible and not the usual potato salad and cold cuts one would see at a picnic. We decided that the food was probably fine, but our fear of the unknown suggested otherwise. Our imaginations took over, and we conjured up the possibility that perhaps the food had been drugged or laced with something. We would be thrown into the back of a van at any moment, delirious and trapped in a cult we knew nothing about and had no way to get out of; therefore, we would be impregnated by the cult leader, and our families would have to come and deprogram us. Although unrelated, I still remembered my close call with the man in the truck who picked me up at the bus stop in Palm Springs. Even though I willingly got in, I learned my lesson and would be more prepared next time—if there was a next time, which I highly doubted.

After a few bites of the bland, flavourless food items, in unison we folded up our blanket and crept away from the crowd. Dispensing of our uneaten paper plates heaped with a mass of soggy vegetables in the nearest garbage can, we made our way back to my car.

Driving back over the Lions Gate Bridge and up toward Cypress Mountain, I experienced feelings of melancholy. On the one hand, I was happy to be with my friend Dawna, independent and living together in our North Vancouver apartment. On the other hand, I was filled with sadness when thinking about John and how I often missed him. My perpetual dream and fantasy of the day that we would be married periodically waned, going stale with each passing day or new experience that I inevitably had without him. I missed him.

The same questions often circled my brain. Why was the storybook romance taking so long to achieve? When would I be safely encompassed by the white picket fence, marriage, and motherhood?

We drove halfway up the mountain and pulled over at the scenic lookout. Getting out of our car and finding some boulders to sit on, we gazed down at our beautiful city. The sun-kissed water lightly rippled, luminously meeting our eyes as we continued to look down from our viewpoint near Cypress Mountain. The puffy clouds overhead and beyond allowed fragments of blue to escape in between the cotton ball whiteness, reminding me that everything was going to be okay. It was a beautiful day in Vancouver.

CHAPTER 5

"Leather and Lace"

1983

"There is a time for risky love. There is a time for extravagant gestures. There is a time to pour out your affections on the one you love. And when the time comes— seize it, don't miss it."
-Max Lucado, Writer, Preacher, Speaker

JOHN'S INTELLECT AND DRY SENSE OF HUMOUR WERE ALWAYS appealing to me. However, his drive and determination to succeed with his education and eventual career intermittently made me feel small and vulnerable. My low self-esteem was not a match for John's self-confidence, and inevitably, the more anxious I became about my career and our relationship, the more confident he became with his.

I had been an average student with average grades. Neither of my parents or siblings had gone to university. Therefore, furthering my education was never spoken of, or even suggested. My father had a grade seven education because his family was impoverished, and he ran away at the age of thirteen during the

Depression era. Even though he became successful later on with a small bulldozing company, it never crossed his mind that life could be any easier or more profitable. He was always seemingly happy.

I had one guidance counsellor at high school say to my mother at a parent-teacher meeting, "There is no point for Karen to even think about university after grade twelve since she is in the general math program." To this, my mother nodded, and out the door we went.

Taunting me was an internal message of my own, "Why would such a good-looking, smart guy like John be interested in you?" and "What's the deal with the white picket fence dream? You are not getting any younger, so what are you waiting for?" Regardless of these negative thought patterns running through my brain, I forged on and displayed to the world a happy, positive twenty-one-year-old attitude.

When we were together, I gladly let John lead and, figuratively speaking, I would happily sit in the backseat while John drove.

Neither John nor I were following any religious doctrine or spiritual practices, even though unbeknownst to John, I had become a Christian many years prior at summer camp. It was in the wake of my camp counsellor's outwardly spoken prayers and regular requests to invite Jesus into my heart that I did so.

I truly wanted the forgiveness and blessings that were promised to me, with safety and protection from the devil, so it made sense to throw all caution to the wind and ask my Lord and Saviour to take the reins and save me. I was relieved to know that I could now end up in Heaven when all this world had to offer had ended, and the people left behind would be cast into the fiery pit of hell.

Even though I was living the secret life of a Christian and did not know anyone who followed any Biblical teaching, I was surprised when John told me about a Christian man named Max

Lucado. John had come across him while studying children's books as part of the curriculum for his teaching degree.

John dug a little deeper into this author, and he was inspired. His ideology was palatable for John; he liked how Max pondered the love aspect of religion, and John shared with me how Max Lucado spoke of love, hope, forgiveness, and dealing with grief.

Soon after, I noticed a shift, more of an openness with John. He was still headstrong about school and worried about eventually finding a job. Yet, he was developing a tendency to look at life a smidge differently after his discovery of Max Lucado. He seemed more flexible and seemingly more attentive. I noticed and liked the subtle changes in John. It made me feel calmer and more secure for a time.

When we were able to squeeze in some time together, one of our favourite pastimes was watching television. John rarely came over to my apartment, so it was at his house that we gathered around the TV with his mom or brothers. Our shows were *Hill Street Blues*, *Cheers*, and *M*A*S*H*. One movie we particularly enjoyed was the epic miniseries, *The Thorn Birds*, with Richard Chamberlain and Rachel Ward, adapted from the book by the Australian author Colleen McCullough.

The storyline and sweeping saga of the Cleary family were intriguing, with tragic consequences. We were both struck by the romance and entangled relationships that, as fate would have it, were not meant to be. I often wondered if John and I would end up like the characters Meggie and Father Ralph, desperately longing to be together, yet having it not turn out the way we had hoped.

My parents had met at The Cave Supper Club in 1945, and almost thirty-seven years later, for one of John's well-orchestrated dates, we went to the Cave Nightclub to see a popular Canadian singing group called Doug and the Slugs. Coincidently, my older brothers and their girlfriends were going to the performance, as well, plus a multitude of John's buddies. I adored my brothers, and I was thrilled to be spending time with them.

The Cave (1937 – 1981) was an establishment like something out of Bedrock City in the hit cartoon and comic book series *The Flintstones*. The Cave Nightclub was eclectic and unique, with stalactites made from burlap and plaster hanging from the ceiling. The whole place, walls, and pillars were made to look cave-like and were initially a supper club in the early days, with floor shows and a full orchestra. Later on, it became a popular nightclub with bands, drinking, and dancing.

On this night, in particular, the alcohol was being poured as fast as we could order it, and the sweat poured off us in buckets, stinging our eyes as we danced the night away to the band. No thought was given to smeared makeup or our curly perms becoming even curlier. We thought only of being front and centre on the dance floor for every song.

I had an immediate crush on the lead singer, Doug Bennett.

In my books, Doug Bennett was a born entertainer. He had a stage presence like no other, and I could hardly wait for the band to take a break so I could seek out this animated, comical frontman. I felt that I just had to meet him.

Without a jealous bone in his body, John encouraged me to search out the lead singer. So, off I went backstage to fawn over my new cherished musician. Finding him sitting alone in the darkness pounding back a beer and catching his breath, he was all ears for a ridiculous fan such as myself dishing out compliments and star-struck antics oozing from my mouth like floral-scented diarrhea. The vodka and orange juice that surged through my veins helped to fuel my monologue significantly.

As per usual, we stayed at the nightclub until all the lights came on, and the band packed up. While newly introduced couples were leaving hand in hand, I applied my token application of fresh pink lipstick to bid farewell to Doug Bennett and say hello to my new-found title of "Groupie for the Band."

Days later, John told me about a play that Doug Bennett was starring in and asked if I would like to go. Without skipping a beat, I wholeheartedly responded with an enthusiastic "Yes!"

John found out that if one volunteered at the East End Cultural Centre, we could see the play that Doug was starring in for free. With John being a frugal student and me a starving fitness instructor (literally), this was our ticket to enjoy the show without breaking the bank. Adding another layer to our relationship by volunteering together, we took tickets at the door. Feeling like I was part of the performance, I relished welcoming and greeting the patrons while ripping their ticket in half.

The play was a musical called *Rock and Roll,* about five friends, the dating scene, songs, and dancing from the era and took place in the 1950s and 1960s. I loved every breathtaking second of it, overly applauding and laughing at just the right times!

My mind played the event over and over. I talked about my obsession with Doug Bennett and the play with anyone who would listen. John and I both became fans, and he thought my passion was cute. We were fixated and enthralled by Doug Bennett's wit, sense of humour, and talent in both singing and acting—a natural-born talented performer.

As romantic as it could get, John and I had a song that reminded us of each other titled "Leather and Lace" by Stevie Nicks and Don Henley. The lyrics seemed to truly reflect our very different upbringings, with me being from the country and owning a horse and him being born and raised in the city. However, and noticeably so, our roles seemed to be reversing, as I had become a city slicker, and John often spoke of one day settling down to live in the country.

It was clear to me that my prince charming had arrived. I was happy but often felt that I should be happier. I was content but periodically found myself searching. I could not quite put my finger on what was missing.

The Circle Craft Fair at the East End Cultural Centre was an activity that John introduced me to before Christmas one year. He suggested we attend and do our Christmas shopping there. The ambiance and festive surroundings were magical. Artisans, potters, knitters, woodworkers, and painters were all in one place, selling their wares. Crafts of every description were displayed while Christmas carols played, and the aroma of cinnamon and mulled apple cider filled the air. It was a heady, festive, and romantic experience.

That year for Christmas, John gave me the record album *Leather and Lace* by Stevie Nicks, featuring Don Henley, combined with a beautiful lace blouse and a leather-bound journal—all purchased at the Circle Craft Fair. My gift to John was a bottle of Stetson men's cologne because he had just bought himself a pair of cowboy boots.

It was evident that John and I had grown closer. Feeling more self-assured in my relationship, I was able to shift gears and think about my career in the fitness industry. After making lists with the pros and cons of my European Health Spa job, I determined that I liked the exercise class component and disliked high-pressure sales. I questioned where my job was taking me and if I could stand the corruption any longer, of taking people's money in the expected ruthless fashion.

The late nights of disco dancing had started to become mundane, leaving me wondering how many more Harvey Wallbangers and rum and Cokes I could consume. And even more so, how many more dance partners I could endure, especially since I only had eyes for John.

Going over other possible career options, I examined the possibility of opening up my own fitness studio, a place separated from high-pressure sales that focused only on a variety of aerobics classes without weight-training machines.

I concluded that I needed some concrete advice, so I decided to call and ask to meet with my first exercise mentor, David Bogoch, from the very program I had initially become certified in.

Approximately ten years my senior, David was well educated, both academically and in business. In addition to being outgoing, fit, and energetic, he had been ahead of the game, offering fitness classes back in 1979 and onward for a drop-in rate at a local community gymnasium. Taking it one step further, David had also written and published a book.

He had another niche, and that was offering training classes and a certification program for other fitness enthusiasts who also may want to teach safe and effective exercise classes to the public.

Before my job at the European Health Spa, I attended his weekly classes, and then much later, I enrolled in his fitness training courses. He was a great facilitator and offered me uplifting, encouraging feedback about my teaching style. As a class, we learned other methods of performing the moves, transitions, anatomy, and what the term "Aerobic" stood for. He gave me rave reviews on my fitness teaching abilities. He was an extremely intelligent, encouraging, and kind man.

David Bogoch was the first person I thought of when I was looking for advice, someone to talk to about my career, where it was going, and how I was going to get there.

I decided to reach out to David because I was in a stagnant place. Dawna had made her way up the ropes and was now the Assistant Manager. I was holding the status of Head Girl, a title that none of us knew the meaning of, but it was up to me to direct my co-workers when to take new clients on tours, clean the bathroom, polish the equipment, put chlorine in the Jacuzzi, and so on.

A real sign of boredom at work is when one is less than enthusiastic about their duties, sometimes slacking off and pushing the envelope with what one can get away with, which is precisely what Dawna and I had started to do. Perhaps not purposefully, and in our defence, we trained the staff beautifully. They liked us and did their jobs well. On the other hand, we started to take extra-long lunches because we did not need to hurry back, knowing full well that the spa was in good hands.

A restaurant by the name of Bridges at Granville Island had just opened, and it had become the hot spot for lunches and dinners, especially with the boating community in the Vancouver harbour. All one had to do was moor their boat and climb up the ramp from boat to dock to enjoy a fine dining experience at Bridges Bistro.

It had become a habit for Dawna and me to leave the club at 11:00 a.m. for a long lunch at Bridges Bistro. We managed to make it back to work sometime before 2:00 p.m. Our preferred lunch entrée was a glass of chilled white wine with cheesy Quiche Lorraine, accompanied with a fresh side salad and warm crusty rolls served in a basket with pats of hard butter.

While lingering over lunch, we chatted with wealthy and retired millionaires, who were languishing on their yachts, sailing and manoeuvring the inner harbour of Vancouver, making a stopover for a beverage and light fare at Granville Island.

It felt glamorous associating with the high rollers, but not enough for Dawna or myself to take up any offers of setting sail on the wide-open seas with our new leathery-skinned sea rover friends.

Frequently on our way back to work, we would stop for a little shopping on 4th Avenue and then pick up some baked treats from the Lazy Gourmet for the staff back at the spa. All was well that ended well. Our bosses were none the wiser, and life went on.

However, I knew that our daily routine could not last forever, so I made arrangements to meet David Bogoch for lunch. I wanted to get his opinion on my job prospects, and I was hoping that he would give me his professional advice on the feasibility of opening a fitness facility of my own and if it could be successful.

The year was 1982, and my mother was in full support of me venturing out on my own. She was willing to offer me financial backing, and her faith in me was outstanding. But as a confident fitness professional, it was the business side of things that made me wary. My number-crunching days at the bank pointed out my weaknesses in the area of finance.

David unhesitatingly offered to pick me up, something I was not used to, as John did not have a car. Any picking up was always done by me, as I was the one with a vehicle. David showed up in a cute little Mazda something or other, and we drove to the much-talked-about and coveted Bridges Bistro.

Over lunch, David highly recommended that I not start up my own fitness business. He said, "The larger organizations, such as Ron Zalko, Fitness World, The Fitness Group, and the European Health Spa would eat you alive. Lesser facilities, smaller businesses, are no match to the flourishing fitness clubs that have already made their mark."

He went on to emphasize that I would become a small fish in a big sea of sharks.

I thanked David for his well-qualified, wise words and made the decision right then and there to seek out another career path. Finishing up our meal and looking across the table at this fitness guru, I thought that I might be slightly infatuated with him. He appeared suave and debonair, and I was flattered to have been picked up, treated to a meal, and given concrete professional advice.

I was not exactly floundering, but I was also not going anywhere. My dreams and desires revolved around my life long dream, and my life would be perfect if only I could get married.

In the meantime, it did not take me long to figure out the age-old saying, "It is not what you know, but who you know." It reminded me of how I got my job at the Bank of Commerce through my sister's bank manager and well-loved cat enthusiast. Without an ounce of experience in the banking field, I was eager, charming, and willing to try.

When all was said and done, I learned that banking was not for me. The outcome was experience gained, and friends made. I was taught the ropes and decided that I did not want to climb the corporate ladder after all.

Coincidently, the bank manager just happened to have an influential wife, a lovely woman who was also the head dietician at the Abbotsford Memorial Hospital. All it took was a request in the way of a phone call, and a raving reference came forth for another job that I had no experience in.

After a brief interview and drop off of my small but adequate resume, I soon became a full-fledged Food Services worker at Vancouver General Hospital.

I quit my European Health Spa job, front desk and sales, but kept teaching classes.

In 1886, The Canadian Pacific Railway first opened a nine-bed tent to treat railway workers. After the tent burned to the ground, a one-story building was erected. Shortly after that, the City of Vancouver took over the facility, which became the City Hospital. Located at the southern edge of the original Gastown settlement, a thirty-five-bed hospital opened. The upstairs ward was for female patients, and the downstairs was for males.

In 1899, the Vancouver City Hospital Training School for Nurses was opened. By 1902, it had been renamed Vancouver General Hospital. Shortly after that, the hospital expanded, and in 1906, in an area overlooking False Creek, a new building was erected called the Heather Pavilion, which began housing staff and patients. In 1950, The University of British Columbia Medical School opened clinical facilities at VGH. In 1959, the Centennial Pavilion was added, named in commemoration of the centennial of the founding of British Columbia as a British Crown colony. In the 1960s, VGH built Canada's first intensive care nursery, equipped with the first capable apparatus used for natural breathing in infants with respiratory failure. It amazed me that I would be working at this historic site.

I was given three uniforms and a locker and told to wear white nurse shoes and pantyhose stockings. A hairnet was supplied, which was mandatory. After three days of training, I began my four-hour shifts five days a week.

I was the low man on the totem pole. There was a lot of grunt work, expectations, and schlepping around with extra jobs which were passed down from my superiors, the women who had made a lifetime career in food services.

During the training, I quickly noticed that there was an initiation process and pecking order. The old-timers (gals who had been working there a long time) were authoritative types, who showed me the ropes and a few tricks of the trade: how to wear my hairnet, and where to hide when our duties were done but the shift was not.

Other employees were not quite so helpful: food service workers who sat squarely in the driver's seat and made me wash all the pots and pans, even when it was not my turn—not delightful at all. Colleagues that were supposed to oversee me took longer breaks than allowed and smoked cigarettes behind the linen closet. I could not help but see them slip ketchup, peanut butter, jam, and crispy bacon into their purses. Of these women, I tried to stay clear.

I did make a friend. Stacey knew her way around the kitchen like nobody's business and took me under her wing. She told me who to trust and who not to trust; who to listen to, and who to ignore. She was not openly friendly and showed little emotion except that I could often detect a slight smirk as if she was holding back a smile.

Stacey was my age, tall, slim, and blonde with wild hair that she wove into a thick braid down her back. Fresh-faced, with penetrating blue eyes, she proudly wore a thin gold chain around her neck with an adjoined broken heart. Instead of pantyhose, Stacey kept her legs bare, and rather than practical nurse shoes, she wore red high-top running shoes. She drove a black Jeep.

Stacey was confident and rebellious, the opposite of me. She would not stand for any guff from our co-workers or the patients; this job was just a stopover for her. She was trying to save money for university and by no means was she going to become a lifer in the VGH food services department, as she often very eloquently lamented.

The work was arduous and taxing, but the pay was great. I had started at Bootlegger making $3.00 an hour, my wage moved up to $6.50 an hour at the bank, the European Health Spa brought my income down to $5.50 an hour, but at the hospital, $10.00 an hour was the going rate, and when payday rolled around, I felt none other than loaded.

With my new friend came a different social life. Amidst the early '80s, there was another music scene. Disco was becoming less popular, while new wave and punk music were hitting the clubs. It was Stacey who introduced me to a place called Luv-A-Fair. In the late '70s and early '80s, Luv-A-Fair was a Vancouver institution, a giant warehouse that could hold 300 to 500 patrons on any given night.

The club had once been a gay disco that had a reputation for wild antics, colourful characters, and full-throttle disco music.

When the format switched to new wave music, the partygoers did, too. However, management kept the sign on the door that read, "You are entering a gay establishment," in an effort to keep the tourists out.

By the time I started attending Luv-A-Fair, it still attracted its original gay clientele, but now also party kids, artists, hairdressers, and designers filled the establishment. Hairdressers in the '80s were considered the most trendy and stylish people to emulate.

New wave music's common characteristics brought a wide variety of styles, which often shared a quirky sense of humour, in opposition to punk, which was raw, rough-edged, and political compared to mainstream "corporate" rock. The basic principle behind new wave was the same as that of punk – anyone can start a band – but new wave artists were influenced by the lighter side of the 1960s, pop music, and 1950s fashion. New wave was more commercially viable than its more abrasive counterparts.

Luv A Fair delivered an edgy new trend for young people looking for something different. One of the waiters wore roller skates, and the speakers that blared the music were so large some of the patrons would climb on top of them to dance like the '60s go-go dancers. The bouncers were harsh, and their purpose was to keep any troublemakers out. All of this only added to the uniqueness of the environment. It was flamboyant, wild, and individualistic. I felt very avant-garde, strolling around the high-top tables and the surrounding darkened club scene.

Times were changing—jobs, friends, apartments, and music—but my relationship with John was steadfast and strong. Still flitting about independently while working at the hospital, I was able to keep teaching fitness.

Dawna and I remained friends, but we decided to move out of our North Vancouver townhouse, as she was moving home to save money for university and then going up north to work. I, on the other hand, wanted to live closer to VGH and John.

My brothers and father packed me up and loaded everything into my father's pickup truck, making it the fourth time I moved since initially coming to the city after high school. My new apartment was located at 70th and Osler in South Vancouver.

Sarah and I stayed in contact, but she had plans to move to Palm Springs to attend the College of the Desert and to live with her grandparents. So now, Stacey took up more of my time at work and on the weekends, introducing me to another world entirely. I dyed my hair purple and cut one side shorter than the other, paying exorbitant prices for hair treatments, facials, and tanning beds. I was following the direction and progression of city life in Vancouver, along with other twenty-two-year-old young women in 1982. I felt on-trend, contemporary, and professedly happy.

My brand-new one-bedroom apartment was only a year or two old and felt clean and modern. It came with four appliances, was located just off Granville Street, and at $450 a month, it was the most expensive dwelling I had lived in thus far.

The only drawback to my new digs was the necessity of dodging my creepy landlord. He seemed exceptionally old to me, at least forty, and he lived across the street with his mother in a run-down building.

His appearance was dishevelled, his hair long, unkempt, and greasy. He was unshaven and often wore a perpetually dirty dress shirt partially buttoned, or not at all. Glimpses of his swollen belly were hard to ignore as it emerged and poured over the top of his baggy trousers. His thick-lensed glasses appeared dirty and smudged, his dark eyes behind them darting to the side and avoiding eye contact. Yet I could feel him glance all over my body when he thought that I was not looking.

I was pleased that my mother had gone with me to fill out the initial application and to act as my reference. However, surprisingly she did not notice how oddly my landlord represented himself, or at least she never brought it up, so we did not speak of him and his creepiness.

Shortly after I moved in, I lost my keys, so I had to contact my sinister-looking landlord to request a replacement. He insisted that he meet me in the lobby of my apartment building to give me another set, as he wanted to ensure they worked. We met outside of the building that same day after work, and together we took the elevator to the third floor. While the elevator slowly made its progression up to my floor, it felt like an eternity. Once the doors opened, he lumbered behind me as we walked to my suite. Pausing outside my door, he tried the new key in the lock, and it worked. Before I could grab the keys and scoot inside, he awkwardly leaned in and tried to kiss me.

Taken aback, shocked, and repulsed, I put my hand up and turned my face abruptly to the side. Flustered, I grabbed my keys from his pasty white hand, entered my suite, and immediately locked the door behind me. The sound of the bolt clicking was almost deafening, as if to ward off any further advances.

Strangely, I told no one, later thinking that perhaps there had been a misunderstanding; had I been misleading, did he think I wanted him to make a move on me? Everything happened so fast, and going over it in my mind, I wondered if losing one's key was an invitation of some sort?

The incident with my landlord brought back a similar memory of when I was fifteen years old and caught off guard by another older man while taking driving lessons through an organization called Young Drivers of Canada. During my last lesson, my instructor, a rotund, loud-breathing older man with perpetual beaded sweat on his forehead, turned to me and said, "My, what a lovely tan you have. I bet you look great in a bikini." My eyes widened, and with a nervous smile, I said, "I suppose so," while slightly turning my body away and hesitantly shifting my weight to look out the window. I felt myself become an inch or two smaller in the seat next to my driving instructor, a seat that immediately felt uncomfortably close.

I did not tell anyone, especially my parents, of what seemed like an inappropriate comment that was made to me by my driving instructor. Still, I passed my test and became an excellent driver regardless of the pervert who taught me.

It also brought my mind to a more recent encounter in Palm Springs when I accepted a ride from a stranger, and again, never told anyone. It still made me shudder to think of the possibility of what could have happened, knowing it was a stupid thing to do in the first place but glad that I had the wherewithal to escape unharmed.

I did not always have the opportunity to work with Stacey, but when I did, our shifts together just flew by. Her strategy was to work brutally fast and then have more time for an extended break, giving her extra time to study for her grade twelve diploma.

Quickly but competently, we took the prepared food and placed the stainless-steel containers into heated carts. It took two of us to wheel the enormous carts onto the elevator. Once on the correct floor, the cart was plugged in, and we would dish out the food according to the dietary plan for each patient. The nurses and nurse's aides would help us deliver the food.

Stacey's curtness could be intimidating. She was direct, a no-nonsense type of gal. When working next to her, I could feel her tension mounting if the food was not going out fast enough, which made for an unpleasant environment to be in, even if it passed quickly.

Shortly after my landlord kissing incident, I accidentally served minced meat instead of pureed meat to an elderly patient. When the nurse detected my mistake, she lambasted me, stating that I could have killed the older woman who had no teeth, and she could have choked on the foreign ground round. My take on the situation was that it would have been curtains for the patient and me, I could only imagine the late-breaking news making headlines in the *Province* newspaper:

"Neglectful Death of Helpless and Fragile Alzheimer Patient at Vancouver General Hospital Caused by Careless Food Services Worker—Family and Friends Left Horrified."

I immediately wanted to retaliate against the nurse, boldly exclaiming that I had been accosted by my creepy landlord only a few days earlier. Instead, I apologized, holding back tears while Stacey held her usual hidden smirk and kept on working.

After working the late shift one night, Stacey suggested we go to Luv-A-Fair. Nightclub conditions and practices had changed since my patronage at Richard's on Richards, and flashing a membership card at Luv-A-Fair was not an option. Getting past the bouncers was the hard part, but once inside, and after one's eyes adjusted to the black walls, neon signs, and flashing strobe lights, it was everyone for themselves.

I was always open to trying something new, and I admired the individuality of the people dancing by themselves, marveling at the aloofness that others carried. It was odd to see people swaying, jumping, and twirling all by themselves on the dance floor, but it seemed appealing and freeing. However, the first few times I tried it, I was a tad embarrassed and felt that I stuck out like a sore thumb. Despite the expressionless faces of the patrons, I hung on to my friendly, outgoing nature. I could never quite get the hang of bringing myself to be as introverted and downtrodden as my new counterparts.

Cocaine, which I had only seen glimpses of in Palm Springs, could be seen laid out on the tables. As the long white lines went up people's noses, I chose to abstain. Instead, I found myself standing in the long lines waiting to use the bathroom, which turned into a meeting spot for women of all shapes, sizes, attire, and personas. The darkness and pounding beat of the club were muffled and replaced with bright lights, bathroom stalls, and graffiti. Camaraderie, screeches, and giggles, sharing lipsticks and phone numbers, made for an enjoyable pee break and an event all on its own.

Nothing seemed to stay the same, and as the venues were changing, so was my taste in fashion. Le Château was my go-to store, and my most treasured purchase was a pair of hot pink and black checkered hip-hugging pants, a black V-neck men's sweater, and black velvet high heels. I completed my look with hot pink neon lipstick, fluorescent purple eyeshadow, and enormous hoop earrings that all tied in nicely with my purple hair, which was cut short on one side.

Not only did Stacey introduce me to the underground world of Luv-A-Fair, but she also popularized a term and unknown activity called the "after-party." Leaving Luv-A-Fair after a night of individuality and making statements, Stacey suggested an after-party at a friend's house near UBC. Feeling adventurous, I enthusiastically accepted.

Having gone to many fraternity parties at UBC with John and visiting his friends at their Point Grey and Shaughnessy homes, I felt well-versed in what to expect, which completely unprepared me for a darkened, dilapidated house on the UBC endowment lands. Once inside, the small dwelling was barren, with no furniture except a few mattresses on the floor. Garbage and empty whisky bottles lay strewn about, along with the people whom I assumed to be the inhabitants. As the partygoers lay around, staring off into space, I thought that everyone was either stoned or high, or just exhausted. Music was blaring, songs that were unknown to me, and I felt oddly out of place and uncomfortable.

Stacey flopped down on one of the box springs minus the bedding to chat with a few of the guys. As she shared a joint with them, I stood demurely nearby, arms folded, looking around with only one thought on my mind, and that was getting out of there.

A turning point was the realization that I had created an image of Stacey, and she was not as cool as I thought her to be. Her lifestyle felt uncommonly depressing.

As I looked around at the doom and gloom in the "after-party" house, I began to take stock and assess my situation. I was dating a fantastic guy, working in health and fitness, which I loved, but at the same time hanging out with socially awkward strangers who were turning out to be deadbeats living in a dilapidated house, with few life goals and fewer furnishings. I pondered not belonging, and realized that I had choices. Walking out the door, I got in my car and drove home by myself.

After sweating it out washing pots and pans, and walking on eggshells worrying about making another life-threatening mistake in the food services department, I decided to look at the job board for another job.

The employment postings at VGH were on a glass-encased corkboard with an array of thumbtacked notifications of available positions. These were listed only for the internal staff at the hospital. It all depended on seniority, availability, and qualifications. If you were right for the job and had enough seniority, after applying and enduring the waiting period, if eligible, you would get an interview.

Office administration work was out of the question, which I learned from my uninspiring job at the bank.

The position that did catch my eye was as follows:

Admitting Messenger

Must have great people skills, be able to follow instructions, easygoing, friendly, and hospitable.

An asset to know the tunnel routes from the admitting department to the Heather and Centennial Pavilions.

Copying down the job code, I applied immediately. A few days later, I was telephoned and asked to come in for an interview. I undoubtedly knew that I was perfect for the job. I just hoped that the HR department felt the same way. Subsequently, I left the interview and drove home to wait for the call, which came later that day, informing me that I got the job. I would start the next day, and I was to wear regular, everyday clothing that was neat and tidy. I could pick up my name badge, hiring information, and show up for training at 9:00 a.m. the following morning.

The interview process reminded me of an audition; if I could read into what they were looking for, acting the part was natural.

I never saw Stacey again but periodically thought of her, sincerely hoping she had made it out of food services to accomplish her dream of a university education.

I liked my new job as an admitting messenger at Vancouver General Hospital. Duties included greeting patients for their day surgery appointments, assisting them in a wheelchair, and rolling them off to the appointed area. I also routinely took people to their rooms, who would be coming into the hospital for overnight stays for whatever was ailing them.

When not escorting patients, our pool of girls (never did I see a man in this position, or in food services) sat in a suffocating tiny cubicle, waiting for our next duty. Sometimes we would be instructed to file or rearrange clipboards, but mostly during the interim, we talked, shared stories, and anticipated Lady Diana's wedding to Prince Charles.

My job was social and fun, much like a hostess or camp counsellor, but instead, I greeted sick people. I was getting my carefree spirit back, emerging from the doldrums, and was relieved to be out of the too-bright, damp kitchens and the dark and smoky nightclubs.

Instead, I was whizzing through the underground tunnels at VGH, delivering patients. The underground was scary, yet fascinating, and eventually, I learned the routes and how to step aside if there was an emergency coming. Just knowing the general public was completely unaware of what went on in the bowels of the oldest hospital in Vancouver was enthralling.

Once I had escorted the patient to their room, I would hospitably show them around as if they had just registered as a guest in a resort hotel. But instead of telling them where the pool was and offering them a Mint Julep, I would show them the toilet and pour them a glass of water to be placed on their rollaway bedside table.

The critical component of the job was to be friendly, kind, and courteous, which I could readily profess to be. Feeling I had found something else that I could excel at besides teaching fitness, I was now delivering sick people to their required location within the hospital.

The downside to the job, as the girls had already warned me well in advance, was that each of us would take turns, four shifts a month, working in the emergency ward alongside one of the most obstinate women who ever lived.

She could have had good reasons to be hostile, rude, and curmudgeonly. Still, for that matter, her reasoning or life outside the hospital was never up for investigation or discussion.

Ethel Strattle was downright mean, and she ran the emergency admitting department with an iron fist. On the plumper side, Ms. Strattle wore her greying hair in a tight topknot bun. She came to work daily in the same outfit, a navy-blue suit. She wore her skirts below the knee, and the suit jacket buttoned up to her chin. Support hose stockings and shoes called Oxfords, which sounded fitting because an Ox could probably wear them quite comfortably, completed the look. Over her outfit was a white lab coat.

If it hadn't been for her off-putting, bad-tempered nature and unpleasant halitosis, I did not mind her appearance. She could have been someone's dear elderly aunt, doting wife, or endearing friend. but we all very likely doubted it.

The duties for the admitting messenger downstairs in the ER included organizing file folders and medical record charts, plus occasionally escorting a patient to their room.

Ms. Strattle was strict and had an aversion to noise, which included the rustling of papers or breathing too enthusiastically. We all knew early on to sit perfectly still and only speak when spoken to. She often barked orders such as, "Get back to the filing!" or "Take out the garbage!" and oddly, "Dust the cabinets!" Sometimes we would be instructed to peek around the corner to spy on the doctors and nurses and goings-on in the ER, reporting back with our findings expectantly verbatim.

Nothing we did was ever good enough, fast enough, accurate enough, or quiet enough. It was impossible to have a shift go by without incident. All the admitting messengers had to go through it, and we all dreaded when our turn came around. Nobody spoke up, complained, or reported the old battleaxe. Everything that went on in the basement stayed in the basement and was discussed later in hushed tones.

Meanwhile, as an extended part of the ER department, one would be privy to the goings-on there. Ambulances coming and going, emergency surgeries, crying, yelling, and screaming, whatever the case may be, it was a whirlwind of activity and not the calming, sedate atmosphere of the upstairs admitting department. We all dreaded a full moon, as it only increased the havoc.

Shortly after my 19th birthday, without any warning, my mother informed me that my parents' dental plan no longer covered me. I was shocked, thinking how downright ludicrous it was. I had always taken perfect care of my teeth and had visited the dentist twice yearly. Now what? How on earth was I going to afford to pay for my dentist's appointments? I complained and then whined to my mother of the injustice.

As a child and young teen, my experiences were of fear and loathing for my dentist, partly because from a childlike perspective, my dentist was mean. He did not have a conducive bedside manner, and from what I gathered, he also did not like children. His behaviour caused me considerable uneasiness and anxiety.

Now older, I concluded that he was probably a lovely man outside of his dental practice, but as a little kid, I could not get past the stern man dressed in a white lab coat, with a frown and a furrowed brow, coming at me with needles.

When the dentist told my parents that I needed braces, they did not hesitate to begin the proceedings. My father's sister had crooked gnarly teeth, and even though she was beautiful, she never smiled until she was old and could afford false teeth. Both my parents insisted that a person's smile is the first thing they get judged on.

My orthodontist was a gentle, kind man who adored children. Still, memories of the installation and actual wearing of the braces, also known as railroad tracks, bear traps, and cheese graters, came flooding back to me every time I looked in the mirror at my now gorgeous smile and straight teeth. Recollections of being referred to as metal mouth and brace-face will be etched in my mind forever.

After the bands and wires were installed on my teeth, I had to report back monthly for tightening, which could cause massive headaches, jaw pain, and thoughts of ripping the appliance single-handedly out of my mouth when no one was looking.

The learned process for the home maintenance of the braces was associated with pain and discomfort. When all was said and done, after each appointment I was sent home with packets of soft wax to smooth over the sharp parts and prevent the metal wires from gouging into my cheek and rubbing it raw.

The headgear was another component to obtaining a Hollywood star–studded smile. It was another straightening technique that went around the back of the neck and was inserted inside the mouth. It was worn twenty-four hours a day, seven days a week, which I completely disobeyed. I was already a nerd at school and did not need any more assistance in pulling off that persona by adding a noticeable, obtrusive metal object surrounding my face for all to see.

Every time I went into the orthodontist, they raved at what a good job I had been doing, so I continued NOT to wear my headgear because I kept getting praised for the excellent job I had not been doing. "If it ain't broke, don't fix it," soon became my motto.

Tiny little elastic bands added even more bang for the buck. The bands looked like ponytail holders for a Barbie doll, and their purpose was to yet again assist in aligning the teeth, mouth, and jaw. These hurt as well, but the worst part was how they would catapult out of the mouth periodically while I was speaking. So instead of spraying saliva at people, I would fling a saliva-encased small elastic band, always hoping and praying that it would not stick to the face of whomever I was talking to at the time.

The retainer was another torturous device that proved to be just as uncomfortable. The appliance fits in the mouth like dentures. But the slobber would get trapped between the mouthpiece and the roof of the mouth, and one did not know whether to spit the extra saliva out or swallow it—absolutely disgusting—which in turn could cause immediate gagging.

Foods like carrots, sticky candy, coconut, peanuts, and popcorn were off limits, in the possibility that these delicious treats would get trapped in the braces for all of eternity.

After all was said and done, my teeth turned out beautifully. I was delighted and proud of my straight white smile, until years later, as an adult in my early twenties and still without a dental plan, I finally chose to go to the dentist for a checkup.

Much to my dismay, I was diagnosed with receding gums and sent to a periodontist. Gum surgery was suggested and highly recommended, which my mother said she would pay for if I chose to do it. And it was not cheap. If I chose not to go ahead with the surgery, my teeth would apparently fall out by the time I turned twenty-five; not a pleasant thought and a devastating visualization.

The first of five appointments almost was the death of me. The roof of the mouth is a sturdy surface; therefore, having needles in the roof of the mouth is a slow, tedious, and painful procedure. The skin was to be skin-grafted from the roof of my mouth and stitched to my gums for reinforcement.

It was after one of these appointments that John and I had plans to go away for the weekend. Out of respect for his parents, John was still not staying overnight at my apartment. His parents were continuing to pay for his education, and he stilled lived at home, so it was awkward and did not feel right to John. I admired his devotion, but being a woman of the world, such as I professed to be, I always wanted him to stay.

Taking into consideration my wanting and pleading, John came up with a plan. His parents were going to be out of town, and John suggested that we go camping. I was so thrilled with the invitation and excited at the prospect of time away, and alone with John, that I jumped at the chance. I was elated with the fantasies of the snuggling and cuddling in the privacy of our sleeping bag.

I secretly speculated that John would take this romantic time away to propose.

The only catch was that I had a periodontist appointment only hours before we were to leave. But nothing was going to stop me from going, especially since it was John's idea.

The minute John picked me up after my appointment, I realized I was not in any shape to be heading away for the weekend, but *que sera, sera*, whatever will be, will be, I was going, and not even a periodontist could stop me.

It was John's plan for us to do some rustic camping out past Chilliwack Lake. I had never been there, but I remembered that my dad and brothers had often gone fishing there when I was a little girl. Instead of going, I stayed home with my mom, and we went to the movies in downtown Vancouver, a fun activity just the same.

When my brothers and dad returned, their stories about picturesque camping adventures had me captivated. My dad would go on to explain the Gold Rush days and riding the rails to British Columbia from Calgary, Alberta, when he was a boy. The tales of panning for gold and the First Nations people who walked the land before us were information not found in any history books.

I was excited to share with John some of the stories of my father and our forefathers.

In the language of the Stó:lō communities in Sardis and Chilliwack, Tcil'Qe'uk, the name Chilliwack means "valley of many streams."

Established in 1873, the township of Chilliwack is the third oldest municipality in British Columbia, first located along the Fraser River, with the main form of transportation being steamboats between Chilliwack and New Westminster.

Before logging began in the 1920s in and around Chilliwack Lake, a trail was first cut to the Chilliwack River in 1855 by the Hudson Bay Company. There were nine First Nations villages, and the trail helped join Vedder Crossing and Chilliwack Lake. Just before my parents met in 1944 in Vancouver, an army base went up in Chilliwack, BC, in 1942.

My dad spoke about the depth of Chilliwack Lake and how no one had ever seen the bottom. With its beauty came danger. He warned me about boating accidents where the people had gone missing. The lake is a valley-bottom, which is a U–shaped glacial valley made up of old-growth forested slopes and sub-alpine ridges; therefore, objects could get lost or trapped underwater forever.

The area of Chilliwack is filled with lakes and surrounded by mountains. Forty kilometres of trails offer hiking, bird watching, and wildlife.

During my recounting of the history of where we were going, I was having a difficult time speaking with swollen gums, stitches, and a mouth full of cotton balls. I realized that I had never shared with John my knowledge of such things before, and I quietly made a mental note as to how I always considered John to be the smart one in our relationship.

Chilliwack was the perfect place to get away from the city and to explore nature, even in my condition. With John's experience in the Boy Scouts, I felt safe and in good hands, making our way in and around the depth of any wilderness backcountry.

Arriving out in the valley and the outskirts of Chilliwack in the early afternoon, we drove and drove, eventually taking an off-grid side road. Driving up the dusty gravel logging road, complete with switchback turns, we finally found a place to pull over and search for a location to set up a basecamp from which we could explore and hike.

Everything suddenly felt like a more substantial undertaking than I had expected. Still feeling the aftereffects of my earlier surgery, I did not want to miss the only opportunity to be alone with John, his entourage no longer present, or having to cut our date short due to his ever-present load of homework. We were alone, just the two of us.

Parking the van, we grabbed our tent, blankets, and a few other things and traipsed into the forest. Finding a flat, inconspicuous place to set up the tent, I was impressed with John's outdoorsman abilities as he scouted out the flat ground and diligently put up our tent, pounded in stakes, and attached the fly to tent pegs. I had brought my down quilt and blankets from home to make our sleeping quarters exceptionally comfortable and cozy, as I was in charge of preparing our nest for the night.

Eager to start our adventure, we decided to set out for a hike. Feeling a tad woozy from my dental procedure and not my usual self, I was not going to let that stop me, so off I went, falling in behind John. He had found us walking sticks and had peeled the bark to make for a smooth and sturdy hand grip.

It was refreshing to be out in the forest with its old-growth moss-covered trees and low hanging branches that brushed our arms as we meandered past, each fern waving its fronds, greeting, and welcoming us into its untapped secret garden of delights. The scents and sounds enticed us deeper into the trail as we moved forward.

Stopping at one point to take a prescribed painkiller, briefly looking around, as I fell in walking behind John again, a creepy sensation came over me, a prickly feeling encompassing my body. I had an odd awareness of being watched, causing me to periodically look over my shoulder to see if someone or something was following us. I mentioned my inclination to John, but he said that it was just my imagination. We continued onward.

Shortly after that, we both heard a sound, a trampling of branches that had us wondering what it could be. Upon John's cue, we stopped, me freezing in my tracks and John calmly listening and scanning the forest with squinted eyes to see if he could make out something abnormal.

Wavering between trepidation and thinking it was nothing, I wondered if it was my intuition or inventive imagination that brought up images of a hooded killer, a masked man, or a starving hobo looking for his next victim. Or perhaps a hungry animal was seeking out its prey, or a legendary Sasquatch was creeping through the trees and then running to stay out of sight behind the greenery.

My father believed the mythical creature by the name of Sasquatch existed, possibly because there had been so many sightings, and my father questioned, why not? Anything is possible. He believed in UFOs, too, often exclaiming that "There had to be more to life than meets the eye."

In North American folklore, Bigfoot or Sasquatch is a hairy, upright-walking, ape-like creature that dwells in the wilderness primarily in Oregon, Washington, and British Columbia. The word Sasquatch is an anglicization of the Salish word, *Sasq'ets*, meaning "wild man" or "hairy man." Thought to be measuring 2.75 m in height and 360 kg in weight and covered in long dark hair, its footprints are said to be fifty centimetres.

One of the earliest sightings was in 1884 near Yale, BC. He was nicknamed "Jacko," said to be half-man, half-beast, and described as gorilla-like. The creature was said to have been found unconscious on the railroad tracks. Some fishermen reported corralling "Jacko" and dropping a rock on his head, knocking him out. The newspaper ran a letter to the editor about the sighting and rock dropping and ended with, "Truth is stranger than fiction, and facts are stubborn things."

There have been over 1900 alleged sightings of Sasquatches from British Columbia to Northern California. In Harrison Hot Springs, Hope, and Chilliwack, people are still on the lookout for the elusive creature.

My father was always hoping to spot one, and maybe this was my chance. We stood still, waiting for another branch or twig to crack. Keenly watching for a movement of any kind, we glanced at each other, hoping the other knew what to do in case of an animal attack or a Sasquatch sighting. Without speaking to one another, we started to move again, and so did the sound.

Making an executive decision to turn around and head back to camp, we were both in agreement. Dusk was encroaching, and we had enough sense to not be out after dark in an unknown overgrowth forest fifty miles from home and two miles from our vehicle. The rain started to fall the minute we got back to the tent, so we ducked inside to stay dry.

By this point, I was exhausted, and due to the gum surgery, I did not feel like eating much. John tried to light a fire but gave up. I snuggled down into my comfortable bed, falling fast asleep, waking only a few hours later with my pillow drenched in blood. The sticky, ruby red fluid, already turning brown, had seeped out of the stitches in my mouth, matted my hair and was smeared all over my face. Even worse was the metallic taste in my mouth, and the trickling of blood down the back of my throat.

John handled the situation in a calm, orderly manner, telling me that we needed to get in the van and go to the Chilliwack Hospital emergency department. Apologizing for my predicament all the way there, I expressed to John that I should never have gone on a trip in my condition. Unfortunately, following the yearnings of my heart to be with the man I adored was no match for common sense.

Once at the hospital, the intern was annoyed that we did not go to an emergency dentist. He told us there was nothing he could do but give us some gauze to press on the bleeding, seeping area. Leaving the hospital, now exhausted, we went back to our now soggy tent.

In the morning, we packed up and shoved the tent and bedding as a messy, wet heap into the back of the van. My bleeding had stopped, and even though I, too, felt like a messy heap, we drove into the Township of Chilliwack looking for a breakfast place.

Because of me and torrential rain, the trip ended before it began, but all that mattered was that I had been with the man of my dreams, and we made it out unscathed, despite the possibility of a Sasquatch attack.

My takeaway was that my fantasies of a hot night of lovemaking and an even more romantic proposal of marriage were just not meant to be.

I never went back to the periodontist again, and years later, another dentist told me that the gum surgery, combined with unnecessary pain and discomfort, had failed. The work that was done on my mouth had made no difference to my receding gums, and I should never have had it, which only made me roll my eyes every time I thought about it.

My mother had moved to Vancouver from Taber, Alberta, when she was nineteen years old. She found the rain to be depressing but thoroughly enjoyed living near the beach in Kitsilano at 5th and Bayswater. Eventually, she got used to Vancouver's gloomy weather, met my dad, fell in love, and got married.

Kitsilano is a neighbourhood located on the unceded territory of the Musqueam People in the city of Vancouver, British Columbia, Canada. Named after Squamish Chief August Jack Khatsahlano, the neighbourhood is in Vancouver's West Side along the south shore of West Point Grey and Fairview. Like all of Vancouver, Kitsilano is in traditional Coast Salish territory.

In 1940, my mother lived at 5th and Bayswater, a neighbourhood even then filled with beautiful heritage homes, complete with verandas, porch swings, and wisteria wrapped around beams and columns. Her father had bought two side-by-side houses for a combined price of $4,500. She lived with her sister in one, and her parents lived right next door in the other.

Later on in the 1960s, the area was an inexpensive place to live and attracted many from the hippie culture. People from across Canada and the United States flocked to the city with their art, music, and carefree lifestyles. During the time of counterculture, the Soft Rock Café near 4th and Maple was a hotspot for all those interested in easy listening bluegrass and folk music. The Naam Café at 4th and MacDonald provided vegetarian, vegan, and natural foods for hippies and health food nuts. And John and I frequented the Topanga Café, Bimini's Pub, and Darby D. Dawes, as *our* places in Kitsilano.

Kitsilano Beach is one of Vancouver's most popular beaches, which also contains Kitsilano Pool, where I liked to swim and suntan regularly. The Kitsilano Showboat (which is an open-air amphitheatre) has had free performances all summer long since 1935.

My mother, having been smitten with the beachside community, was pleased when I, too, was drawn to the area that she had often romantically recalled.

Nearing the end of John's schooling, we finally started talking about our future as a couple. To me, a wedding and a marriage were inevitable; to John, a future meant moving in together. To this, I agreed. In love and having dated for close to five years, I had known all along that John was the man for me, and moving in was better than nothing. Besides, I realized that people did it all the time. It was 1982, and "Modern Love," sung by David Bowie, was all the rage.

My nights at the discos, nightclubs, and bars had become a thing of the past. The different men I had met along the way were a distant memory and a relief to be able to say good riddance to. John was straight and narrow, had book smarts, and a prospective career on the rise. Everything felt right, as long as I did not think about it too much.

Upon our announcement, my mother, even though she was worldly and well versed in current events, did not appear to be as happy for me as I had expected. In my father's eyes, I could do no wrong, so his opinion and thoughts were "whatever makes me happy," otherwise meaning it was a non-issue that John and I had decided to move in together. As for John's parents, they were old school, and I was sure that they were hoping for a wedding like I was. They supported our decision nonetheless.

Caught up in finding an apartment and furnishing it, I felt like a bride-to-be without the romantic proposal, paperwork, commitment, traditional ceremony, or ring on my finger. As I went through the motions in preparation for the move-in, underneath it all, I was terribly disappointed.

John found a three-storey walk-up at 5th and Cypress in Kitsilano. We shopped on Main Street for an antique table and Pier One Imports on 4th Avenue for dishes, throw cushions, and decorations. A futon from a local futon shop on 4th Avenue worked as a living room couch. I already had a queen-sized bed that had moved with me over the years from apartment to apartment.

John's friends and my dad helped us move in.

I cried myself to sleep on our first night of living together in our new apartment. My behaviour dumbfounded John, and he became a tad irritated.

"Isn't this what you have always wanted?" he repeatedly exclaimed.

Dawna had left the city; she had gone away on yet another adventure. This time she was driving heavy-duty equipment on a section of the Alaska Highway that needed upgrading.

Before I had met Dawna at the European Health Spa, she was working as a hair stylist in Dawson City in the Yukon. I drank up her stories about Diamond Tooth Gertie's, where she dealt cards, and how she was also working toward her pilot's licence. Inevitably, her goal, after she had raised enough funds, was to attend law school at UBC.

Dawna was the most determined person I had ever met. She had a knack for making money and always knew how to have fun while doing it.

For convenience purposes, I was back teaching fitness at the Broadway and Balsam European Health Spa, as it was only a short walk every morning from our apartment. It was late spring, and the tree-lined streets engulfed me, both physically and emotionally. The overflowing maple leaves hung so low they brushed the top of my head, giving me a sense of peace and calmness. Deliberately not ducking, I allowed nature's goodness to wash over me, the leaves touching my head like a priest handing out blessings. At times, I wished that I could make this portion of my day last forever. I never tired of my walk and my fitness class, which I enjoyed immeasurably. I often thought that if exercise were a happy pill, then once a day would surely keep the doctor away.

Sometimes when I was feeling anything but happy, I wondered if my mother's illness had found me. After a month of sharing a place and shacking up with John, my gut was trying to tell me something, but I could not figure out what it was and what was wrong with me.

As troublesome as my feelings were, I superficially laboured through my days. No longer working at the hospital after being laid off, I took on more exercise classes. Apparently, the job of admitting messenger had become obsolete. It would be up to the patients themselves to get where they needed to be, independently on their own.

When not teaching fitness, I moped around, shopped for fresh pasta and Duso's cream sauce at Granville Island, endlessly walked up and down 4th Avenue, read books at the beach, and flipped through issues of *Cosmopolitan* magazine, studying ways to improve my relationship in and outside of the bedroom.

Although I lacked a vision, John continued with finishing his education, working at a group home for disabled children, and sending out his resume in hopes of landing the perfect teaching job, which we both knew he would eventually be hired for.

As luck would have it—or some might call it a mystical intervention—one lazy warm June afternoon, I was startled out of my daydreams by the telephone ringing. Not expecting a call, I hesitantly answered the phone. Taken aback, it was good ol' enterprising Dawna on the other end, who only just left Vancouver a few days prior, calling me from Fort St. John.

All I could make out from her exuberant, breathless exchange was that there was a job opening for me on the Alaska Highway where she was working. She asked if I could get up there as soon as possible.

At some point, before Dawna left Vancouver, I briefly mentioned to her that if there was any kind of job available, to call and let me know. I thought that nothing would come of my inquiry, and I was not sure if I even meant it or wanted to go.

Her call went something like this:

"Hey, how soon can you get up here? There is a surveying crew looking for an assistant. I think you would be great for the job, and the pay is amazing."

I replied, "Oh! Umm . . . hmm. I just moved in with John, but I think I should take you up on your offer. Can I get back to you later tonight?"

"Yes, absolutely, but hurry," was Dawna's excited response.

That afternoon, before heading out to teach another class, I thoughtfully and carefully composed a letter to John and left it on our new-old antique kitchen table, hoping that he would read it and digest it while I was out, so that we could discuss everything when I returned.

Dear John,

As much as I love you and do not want to upset you, I have had a slight turn of events, an opportunity of a lifetime, really, and I am hoping for your support and permission to jump on a remarkable stroke of luck.

I just got off the phone with Dawna, and she has a job for me at the work camp up on the Alaska Hwy near Fort Saint John. I would be employed as a surveyor's assistant; the pay would be great, and I would be working seven days a week for about four months, or until it freezes. I could make somewhere between $3000 - $5000, and who knows, maybe when I got back, I could go to school and make something of my life.

I think that this would get me out of the doldrums. I have not been acting like myself lately, and I know you know that. Plus, I think that this stroke of luck would give me an incredible, unique experience and help me to get my head on straight.

If you say yes, then I need to go out and purchase some work boots and gather up some warm clothes ASAP.

Please think over my idea carefully and tell me what you think I should do when I get home.

All my love,

Karen

When I got back to the apartment, John had the letter in his hands, and he looked at me and said, "First of all, I think that your letter was very well written and very well thought out. I also think that it would be a great opportunity for you to go up north to work. Secondly, let's go out and get your work boots and gear right now so you can get going on this." I threw my arms around John's neck in sheer joy, thrilled to have his support and permission.

CHAPTER 6

"Waiting for a Girl Like You"

1983

"A bend in the road is not the end of the road unless you fail to make the turn."
—Anonymous

SHOPPING WITH JOHN WHEN ALL ATTENTION WAS ON ME FELT like I was out with my dad getting school supplies. He made sure my new work boots fit as he asked all the appropriate questions that one would when outfitting a child. I paid for my boots because we each pulled our weight financially, but I did appreciate John's concern with me getting the right fit.

Being a history buff, even though I would never have considered myself one, I called my dad on the phone to tell him of my plan and where I was going. I wanted to find out where Fort St. John was in relationship to Burns Lake, where he had first started in the logging industry as a young teenager.

He was thrilled to get my call.

My mother had told me that his feelings were often hurt whenever I called home and asked to speak to my mother if he answered, a habit I was unaware of, and one that I was trying to break. My dad's feelings were the last ones I ever wanted to hurt.

He explained that Fort St. John is a city in northeastern British Columbia, a municipality that is in the Peace River Regional District. The city's slogan is "The Energetic City." It is one of the largest cities along the Alaska Highway.

Alexander Mackenzie passed through in 1793, and by 1794 the Northwest Company established a fur-trading post near the present town of Fort St. John. Europeans increasingly encroached on the territory of the Dane-Zaa, who traditionally lived in small nomadic hunting bands of twenty-five to thirty people, but were eventually forced onto smaller parcels of land.

As a means of assimilating Indigenous populations, the Canadian government sent Dane-Zaa children to residential schools, where they and other Indigenous children were not allowed to speak their language and practise their culture.

I had never heard about this aspect of Canadian history, and I felt just horrible when my dad briefly touched on it. As a talker and storyteller, even he had very little to say about it. What he was telling me sounded very hush-hush and wrong.

The conversation ended with my dad not sounding very happy or enthusiastic that I was setting out to work in the Great White North. When reminiscing, it reminded him of the immense loneliness, physically hard labour, and longings for a better life.

I caught an early evening flight the following day. Being alone on the plane was exhilarating. I felt like a modern woman embarking on a new chapter in my life, independent and worldly.

Dawna said that she would meet me at the Fort St. John airport. She told me that she would finagle a ride from one of the other workers, and she would be there come hell or high water, followed by, "Don't worry, I'll be there."

When I arrived, the small airport was empty; no one was there to meet me, not Dawna or her supposed driver. I sat on a bench, contemplating what I would do if no one arrived, never thinking beforehand to have a plan B.

Moments after the debate in my head started, Dawna was flying through the door of the darkened waiting room, breathless and cute in her faded blue jeans, work boots, plaid jacket, and puffy vest. Dawna, my fashion plate friend, was always stylish without ever trying, even here in the cold, rugged north. In a flash, I couldn't help but recap the history of our friendship from the aerobics floor to the disco floor and now out in the boondocks in Northern BC.

As she helped me with my gear, we made our way out into the crystal-clear starry night. She led me to a truck that sat idling, with a Grizzly Adams–type man seated behind the wheel. We threw my stuff into the back of the pickup truck and sped off to embark on a one-hour drive into what seemed the northern abyss.

Dawna chatted enthusiastically about how beautiful the weather was, how we would be sharing a room, and the ratio of men to women being ninety-six to four. Intermittently throughout her one-sided conversation, she kept having to tell the driver to slow down, going from hushed enthusiasm to a deep-voiced demand in the driver's direction. Aside from Dawna's adventurous spirit, she was a stickler for safety, even buckling us both into the same seat belt because the truck only had one.

The road was long and poorly lit, with shadows dancing in the darkness and playing tricks with my eyes. Never had I experienced such deep black stillness. Our vehicle moved along the deserted road in a ghost-like silence, the sound of Dawna's voice echoing in my head with the hum of the truck engine. There was a droning comfort to my friend's chatter as she sat snuggled up next to me in the confines of our safety belt. The burly stranger silently drove on.

Just as I thought that I might doze off, unexpectedly out of the darkness came an earth-shattering thud. We had hit something.

The truck shook, banging the three of us abruptly from side to side. Stunned, the driver pulled over. Looking out the back window, straining our necks to see past the gun rack, we saw that we had hit a big black bear.

The city girl in me was devastated. My first thoughts were an immediate concern for the bear as I blurted out to the silent cab, "Is the bear okay? Is there any way we can help him? Can we take him to the vet?" My questions went unanswered. Finally, I said, "There must be something we can do." I pleaded with Dawna and the unflinching driver. The country girl in me knew the inevitable outcome would not be on behalf of the bear.

Conclusively, the driver smoothly responded, "No, we cannot go back. A person must never approach an injured wild animal." As he started to pull out and away from the dying bear, I shouted: "Please can you at least shoot it with your gun and put it out of its misery?" Silence and driving ensued. Tears stung my eyes as I wondered if I was prepared for what lay ahead.

For the rest of the drive, we all were quiet. Even Dawna's talking had broken off. I wondered if I had made a mistake. Was hitting the bear the handwriting on the wall for what was to come? Or was it just an unlucky throw of the dice? Perhaps it was kismet that we did not swerve off the road and all die in a fiery truck crash.

I found out later that the driver had a glass eye, which was unsettling to find out after our near-death experience.

Fear of the unknown crept into my thoughts, and I realized that this was my new reality; there was no turning back. I had committed to the job and my time in the unforeseeable future.

Pulling into the camp well after midnight, Dawna gave me a brief tour of the facility. It was pitch dark outside, so all I could see was the outline of what looked like a bunch of mobile home trailers joined together.

As we entered, she began with a glimpse into the communal TV room. Three or four guys were sitting on well-worn couches, gazing wild-eyed at a large-screen television on which explicit pornography vividly spilled out into the bleak room. Hiding my grossed-out astonishment, we left almost as soon as we had arrived. The tour continued.

A drunken man approached us in the cramped hallway, and as he swayed to and fro to get past us, Dawna stopped him to introduce me. Shaking my hand, he smiled bleary-eyed with a toothless grin. With my mouth agape, we exchanged pleasantries. Saying goodnight, we carried on down the long corridor.

Exhausted and trailing behind her at a much slower pace, without missing a beat, Dawna cheerfully prattled on; me not so much.

We made our way to our small room at the end of the three adjoining trailers that made up the sleeping quarters. I noticed rooms on either side not very far apart.

Dawna explained that the bathroom was outside in another trailer and to try not to use the soap as it was chemically hard on the skin. After seeing the likes of my new co-workers, I could understand why.

Once in our room, I settled into the top bunk. The mattress was hard and crackly, and the one wool blanket was rough and scratchy. Relieved to be in a bed, any bed, I pulled the covers up to my neck, still fully clothed. I felt like crying but instead drifted off to sleep dreading the next day.

Six a.m. came quickly. Waking up to Dawna's blaring clock radio, the tinny music brought me to life. I could instantly see out the small window that it was already a clear, bright sunny day, even at this early hour. Still lying in bed, Dawna explained the order of what was to come and what I could expect for the upcoming day's events.

First, we would make our way to the breakfast trailer, eat, and then pack lunch to take with us. We had a ten-hour day ahead of us, and a bus would pick us up at 7 a.m. to transport us to the worksite. Jerry, the foreman, would hand out the day's duties. I knew that we might not see each other very much, but Dawna said that she would look for me during our first coffee break. At 6 p.m., the bus would return to pick us up, signalling the end of our workday. Then it would be back to the camp for dinner.

Quickly getting dressed, I felt a glimmer of optimism as I pulled on my new work boots, dressed for the occasion of being an Alaska Highway worker.

Dawna, being the smart cookie that she was, adored asking questions; she loved digging for answers and finding out the history or the backstory. Dating back to when she worked in the Yukon, she had met some very influential people over the years and had retained everything she learned, from cutting hair to teaching fitness to working construction.

Never at a loss for words, after we brushed our teeth and made our way over to the trailer for breakfast, Dawna explained how it all began by recounting her research. She told me that the highway began as a dream in the 1920s when the United States wanted a route through Canada to connect Alaska with the forty-eight states south of the 49th parallel. Approximately 800 kilometres of land lay between Alaska and the rest of the US. With no overland way across Northern BC and the Yukon to Alaska, the northernmost US state was reliant on air and marine transport.

She further explained that back then, Canada was not interested, as they felt there was little to be gained, and the next decade brought the Great Depression. When the Japanese bombed Pearl Harbor, Hawaii, on December 8th, 1941, everything changed. The US entered the Second World War, and a supply and defence route became crucial to both Canada and the United States. Canada agreed to the building of the Alaska-Canada highway on the condition that the United States foot the bill, and the route be turned over to Canada after the war.

In March of 1942, hundreds of pieces of construction equipment arrived by train to Dawson City in the Yukon. More than 10,000 American soldiers went there to build the highway, starting from different locations. How Dawna remembered the historical facts was mind-boggling.

We made our way into the dining trailer. The cookhouse was two large trailers made into one. On one side of it were rows of tables for eating, and on the other side was the kitchen, appliances, prep counter, and a cafeteria-style, serve-yourself buffet.

I tucked in behind Dawna to copy her actions. Filling up our trays as she continued to talk, it did not take long for a small group to gather, and a few of the guys began to listen in.

We filled up our plates with eggs, sausages, hash browns, and toast. At the same time, we each loaded up a brown paper lunch bag to the brim with baked goods, sandwiches, and fruit for later.

As we made our way to the dining tables provided, Dawna kept explaining in storytelling fashion, how across the untamed sub-arctic wilderness of Alaska and Canada, thousands of American soldiers began one of the most significant and most demanding projects, the building of the Alaska Highway.

Young soldiers battled mud and mosquitos, endured ice, snow, and bitter cold to cut pathways through dense forests and some of the world's harshest landscapes. Winter temperatures were hard on the soldiers and the equipment. The summer brought sweltering temperatures and choking dust, blackflies, and mosquitos that could cause one to go stark-raving mad.

The most frustrating and challenging part of the project was the muskeg, decaying swamps of vegetation that swallowed roadbuilding equipment whole. Attempts were made to fell trees and use them to fill the soggy ground, but some sections were fifteen feet deep, which made filling holes next to impossible. They then changed the process and used fill to cover up the gaps and holes. However, after the permafrost would melt, the road would sink along with the machinery. They persevered, through.

About a third of the US soldiers were African American. For them, the hardships were far worse due to being segregated from the other soldiers and local communities. They did not receive the same calibre of equipment and had to use hand tools instead of machinery. They mostly slept in tents while the other soldiers had wooden housing. Despite the discrimination, three African American regiments made an outstanding contribution, and their efforts were the catalyst for the desegregation of the US military in 1948.

Eventually, in 1948, the road was opened to the public, but lightning and hail storms turned everything into a paste. Things improved in the 1960s and '70s when the provincial government paved from Mile 0 at Dawson Creek, to Mile 83, followed by the route to Delta Junction.

The Canadian portion of the highway is now managed in sections by the BC Ministry of Transportation and Infrastructure, the federal government, and the Yukon government. Today the Alaska Highway is fully paved, and gone are the many switchbacks and gravel surfaces, except for areas that are periodically under construction. Many tourists purchase T-shirts and bumper stickers that proclaim, "I Drove the Alaska Highway and Survived."

I could hardly believe how important my job sounded, that I, too, would be a part of making history. I wondered how I could get one of those T-shirts for myself, all the while assuming that Dawna probably already had one that she cut the neck or sleeves out of to make it look more fashionable. Before I could ask, we were interrupted by Rosie, the camp cook.

Rosie took an instant liking to Dawna and me. His cheerful, rosy face was what apparently gave him the nickname. His shaggy beard, rotund body stature, and wide smile, gave me the impression that he was a kind, generous soul.

I was taken aback at how friendly he was to us girls, eagerly loading up our plates as if he was trying to fatten us up like a Thanksgiving turkey. His response to us was opposite to how he spoke in clipped, gruff tones to the others, telling them to move along, which caused Dawna and me to smile inwardly and share the camaraderie of being the only women around.

After wolfing down our breakfast, with sack lunch in hand, we made our way outside and piled onto the bus. While finding our seats, all eyes were on the new girl, as Dawna comfortably laughed and joked here and there with a few chosen lucky contenders who were hoping she would prefer to sit with them.

Finding an empty seat, Dawna scooted in beside me. Scanning all the men sitting on the bus, I noticed their friendly faces and how they all appeared to have an affectionate eagerness toward Dawna and myself. Even though outnumbered, it was fun to feel sought after and be well received.

Pulling up just outside of a place called Pink Mountain, Mile 143 of the Alaska Highway, my father's stories of his work in the logging camps back in the 1930s and '40s flooded my brain. His tales of the harsh winters and back-breaking work were now more real to me; I felt a connection to my dad as I disembarked from the rickety old school bus.

I couldn't wait to describe to my father what had transpired thus far, minus the satellite TV room. I knew that he would be excited and proud, if not worried to death for me. Back in my father's day, the deep wooded north was not a place for women.

Since the work that I was involved in was part of a restoration, rebuilding, and reconstruction of the Alaska Highway from Mile 143 north, I could not imagine what it was that I would be doing.

In anticipation of what my duties would be, Dawna told me that she would be driving a ride-on packer all day. She had her

Walkman all set up with her taped music, snacks nearby, and at every coffee or lunch break, she would need to stand and walk around, as sitting all day was not an easy feat, especially for someone as energetic as she was, she concluded.

Having met my father, Dawna suggested that my dad probably knew what a packer was from owning his own bulldozing company. Also known as a road roller (sometimes called a packer, roller-compactor, or just roller), they are a compactor-type engineering vehicle used to flatten soil, gravel, concrete, or asphalt in the construction of roads and other foundations.

She said that the first road rollers were horse-drawn and were used as an agricultural tool. Starting in approximately 1910 and onward, steam rollers were used for the compressing and rolling of hot-laid surfaces, and were sometimes referred to as "chip chasers" because they followed behind the laying machines for hot tar and chipping material. All types of road rollers use the weight of the vehicle to compress the surface.

The whole idea of driving heavy-duty equipment was familiar to me, having grown up immersed in my father's bulldozing business, so I was prepared mentally for anything thrown my way.

Once off the bus, I immediately noticed new terrain. The landscape was dry, and the trees were not as big and thickly forested as I had imagined, with the lush west coast of BC being my only reference.

When I offhandedly glanced down to my brand-new work boots, a rightness came over me. For the first time in a long time, my feelings were that of confidence and excitement, like I belonged. Standing on the side of the Alaska Highway, I was ready to start my day.

Jerry, the foreman, introduced himself to me and then handed me off to one of the three on-site surveying crews.

Crew number one, the government surveying crew, looked very official with orange vests, hard hats, plumb bobs, and intricate surveying tools: three young men in their early to mid-twenties, who carried well-educated confidence and calm demeanour. They smiled as I said, "Hi."

Crew number two was the surveying crew that was part of a private company—three handsome, cool guys from Alberta. Sporting sunglasses, long hair, jeans, and puffy jackets, they were smiling and joking around, carefree and confident. They, too, were in the mid- to late twenties, and gave me a friendly hello.

Crew number three, my crew, seemed to be a haphazard bumbling team made up of the foreman's seventy-eight-year-old father and sixteen-year-old juvenile delinquent nephew. As luck or misfortune would have it, I was thrown into the mix, a twenty-two-year-old girl utterly unversed in road building, unskilled, and someone who hated math and calculations of any sort. Neither of my new co-workers said hi.

Thus began an adventure and education that was not available in any teenager clothing store, corporate bank, glitzy nightclub, steamy fitness studio, hospital employee job, or monthly edition of *Cosmopolitan* magazine.

On that crisp, late spring morning, I was up for the challenge and ready to get started.

Dawna and I were both escorted in separate directions. She to a heavy-duty machine that she effortlessly climbed upon to rev the engine as if she had been born to do so, and me to my crew that would soon be teaching me the ropes; Road Surveying 101.

My crew leader was Sid, a kind man way past the age and capabilities of the younger crew members on the other teams. He was perhaps waiting for a long-overdue retirement, unshaven and reeking of alcohol, which I noted when he reached out to shake my hand weakly. I could not help but also notice a slight tremor in his dry, chapped grasp. Immediately I felt sorry for him.

Sid introduced me to Darcie, the soon-to-be thorn in my side, regardless of being the boss's nephew. He was shorter than me, with a slight build, light brown shaggy hair, and an off-putting sarcastic grin. Wearing jeans, running shoes, and a hoodie, he looked more like he was hanging out on the street corner with his buddies, up to no good, than doing serious road construction on the Alaska Highway.

Thankfully my duties were simple. Sid would measure out the distance from one stake on the side of the road to where the next one would be. Darcie would pound the stake into the ground, and I would follow, tying orange flagging around each stake.

Monotonous work, but I liked it thus far and was relieved that it was somewhat mindless.

As I meandered along on my first day, I was in awe of my surroundings, especially the cloudless sky. Dawna said that it never rained, and without an ounce of precipitation, the brisk morning gave the landscape a feeling of alertness. It was on this day that my love affair for the outdoors, with its crystal clear, wide-open sunny skies, took root. I took a deep breath, realizing that I did not miss the rain, dampness, and socked-in cloud coverage of Vancouver in the least.

After the first two hours on the job, we broke for a cookie and coffee break, and then two hours later, we stopped for lunch. I was able to wave Dawna down, and we sat on the berm together, eating our thick sourdough bread, ham-and-cheese sandwiches that were laden with butter, mustard, and mayonnaise.

Not thinking or concerned at all about the extra calories and possibilities of weight gain, it felt liberating to sink my teeth into food with substance. Soon I discovered that I did not miss my usual empty stomach and calorie counting back at home.

By the end of the day, as dusk was creeping in, the mauve-and -gold-hued skies were an artist's masterpiece. Heavy-legged, we climbed aboard the bus that would take us back to the dining hall and bunks for the night, only to start all over again the next day.

Three days into our routine, Dawna said that she had some ideas brewing, some activities that we could do for a little extra fun. Not surprised, I listened intently to her proposition and had to admit that her ideas were pretty good.

She had noticed that there was a riding stable a few miles outside of camp. Since we did not have a vehicle, she suggested that I ask the surveying crew with the three cute guys if they would like to go horseback riding with us. She would ask the other surveying crew with the engineer guys, and hopefully, between the two groups of six men in total, someone would be interested in going with us.

The next day at work, we would each separately approach our appointed groups. As nerves started to get the better of me, I quickly concluded that I had nothing to lose. During the coffee break, I went up and introduced myself and soon met Dale, Ray, and Clay. Before I could finish my invitation, all three men in unison eagerly nodded their heads up and down to my request, responding "Yes, for sure" to horseback riding on the upcoming Sunday.

After meeting up with Dawna at lunch and sharing our findings, we laughed in hysterics that she had the same response from the surveying crew that she had asked. Now having six escorts to go horseback riding with, we couldn't have been happier at the prospect of some exercise and socializing.

I found out that Dawna's friend Merv from Whistler was working at the camp, too, so she suggested that he come along as backup.

Getting through the rest of the week knowing that we had a day off coming up, revitalized us, as our days were long, and our nights were short.

We caravanned to the stables in three vehicles, Dawna and I with Merv, and our six suitors forming a line behind us, the three engineers in their service vehicle and Dale, Ray, and Clay in Ray's big silver pickup truck that proudly held the name of Sluggo.

Having owned a horse as a teenager, I was thrilled at the opportunity to be riding again. I registered with the stable as an intermediate rider. I didn't know if Dawna could ride, but one never questioned what she could or could not do because it was inevitable that she would fall into it as effortlessly as falling into a lake on a warm summer day regardless.

Once we were all saddled up, each rider and horse fell in behind the other.

Our guide was Laura, not just a ranch hand, but one of three daughters who lived and worked on the horse ranch. Only sixteen years old, her worn cowboy boots and finesse with leading our trail ride told anyone who observed that she was a pro and wise beyond her years.

I thought she might get cold wearing just an old worn sweater, Levi's jeans, and a sturdy white cowboy hat, but Laura's tanned skin told me she was used to the extreme outdoors. Her straw-like blond locks were noticeably spilling out from underneath her hat while cascading down her back. I instantly liked her and thought her to be prettier than any girl I had ever seen back home in the city.

Traversing along old abandoned logging roads, the sights and smells of nothing but wilderness took my breath away. After only one week, while immersed in my new surveying job in the northern reaches of British Columbia, I was back in the saddle again. Life felt great.

Wildflowers painted the landscape with a rich palette of colours to guide our way. A variety of trees bristled in the breeze, welcoming us with their branches that looked like open arms: white and black spruce trees, golden aspen, and alders, with their tall slim bodies and leaves that flipped from silver to green. The scent of lodgepole pines filled the air and offset the radiant blue sky with shifting shade when the wind nonchalantly picked up speed. Dead branches could be felt and heard crackling under the weight of our horses' sure-footed hooves. All of this created an element of scent and sound. The buzz of insects added to the melody, clicking and snapping in unison as we lazily plodded along.

Taking stock and cataloguing the moment, I did not want to forget the feeling of peacefulness that surrounded me. We were like nomadic travellers along the un-used trail, and as we wandered, my mind also wandered and was taken back to thoughts of John at home in our quaint, sunny Kitsilano apartment and the unknown future that lay ahead.

Picture-perfect memories from my past were intermingling with my present, making me appreciate the moment.

As I pondered, I realized that I was pleased with my decision to accept Dawna's offer to join her up north, especially on this day. There was nowhere else that I would rather be.

Lost in my thoughts, I was shaken back to attention by a loud thundering sound coming up from behind me. I could feel the earth move beneath my horse, and the presence of something encroaching. Startled, and before I could grasp what was happening, I glanced over my shoulder to see a horse that had broken free from the chain of ambling riders. Now at a full-on gallop, the getaway horse and rider were rapidly coming up alongside me. I recognized Dale, wide-eyed on the wild snorting animal, with his feet out of the stirrups and flopping from side to side. I immediately gathered that he was in trouble and had no control. Dale was holding on to the saddle horn for what seemed like dear life. I steered my horse out of the line and trotted after horse and rider.

Clicking my tongue, instructing my horse, Marley, to break into a full-on gallop, I caught up and told Dale to reach his hand up the reins near the bit of the harness by the horse's mouth and pull down hard, yelling "whoa" in a loud firm voice. Doing just that, Dale's mare did what I had hoped it would do. The horse and rider came to a grinding halt.

Slightly embarrassed and yet immensely relieved, Dale thanked me as his buddies caught up to rib him as only guys instinctively do. Deep down inside, they had an underlying sense of relief that it was Dale and not them who had gone for an unexpected, uncontrollable jaunt.

I shortened Dale's stirrups and told him how to grip the horse's girth with his thighs while keeping a slack, controlled hand on the reins. Laura had heard the disturbance and had turned from the front of the line to circle back. By the time she reached us, all was well.

After my brief moment helping Dale out on our trail ride, we became immediate friends. Never having been the "take charge, leader type," I felt resilient and pleased with myself that I could rescue a guy instead of the other way around, as every storybook or folk tale often described. The damsel in distress was always rescued by a man, except this time it was reversed.

Once back in stride, the horses and riders carried on, the horses knowing well the route and their duties. As the lazy afternoon turned into an early sunset, we made our way back to the ranch, our vehicles, and home for a camp supper.

As if Rosie the cook had been waiting for us, he eagerly dished up a hearty meal for Dawna and me, of salad with Thousand Island dressing, thick greasy pork chops, mashed potatoes smothered in gravy, thick white bread, and dense chocolate cake for dessert.

After only one week at the work camp, my jeans had become more snug.

In the closed, confined space of a work camp, it does not take long to get to know your neighbours.

Dale was proving to be one of the sweetest, kindest men I had ever met. Standing five feet seven inches, with a muscular yet slight build, his tanned and weathered complexion offset his bright blue eyes, and his polished white teeth gave him a handsome prettiness. With shoulder-length wavy blond hair, I was not surprised when he told me that he had been nicknamed Jesus by the locals while travelling in South America.

Through the usual banter of introductions, I learned that Dale was originally from Saskatoon, Saskatchewan, but was now living in Calgary, Alberta, and working as a surveyor in Northern BC and parts of Alberta. When I told him that I was from Vancouver and had a boyfriend back home, he said that he was not surprised. I was flattered with his response and intrigued by this new prairie boy who had entered my life.

Dawna and I never ventured into the TV room for obvious reasons, but she had gotten wind that there were board games available inside the R-rated hangout, which we could thoroughly enjoy.

Instinctively plugging our nose as if running into a smelly room, we instead covered our eyes and ran past the porno movie on the big screen that never ceased to play. Grabbing the first game we saw, we quickly exited as fast as we could. The box we grabbed just happened to be a brand-new, unopened game of Trivial Pursuit, a game with which I was familiar, as I had played it many times with John and his friends and my own family at Christmas time.

It was a well-known fact that two Canadians had invented the game of Trivial Pursuit in 1981. The two friends came up with the basic concept while they were playing a game of Scrabble and drinking beer. They decided right then to invent their own game.

The basis for the game involves six different categories: Geography, Entertainment, History, Arts & Literature, Science & Nature, and Sports & Leisure. The winning team acquires the most answers and collects the most pie pieces.

For me, fond memories of my father's stoked fireplace, ripple potato chips with French onion dip, and Christmas carols playing in the background, were prevalent when the game of Trivial Pursuit came to mind.

Dawna's idea was to host a Trivial Pursuit game night in our room. So, we made posters to promote the event, and word spread quickly.

Join Dawna and Karen for a game of Trivial Pursuit

This Sunday at 2:00 p.m.

Knock on our door for entry

Making our room presentable, we used crates the cook gave us as a makeshift table for the potato chips and cans of pop that were our entertaining props. When the day arrived, and we opened our door to see if we had any takers, much to our amazement, we were pleased to see a long line had developed down the entire hallway.

The drunk men were passed by and sent away. Dawna and I had previously discussed that there would not be any alcohol allowed or given out. Due to the nature of the job, being six days a week, ten to twelve hours a day, many men drank every night after work and all day Sunday. With the game taking place on Sunday, we were leery of what we could expect.

Our work hours were long and lonely, and I assumed that some were addicted; the alcohol got the better of them. It was not the actual drinking we minded. It was the aftereffects that turned average, mild-mannered men into sloppy, incoherent drunks that we loathed.

Some of the guys brought us gifts, which we welcomed: bottles of liquor (we only accepted the unopened bottles), bouquets of wildflowers, and offers for rides in their pickup trucks to check out the Northern Lights. The afternoon proved to be fun for all and gave Dawna more fuel for ideas and other upcoming special events that we would be sure to organize in the future.

Dale's two co-workers, Ray and Clay, were a barrel of laughs and made me look forward to every coffee break, lunch hour, and meet-up to sit together for dinners.

Clay was astute with a dry sense of humour. Not very tall with short dark hair that was perpetually greasy, he wore wire-rimmed glasses that often slipped down his sharp nose. His flannel shirt, work pants, and boots seemed too big, like a little boy in his father's clothing. If it weren't for his wisecracking playfulness, I might have found him unattractive.

Ray was almost as funny but more ponderous in stature. His oversized down-filled puffy jacket gave him a teddy bear appeal, and his feathered blond, fluffy hair would have fit perfectly into the latest *Teen Beat* magazine. He was a wise guy and wore it proudly.

In amongst the friendships made, I could feel the chemistry brewing between Dale and myself, but I made a conscious choice not to let it go any further, although I was having a difficult time. A fellow by the name of Mark from the government surveying crew had taken a liking to Dawna, and they were gradually becoming an item. Needless to say, sparks were flying all around.

I wrote letters home to John, sharing with him about my job and the gorgeous scenery, and yet was getting to know Dale on a friendship basis, which I chose not to share with John.

At work, I found myself aware of Dale's presence at all times, often craning my neck to see if he and his crew were on another stretch of the highway up ahead.

Dale, Ray, and Clay would take it upon themselves to occasionally loop back to see if we had made any mistakes, giving Sid time to rest, catch his breath, and pound back more booze. Any miscalculations could be detrimental, and Sid was making quite a few. Rather than report him, the boys took care of it.

Dale was aware that my job was tying the orange flagging around the stakes, so if they were working up in front of us, occasionally, he would leave me notes on a stake with his black jiffy marker, hoping that I would find his message. Sometimes I would find a "Hi Karen," and other times, I would find cute little drawings of flowers or cartoon characters; his small artistic gestures thoroughly warmed my heart and made me smile.

I speculated that Sid, Darcie, and I got hired as a bunch of charity cases, much like a calamity of fools. Sid often made miscalculations, omissions, or oversights, and for the first time, I was never embarrassed or worried what the other people in the camp were thinking. At most times, my fellow workers were oblivious to everything around them unless a deck of cards or a whisky bottle played a key role.

Rather, I felt sorry for Sid, as it was evident that he was partially blind and indisputable that he drank coffee from a thermos with something added other than cream and sugar.

Even though our paths rarely crossed, I got the feeling that Jerry was a good guy, and I was impressed that he had hired his father to keep him gainfully employed, for some source of income and self-worth, aside from his dependency on alcohol.

Working ten-hour days, Darcie and I spent a lot of time together talking and walking the gravel Alaska Highway. Eventually, it came out that Darcie had quit school, and his mother, Jerry's sister, had begged her brother to hire his nephew to keep him out of trouble.

To help me cope with my insubordinate co-worker, I referred to him as an EGR, which stood for "extra grace required." He had a definite chip on his shoulder and could be considered a royal pain in the butt. His flirting was bratty more than it was cute or wrong. Darcie was always coming on to me, trying to kiss me on the job or standing abnormally close. His sixteen-year-old high school dropout mentality was no match for my twenty-two-year-old woman of the world's way of thinking. Completely uninterested, I was also not frightened by his advances, just annoyed.

What made matters worse is that he never started work on time and slept in daily, missing the bus, so it became Jerry's routine to pick up his underage nephew and drive him to the job site. None of the other workers had any patience for Darcie; they scoffed at his laziness and, most times, did not give him the time of day.

Last but not least, to round off the crew, there was me, hired as the popular, persuasive girl's friend, brought up from Vancouver. I enjoyed every aspect of the job, and when not warding off Darcie's advances, I skipped merrily along. I was meeting new people and making money just the same, often whiling away the hours daydreaming and calculating what I would purchase with all the cold hard cash I would receive when the job came to an end.

I was also procrastinating as to how I would spend my life upon returning to Vancouver. Avoiding the fact that I was supposed to be using my time away to ponder furthering my education and my future, I found myself pondering my relationships with John and Dale instead.

A barbecue picnic at the river was Dawna's next grand idea. However, Rosie the cook advised us against it because he had seen some grizzly bears down there only a few days before.

Our plan was to ask Rosie for some steaks, potatoes, pop, dishes, and cutlery. We would build a bonfire and have a good old-fashioned cookout.

Dawna explained to Rosie that our vehicles would only be a few feet away, and the fire and loud partiers would be a deterrent for any bears. Besides, building camaraderie and getting the guys away from gambling for a night made for a win-win situation.

In the end, he agreed, and the party planning committee, Dawna and I, carried on full speed ahead with our plans. Once the invitations were handed out, Rosie handed over the supplies.

We loaded all the provisions into various trucks and headed down to the river late one Sunday afternoon. It was mid-summer in Northern British Columbia.

We did not take into account that most of the guys would be half-corked when they got there. As they had already been drinking for the better part of the day, we were not prepared for what ensued, which was total mayhem.

The men rarely left the camp and the confines of their rooms. Work, the dining hall, the TV room, and gambling consumed their existence, some for at least five or six months at a time.

On this particular day, it was comparable to chickens let out of the coop, caged birds being set free, or cattle emerging from the barn after being locked up all winter. Down at the river, everyone seemed to be running amok, hooting and hollering, play wrestling, and daring each other to jump in the cold, frigid river. I went to Dale, looking for some guidance.

Dale immediately took charge and grabbed an axe from the back of the truck to chop up old dried logs to build a fire. He taught me how to gather the kindling in the form of twigs and branches, and together we created a raging bonfire. On Dale's instructions, we went around setting up a few lawn chairs and assembled logs for people to sit on. Once the fire was hot enough, Dale threw foil-wrapped potatoes into the burning embers at the base.

We set up the condiments, cutlery, and plates, and created an eating area. When the potatoes were forked, indicating just the right softness, Dale placed the steaks on racks the cook had given us and started barbecuing them. Watching Dale and the whole process of pulling the dinner together gave me comfort and a sense of being taken care of. I was impressed by his outdoor skills and know-how. He reminded me of my dad.

The men ravenously ate the prepared food, and everyone simmered down once their bellies were full.

Dawna and Mark managed to organize a few rounds of charades, and they looked cute during the guessing game antics. Dawna's slim body was bundled in plaid, faded jeans, and running shoes with work socks over the top of her narrow blue jeans like leg warmers. Mark was standing at her side with his lumberjack appearance in full beard, dark matching hair, and muscular build. While watching them, I briefly thought if they were to marry, their children would probably be tall and perfect like them.

I, on the other hand, suggested the beer kegs get put away. After a brief silence, there were no takers; everyone rebutted my suggestion, and I almost started World War Three. I soon realized that this group only put the liquor away down their gullets. The party would not be over until every keg and bottle had been consumed.

When the fire finally began to burn out, darkness invaded, with the moon and stars being the only form of light. Finally, when the food and alcohol were all gone, we started to pack up.

Dale explained the importance of ensuring the fire was completely out before we could leave. So we doused the last few flickers from the glowing coals with water taken from the river. The sound of steam combined with truck engines revving filled the night. The echo of screeching tires in the direction of the camp left us standing side by side, silently waiting and watching the smoke curl up toward the star-studded night.

Once we were alone and silence engulfed us, Dale leaned in and kissed me. I let him. It wasn't the kind of kiss you see in the movies, and all I can remember about the moment is that when our lips touched, I knew the memory would last forever.

Soon we were to become more than friends.

I am not sure how everyone made it back to the camp unscathed and all in one piece, but everyone showed up for work the next day, even if the bus ride was more quiet than usual.

Dale, Ray, and Clay were a team and worked for a private surveying company. So they had a different work schedule than the rest of the camp employees. They worked three weeks in and one week out, and it was time for Dale's one week off. I was sad to see him go. I knew that I would use our time apart wisely now that I had more thinking to do than ever.

In Dale's absence, I managed to write a few letters to John, and because Dawna was keeping busy with Mark more and more, I found myself alone in the evenings, which was a welcome change.

I made a pros and cons list. In one column, Dale's name was at the top; in the next column it was John's.

A couple of days after Dale had left, I was in my room reading one evening when I heard a knock at my door. Answering it, I found Merv standing there. He had been kept busy elsewhere on the job site, so I was only seeing him here and there from a distance. He had taken to spending more time down at the horse ranch with the farmer's daughters, visiting, cleaning the stalls, tending to the horses, and spending dinners with the family. None of us questioned what else was going on, but we sure noticed a happy Merv every time he returned to camp.

I liked Merv and all the fun times we had up at Whistler, skiing with Dawna. He had a propensity for being generous and kind, always interested in everyone and everything around him, caring and conscientious.

Standing in my doorway, he said, "Come on, there's something that I want to show you." He then told me to grab my coat, and out the door we went. He led me to his truck and instructed me to get in.

The night sky and surroundings were pitch-dark in this wilderness region, the air cold but not freezing. The complete and utter darkness reminded me of my parents' many Mexican black velvet paintings, minus the flamenco dancers or wide-eyed child with tears streaming down her face.

Leaving the confines of the camp, I wondered where we were going and what Merv had in mind. Neither of us spoke, but I felt safe and at ease, taking the time during the silent drive to ponder and reassess my time thus far, my new friends, the job I was doing, and the vastness of the northern wilderness that was quickly becoming my home. Going into my fourth week at the camp, I had not seen a drop of rain nor a cloud in the sky since I left Vancouver. This night was no exception.

Fifteen minutes later, Merv pulled over, popped in a cassette tape, and said, "Come on," turning the volume up as high as it would go. We emerged from the truck accompanied by Frank Sinatra's voice crooning the old-time classic "Fly Me to the Moon." On that dark, clear summer evening, Merv taught me how to waltz under the stars smack dab in the middle of the Alaska Highway.

It was not a romantic gesture but sweet and charming, just the same. I laughed at myself, learning the steps as I trampled on Merv's toes in the process. He told me stories of his youth and how his mother taught him the old-time dances in their kitchen every morning before the school bus came.

After my attempt at trying to follow and not lead, the song ended, and Merv said that there was something else he wanted to show me. Giving me his hand, he led me up into the back of his pickup truck. He told me to lie down and look up. Following his instructions, taken aback, and in awe, I relaxed and was mesmerized by what I saw—flashes and stripes of purple and pink that streaked the galaxy above.

The magnificent ebony backdrop set off what I had only ever heard about, the Aurora Borealis, also known as the Northern Lights.

Laying face up in the back of his pickup truck, Merv quietly explained that the light show comes from the magnetic poles of the northern and southern hemispheres. This display of bright dancing lights is a result of disturbances in what is called the magnetosphere, caused by solar winds that change the direction of charged particles, mostly protons and electrons, sending them to higher atmospheres, causing the variation of colours.

He pointed out how the lights appear in many forms and colours. Pale green and pink are the most common, but shades of red, yellow, bright green, blue, and violet are documented, too. They come in designs from patches of scattered clouds of light to streamers, arcs, rippling curtains, or shooting rays that light up the sky with an eerie glow.

The Northern Lights we were looking at were bright purple streams, interspersed with hot pink, comparable to my favourite shade of Clinique lipstick, which I had not applied since I was in Vancouver.

We drove back to camp, neither of us talking and just being. I realized that Merv was my first male friend who was not a love interest. I liked him for that very reason.

The Sunday Dale returned from his week off, I found that I was more excited to see him than I thought possible. When he left, Dawna and I gave him a list in hopes that he could bring us back a few things from the city. We were desperate for reading material and civilization, so we requested magazines, *Glamour* and *Cosmopolitan*, plus a bottle of Halston perfume each. He insisted that we not pay him back. I felt royally taken care of, like a princess, and he a gentleman.

I had started to take inventory in my head, comparing John, my university boyfriend of five years in Vancouver, to my new, hardworking, kind-hearted friend Dale from the Prairies. The men were the opposite of each other. With John being a frugal student, he was not in any position to lavish me with gifts, which I fully understood. However, Dale, as a hardworking, gainfully employed surveyor, could. He was older and had a different mindset.

I was perplexed and in a perpetual state of comparing the two men. I summed up that in the long term, John was a safer bet for husband material, and soon he would be graduating as a full-fledged teacher. We had a history together. He was satirical and witty. I admired him and marvelled at how smart and well read he was.

Dale was smart, as well, but in a different way from John, being intelligent in the lay of the land, and he displayed a knack for physical labour. He carried a softness and generosity in him that reminded me of my dad. I was getting used to his laid-back ways and how friendly he was to absolutely everyone. The familiarity I felt toward Dale was down-home goodness that made me think of family, settling down, and having babies.

Dale often talked about his older brother, who was attending art school, and his twin younger sisters who were identical in looks but different in personality. His parents lived in Saskatoon; his mother was a great cook, and his dad was a hairdresser. They went to church, and family was first and foremost in priority. He especially adored his grandfather in Moose Jaw, whom he referred to as Grandpa Pete, and who loved to garden. Dale shared how he would trail after his grandpa as a little boy and family referred to him as "Grandpa Pete's little shadow."

As I feverishly considered my two options, Dale or John, John or Dale, I felt a forewarning worming its way into my reflections. I could not pinpoint a solution, so over and over in my brain, I flipped back and forth, never sharing my dilemma with anyone. I was reminded of the song "Torn Between Two Lovers," by Mary MacGregor and I felt like a fool, breaking all the rules.

Dale introduced me to his music. I had already heard of Neil Young; in fact, my oldest brother had often been compared to Neil Young when he was a teenager (in looks, personality, wardrobe, and stature). Still, I had never listened to or taken note of the heartfelt melodies and political lyrics, as Dale had done.

Dale's homemade tapes had the song titles neatly printed on the outside cardstock encasement, in addition to his artwork, so each cassette looked like a masterpiece encased in its plastic cover.

On our day off, and sometimes late in the evenings, we would sit together on the edge of his bed in his small eight-by-ten-foot room. Dale would play me song after song, patiently explaining such things as the political stance Neil Young was taking in his 1970 hit "Southern Man," which initiated one of the most legendary feuds in rock 'n' roll history. It started when Lynyrd Skynyrd took issue with Neil Young's blanket indictment of Southerners as blatant racists and continued with Skynyrd later name-dropping Neil Young in the song they chose as their reprisal, "Sweet Home Alabama." The lyrics argued, "Southern man don't need him 'round anyhow." Young laid it on thicker with his 1972 song titled "Alabama," which included a blanket indictment of the namesake state's history of racial persecution and its reluctant embrace of civil rights.

I was fascinated and impressed with how much Dale knew and how passionate he was about the world, primarily through music.

His number one band was the Grateful Dead; the name to me, sounded demonic or like heavy metal. Dale laughed and told me that Jerry Garcia was far from evil or hard rock and roll. Garcia spotted the phrase "grateful dead," which the band later discovered to be from an Egyptian prayer, in a dictionary, and it stuck as the band's name. I kind of liked that Dale used the word *prayer*. He went on to tell me that they mixed genres such as psychedelic, blues, folk, country, rock 'n' roll, and jazz to create their incredibly unique rock sound. Dale felt the band's poetic formulas and lengthy jamming rifts were what made them so great. I realized at that exact moment that my treasured disco music had been replaced.

Bob Dylan, Joan Baez, Joni Mitchell, and Van Morrison were also on Dale's playlist. After hearing Van Morrison, I decided that I liked his songs, lyrics, and style the best, especially the song "Brown-Eyed Girl."

Getting to know Dale better attributed to the sickness and uneasiness in the pit of my stomach every time I received a letter from John in the mail. His letters were long and filled with sentiments of missing me terribly, how he adored me and there will never be another . . . as the saying goes, "Absence makes the heart grow fonder," rang in my ears. I would have given anything to hear John speak these words at any given moment during our five-year courtship.

Now here I was out in the Northern British Columbia wilderness at a work camp, so far away from the love of my life. Sometimes I could not even bear to read John's heartfelt words. Reluctantly, and yes, negligently, while biting my lip, I placed his sometimes unopened letters at the bottom of my suitcase.

My life had taken on a different meaning. I was learning so much about myself, making new friends, living in nature, and listening to and learning the lyrics of songs that were powerful and political. I worked day in and day out from sunrise to sunset. I missed John but was taking on a life of my own.

At the end of August, the weather had changed, and work was winding down. Some of the crews and various machine operators were packing up and heading off to other job sites in and around BC or Alberta. Once the ground would freeze at night and not thaw by early morning, everything would come to a grinding halt. A complete job shutdown would take place sometime in the next two weeks.

Dawna and I thought that we should organize one more special event, a party to bid farewell to the North and our workmates, as one last hurrah.

We had noticed a bar in the Township of Pink Mountain but had never investigated. We had heard that the tiny community had a store, a gas station, and a bar, these being the only places to spend money within miles. Realizing that drinks, dancing, and a few games of pool would be a great reprieve to get everyone out of the campsite for an evening and an opportunity to say goodbye, we went ahead and made plans.

With hardly any clothes that fit me anymore, I squished into my jeans like an expanding sausage ready to burst, almost breaking the zipper in the process, and leaving my fingers raw and numb from tugging. I wrapped my pullover hoodie around my waist and tried to adjust my clothes by tucking and hiding various bulges and bumps.

Before my Alaska Highway job, I had hardly eaten anything, with crash diets being common, and wanting to fit sleekly into bikinis in Palm Springs and spandex exercise clothes in Vancouver. The extra calories from the camp food were taking a toll on my figure, and while getting ready for a night out at the bar, I struggled to feel good about my appearance.

As was expected, word quickly spread, and the convoy of vehicles soon proceeded toward Pink Mountain.

There was a lightness in the air, like the last day of school or summer camp had finally arrived, and graduates would be heading off in different directions. But first, the celebrations and goodbyes.

I took my spot in the middle of Ray, Clay, and Dale in the pickup truck. The joking and laughter had begun, and everyone was cheerful. I smiled to myself, noticing that Dale was humming, Ray was whistling, and Clay was singing "Tangled Up in Blue" by Bob Dylan.

"*Early one mornin', the sun was shining, I was layin' in bed, wondering if she'd changed at all, if her hair was still red . . . She was married when we first met, soon to be divorced; I helped her out of a jam, I guess...*" the lyrics sounded familiar even though I had never heard them before.

The now-weathered laugh lines on all three of the handsome men's faces (even Clay had become endearing) was easing my anxiety about how I looked. My mood began to brighten as we careened down the highway, closer to our destination. I felt accepted for who I was and relieved to be in the company that I was keeping.

As we disembarked from the truck and clamoured into the bar, we were all still smiling and laughing. Adjusting my eyes to the dim lighting and smoke-filled room, I spotted Dawna and Mark over by the pool tables. As I approached the couple and their canoodling bodies, Dawna brightened when she saw me. Breaking free from Mark, she moved briskly toward me, clasping her hand in mine, and together we bellied up to the bar to order our drinks.

The haze of smoke in the crowded room was stifling and foreign, causing me to inhale short, shallow breaths and exhale deeply, somehow thinking my method of inhalation would save me from the second-hand smoke that filled my lungs. While pondering the damage to my airways, my eyes narrowed when I spotted Dale nearby, bringing a cigarette to his lips—a nasty habit of his that I had been trying to overlook, telling myself that he had so many other admirable attributes.

Thinking of his kindness brought my heart back to its feeling of fullness, and glancing away, I fell in step with Dawna's chattering to the bartender. I let out a sigh that was a mixture of hope and sadness, joining in the enthusiasm of my friend amidst her suggestion for us to create a signature drink to celebrate the festive occasion.

The bartender concocted "The DK Special," Drambuie and Kahlúa, the initials also representing Dawna and Karen. We all decided that the bartender at the Pink Mountain Bar was signifying a drink in our name. Laughing at the absurdity of it all, we sipped the bitter brown liquid. Initially, it burned our throats, which was followed by the effects of sweet syrupy poison, bringing forth feelings of being on top of the world.

The evening went by without incident, and the feelings of merriment were all around. As the familiar smell of sweat, alcohol, cigarettes, and a few unwashed bodies permeated the air, I realized it was an aroma that, when combined, would always remind me of my time working on the Alaska Highway.

I felt altered—different—and got a sense that there would be more changes on the horizon.

Come Monday, the buzz that turned into gossip on our bus ride to work was that one of the leading Cat operators by the name of Everette had mistaken the Cook's room for the bathroom, entering well after 3:00 a.m. and urinating on Rosie's floor. Everette thought he was standing in front of the urinal, but in reality, having taken a wrong turn, he was nowhere near the bathroom. Consequently, he was black and blue all over from Rosie's hand. When he showed up at the job site, everyone turned a blind eye because he still managed to climb aboard his machine and rev its engine as if it were any other day.

Everette was a small, stocky man with a blond mop top for hair. Holding a continuous furrowed brow and downward scowl, he was a man of few words and fewer friends. Cantankerous and someone to avoid at all costs, he mostly kept to himself unless he was gambling, which was a common nightly occurrence.

It never ceased to amaze me how grown, hard-working men could gamble their entire paycheque away, especially after the day in and day out, and in some cases, hard physical labour. I was astounded when I learned how a select few would spend the entire night drinking and gambling and still manage to work all the next day. When questioning this, Dawna told me that they took pills during the day to stay awake, called Bennies.

I'm not sure if Everette was still intoxicated from the night before or if he had one too many cuffs to the head, but something happened that morning after the urinating incident. When he started up his bulldozer, the earth had given out, and he throttled when he should have braked, causing driver and machine, in slow motion, to slide off the side of the ridge. Onlookers watched Everette and the bulldozer tip and roll from high atop the slope down a steep embankment.

Surprisingly no one was hurt, but in his shock and embarrassment, Everette made a quick getaway to avoid the scrutiny of the others. He jumped off the Cat as it was careening off the embankment, taking off into the bush. Jerry, the foreman, was called on the CB radio, and the entire job and worksite halted for the rest of the day.

Dawna and I, never ones to sit idly by, took the opportunity to chat, goof around, and listen to Dawna's cassettes while practising cartwheels, grapevines, and sit-ups from our past aerobic teaching days. We entertained the troops in the process until the bus came to take us back to the camp. Most of the guys were like our brothers, and we felt like their sisters, all except Mark and Dale.

That night Dale told me that he was leaving the next day for Taber, Alberta. His crew had done all they could do on the Alaska Highway and were being transferred to their next job. We needed to say goodbye. I found out shortly after Dale's announcement that Mark's crew were leaving, too, and Dawna was going to join them. She suggested that I fly out—that maybe there would be more work for the two of us in Taber.

Dale knew that I had commitments and responsibilities back home in Vancouver. He was understanding and prepared that I would be going home to John to sort things out. I owed John that, and I needed to think about him, our future, and what I was going to do next.

Mary MacGregor's song written by Peter Yarrow (of Peter, Paul and Mary) "Torn Between Two Lovers" was reluctantly ringing real in my head yet again.

CHAPTER 7

"It Ain't Me Babe"

1983

I WAS CONFLICTED, WEIGHING THE PROS AND CONS. THE GUILT I felt about deceiving John tormented me, yet the longing to be with Dale brought me solace. I could not focus on anything but the internal combat between my gut, heart, and head. Sometimes I thought neither man was suitable and wondered if it was coming down to the old adage of picking my poison.

I knew that I should have written John more and read his letters repeatedly like lovers did when the miles separated them. It was so unlike me to not be clinging to daily visits from the mail service. In retrospect, a genuinely devoted girlfriend would have placed John's written sentiments under her pillow instead of under her bed zippered into a duffel bag.

In confusion, I felt myself becoming quieter and less animated while I wrestled with my decision to follow Dale to Taber or go home to John in Vancouver. I kept telling myself that I needed more time to know Dale better, which would help me to be sure that a breakup was inevitable with John.

Or perhaps what I had with Dale was just a fling, nothing serious, and John was the man for me.

My thoughts went round and round like a carousel ride at the fair; sometimes, I was on a colourfully painted horse that glided smoothly up and down; other times, I was sitting on a hard, decorative bench that stood still while time waltzed past.

The day after Dale departed, I found out that I could catch a plane to Lethbridge the next morning at 6:00 a.m. and then a bus to Taber to be with him. For the first time since I started work, I decided to go to Jerry with my problem.

A tall, skinny man, quiet and subdued, Jerry was an Albertan hired to work this stretch of the Alaska Highway, overseeing the job and keeping tabs on the camp, workers, and labour, in addition to babysitting his aging father and unruly nephew.

Both Sid and Darcie had left. Darcie had begged for a kiss goodbye, and in my mind, he was lucky that he did not get a wallop to the nose. Good riddance, I thought when I turned my back on the adolescent numbskull, huffing off with arms folded across my chest, my jaw clenched, so wanting to give him a knuckle sandwich in exchange for his months of pestering. Later I thought that perhaps I had been a little harsh with the brat, but unfortunately, I had other things on my mind and bigger fish to fry. True love and a Prince Charming were knocking.

Banging on the door to Jerry's trailer, I felt my stomach drop with a manifestation of dread. Before he answered, I had a compulsion to flee but thought better of it. Eventually, I saw the doorknob turn, and Jerry was there before me with a drink in his hand and a questioning look on his face. Initially hesitant, I quickly realized that if I needed help from this man, that I should look him directly in the eye and assert myself.

Buttering him up, I thanked him profusely for the job he had given me and how it had been a fantastic opportunity. I told him how great he was at managing others and added that I needed to catch the 6:00 a.m. flight the next morning in Fort St. John, heading for Lethbridge. Without missing a beat or taking a breath, I finished by saying that I must leave camp at 4:00 a.m., and could he please arrange a ride for me? Instead of exhaling, I chose instead to hold my breath and stare Jerry right in the eye to wait for his response.

As he swirled the liquid around in his glass, the sound of the clinking ice was deafening until Jerry spoke and casually responded with, "Yeah, I think that Pluto, the parts guy, needs to go into Fort St. John tomorrow. He can take you. I'll make sure he leaves a little earlier to get you to your plane on time."

Before my knees could buckle from relief, I reached out to shake Jerry's hand, then decided to give him a big hug instead. He was taken aback but seemed pleased with my gesture and the easy solution that he had delivered regarding my direct request.

Before closing the door, he said, "Wait a minute." Going back into his makeshift office, he quickly returned and handed me my paycheque. Shoving it in my pocket, I turned to leave and only opened it up while I was walking back to my room. Stopping mid-stride, with widened eyes, I read $4700. Letting out a gasp, my hands rushed toward my mouth as a flush of adrenalin tingled through my body.

Dawna had left behind her clock radio, so I made sure to set it for 3:00 a.m. the next morning. My bags were packed and ready to go, so all I needed to do was shower and somehow try to put on the tiny clothes that I arrived at the camp in. I was sure they must have shrunk with the harsh laundry detergent that we had to use. Unwilling to blame the food, or Rosie, or myself for overindulging, I was excited just the same that I could go shopping soon enough with some of my hard-earned pay.

Waking up before my alarm, apprehension and a sinking feeling told me to get dressed and head over to Pluto's trailer as soon as possible. Within fifteen minutes, I was knocking at his door, and all I could hear was thundering and ear-piercing music that was billowing out from underneath the trailer door and reverberating off the walls. Nobody answered. Desperate to be leaving that morning, I took it upon myself to kick the door as hard as my beautiful steel-toed boots would allow.

Slowly the door creaked open and out poured thick smoke. I had come face to face with pungent-smelling marijuana, smoke so dense that I could hardly see the inhabitants inside the polluted trailer. Finding Pluto through the foggy cloud, I quickly concluded that stoned out of his mind, he might not be able to drive and that I didn't give a crap. All I knew was that I had to catch that airplane!

Grabbing Pluto by the arm, I said, "You are driving me to Fort St. John come hell or high water. Get your boots; we're going!"

With my assertiveness surprising even me, like a bat out of hell, we were off.

It was not yet dawn, so visibility was somewhat of an issue, and only fifteen minutes into the drive, our truck hit the berm. A berm is a raised strip of ground that runs along the side or middle of the road, created by the graders levelling off the road.

With the weather having turned colder, the berm that we hit had frozen rock-hard, so when the truck smashed into the raised ice-covered mound of dirt, a loud thud jolted us, bouncing the vehicle over to the other side of the road. I could not determine if Pluto had fallen asleep at the wheel, or the poor lighting had played tricks with his eyes. Either way, we were both shaken up immeasurably. Neither of us uttered a word. Pluto straightened out the truck, and we continued down the road to my destination.

Another fifteen minutes had passed, and the sun had still not risen, but dawn was slowly coming into focus. Suddenly Pluto screamed, "HOLD ON!" Looking up in slow motion, I saw the most extraordinary sight. A semitrailer was lying on its side across the width of the road, seemingly out of nowhere, and too late to avoid it, we crashed into it.

Even though Pluto slammed on his brakes and tried to turn the wheel, it was not soon enough. We were going far too fast, so the truck slammed sideways, with my side impacting the massive semitrailer that stretched out before us. Upon impact, the sound of crushing metal was earth-shattering.

Stopped almost parallel with the semi, we had smashed and then bounced away. Seemingly timeless, we sat still and silent, confused as dust particles flurried around us. Looking at fragments float past my head and into my eyes, the intense dead air felt dreamlike. I heard Pluto murmur, "Jerry is going to kill me. He said that I had one more chance of not getting into another accident."

With my heart picking up speed, now racing, instantaneously the silence ended, and I became hyper-reactive to sounds, movement, and touch. I could not listen or comprehend anything that Pluto was saying to me. He reached out and grabbed my arm, but out of annoyance or fear, I brushed him off. Vaguely noticing the bystanders running toward us, I jumped out of the truck and with superhero strength, grabbed my suitcase out of the back, stuck out my thumb, and started hitchhiking.

In conjunction were people from all angles hollering at me to wait and to come back; meanwhile, within seconds, a van pulled up. I opened the passenger door and, closing my eyes, I got in. In disbelief of my actions, I made an immediate moral judgment and asked the driver for a ride to the Fort St. John airport.

Settling into the passenger seat, I took a deep breath and let out a huge exhale. It felt like the first breath I had taken all day.

Adjusting myself to my new surroundings, I looked over at the driver. I was taken aback by his appearance. He was an older man, wearing what seemed like a curly wig. Gold-framed aviator glasses perched on his pockmarked nose, and his satin red dress shirt was unbuttoned to his navel. Thick gold chains hung from his neck.

I time-travelled momentarily back to the 1978 disco era, wondering if this man was in costume or if this was his typical attire. All that was missing was a disco ball and Lady Marmalade. Flashing forward to the present time, I instinctively began to check out the rest of the vehicle. Slowly and inconspicuously, I turned to glance over my left shoulder. My facial muscles slackened as the rest of the van came into focus. Stunned in disbelief, all I could see was red shag carpeting throughout the entire vehicle, making its way across the floor and going up the whole inside of the back of the van.

Sitting limply, I eyed dozens of photographs, obviously ripped from magazines, of Canadian singer Anne Murray plastered up on the walls of the van. Then I noticed Anne Murray's familiar gentle voice coming out of the tape deck singing, "We've Only Just Begun."

Snapping my head back around, I observed that the vehicle was creeping along at a snail's pace. Peering out my side window, I calculated that we couldn't be going any faster than twenty miles an hour. Finding my voice, I heard myself whisper loud enough for the driver to hear me, stating that my plane was going to be leaving Fort St. John soon, and could he possibly drive any faster?

The driver's response held a country twang, "I ain't gonna speed for nobody. No girl, or any airplane, will force me to drive any faster than I am already going, you got that?"

Slumping back into my seat, I knew that there was nothing I could do, and I would surely miss my flight. In what felt like minutes, I heard the distant roar of a plane engine soaring overhead. Squinting upward through the windshield, I could see my missed plane above, gaining altitude and headed toward Lethbridge. I was sure I had lost the connection I needed to take me to Dale and my unknown future.

I wondered if the day's events had been an omen of what was to come.

We did not speak for the rest of the ride until the nameless driver asked me to give him twenty dollars for gas, which I did, as we stopped at the airport and I flung open the door to get out. Without looking back, I entered the small waiting area, void of travellers or employees, completely vacant. A sign on the wall indicated that there was another flight leaving at 4:00 p.m. for Lethbridge, so I was hoping to take it.

Spotting a payphone and with time on my hands, I decided that I should telephone John. Surprised that he answered, a mixture of emotions swept over me. Still certain that I wanted to see Dale, I also knew full well that I did not want to hurt John or jeopardize the history that we had shared or the possible future we could have together.

Without hesitation, I told John about the truck accident and my ride with the crazy, eccentric driver. I then explained that I was looking into getting another job, this one in Taber, Alberta, and that I hoped he did not mind. Happy to hear my voice, John was kind and understanding. Stating how much he missed me, he nevertheless assured me that if there was more work to be had, I should go for it. Upon saying goodbye and hanging up, the lump in my throat felt like a golf ball. I was weary and riddled with guilt over wanting to see Dale and not telling John the truth.

On top of everything, my pants were so tight that I struggled to breathe properly. The potato chips and orange pop from the vending machine would be my lunch, which did not make me feel any better. Besides feeling constricted and uncomfortable, I felt a throbbing in my right ankle. When Pluto's truck had slammed into the semi, my ankle became wedged in between the seat and the passenger door. The bump had swollen, and bruising was well underway, turning my whole foot various shades of blue and purple and reminding me of the Aurora Borealis that Merv had so kindly introduced me to.

I started to think that trauma was broadening my perspective of reality but then concluded that trauma was possibly making my perspective a foggy mess.

Later that afternoon, I brightened when the airport started to show signs of life. Two employees arrived, a ticket taker and a baggage handler, followed by people with luggage, and soft murmurs of conversation.

I was able to change my ticket. Missing the plane was a non-issue, and I did not need to speak of the accident that had occurred only hours before. I was planning to use the incident to support my case of why I missed my flight, but it was completely unnecessary. I got on the next flight with no explanation necessary.

As the small plane took off, I nestled in and was struck by another recent out-of-the-ordinary occurrence, a careless mistake . . .

Shortly before I got the call from Dawna, I had had a pregnancy scare with John. My period was late, and we were both panicked. Two to three days of lateness turned into a week and still no sign that I was out of the woods. Even though I desperately wanted a baby, I knew that it was not the right time for John.

When I asked him what we would do if I were pregnant, he responded without skipping a beat, "Well, you will get an abortion, of course." I was instantly profoundly hurt and did not respond to John's blatant statement. His analogy and decision even before it was needed, surprised me, but discerning that he felt that he knew best, I kept my mouth shut at his off-putting remark. Within a day, my cycle had arrived. We were both relieved, but I was left with an underlying feeling of sadness, not able to pinpoint its origin.

Making mistakes, having poor judgment, or just being careless seemed to be in the cards for me because my pregnancy scare ended up repeating itself. This second pregnancy scare would also amount to a late period, and once again my body would get itself back on track.

Throwing caution to the wind, I fell into the excitement of being away from home, the rugged wilderness, and the romance that goes with meeting someone new. The physical attraction took over my senses, and on a late night while listening to Dale's music, the melodies and lyrics of Neil Young, we unexpectedly kissed and, carelessly, without thinking, one thing led to another. Again I was faced with being late, but this time not with my long-term boyfriend of five years, the teenager-turned-man who had been juggling my heart between school and friendships. Instead, my pregnancy scare was with another man.

Almost verbatim to what had happened with John, I found myself repeating my dilemma, telling Dale and asking him what we would do if I were pregnant. His response was immediate and direct. In no uncertain terms, he said with a smile on his face, "Well, I guess we would get married, have a beautiful baby together, and live happily ever after," as if it was the only possible solution. My heart leaped at his sweetness and how easily the answer came to him.

Two men that I cared for, the same predicament, with two completely different responses to an age-old, serious question, "What if I am pregnant?"

Thinking about it, I could not help but wonder if the answer were right there in front of me, a blueprint that would help me pull my needed decision together.

The closer the plane got to Dale and the farther away it flew from John, a song on my cassette tape spoke to me, "Dust in The Wind" by Kansas, and I was wondering if that's all we were, dust in the wind. As the aircraft lowered itself from the cloudless blue sky, I was melancholy as I eased my mind toward the unknown.

After disembarking from the plane, I had no way of communicating with Dale or Dawna that I had arrived. With a new feeling of confidence and independence, I caught a bus headed for Taber, just a thirty-minute nonstop ride from Lethbridge.

The flat prairie and fields that stretched out before me were plain and different from that of the bustling business of Vancouver and the tranquility of Fort St. John. The flatness represented my transition.

Once in Taber, the bus depot was within walking distance to the address of the motel where Dale, Clay, and Ray were staying. Hoisting my duffel bag up over my shoulder and struggling down a few long blocks, I spotted the main office.

Before going in, I noticed an old rusty swing set that I imagined had been sparkling brand-new at one time. Next to it was a seesaw and a sandbox, both lying dormant, no children in sight. The paint had chipped, and speckled rust replaced it. I stood for a moment, thinking about the ghosts from days gone by. The travellers with their excited children had all checked out, probably grown up by now. I speculated that the families all had fond memories of when their parents had stopped at the Taber Motel with its remarkable brand-new playground.

Snapping out of my thoughts, I ran into Dale, Ray, and Clay on their way back from dinner, all three outwardly pleased to see me. After placing my bag in Dale's room, the boys decided that my arrival was cause for celebration, so off to the bar we went.

Dale announced to me that he was expecting time off in a few days and that I shouldn't bother to get a job. If I could hold on for a couple of days, he wanted to take me skiing in Banff. He had some good friends there and offered to treat me to a week of skiing.

Excited at the prospect of going away with Dale on a vacation, I chose not to pursue a job and made the decision to wait until Dale could get away. In the meantime, I decided to check out the Township of Taber so I could finally purchase some larger clothes that would comfortably fit my ever-changing frame.

The next morning after Dale went to work, I stepped outside our motel room, embraced by a brisk wind, not a pleasant fall breeze but gusts that blew signs over and hoods off of one's head. Pulling my jacket tighter around me, I crossed the street and walked through the centre of town in silence, collecting my thoughts.

I stopped in my tracks and was stunned at my failure to remember how my mother had grown up in this small prairie town that I was presently meandering through.

My mother's stories and memories were there at my fingertips, but I could not grasp them. Instead, my brain felt fuzzy and full.

Walking the empty streets, changing gears, and bringing up thoughts of my mother, I felt better visualizing her strolling the streets of this hometown and old stomping ground where she had once lived.

As a teenager, Frances, my mother, was willowy thin with a pale complexion, poker-straight blond hair, and was known for perpetually having her nose in a book and tripping over her feet. She was not petite by any standards and often thought that tall girls were unfairly overlooked.

Her best friend Ruth, on the other hand, was petite, but was also penniless and painfully shy. The two of them were nicknamed the "Gold Dust Twins," even though there was nothing twin-like about them.

As tomboys, they had their fair share of adventure and daydreams hanging out at Ruth's farm, or over at my mother's home at the train station, where her father was the station agent. Bicycles and books were the mainstay all summer long, and my mother notoriously being something of a bully, offered up a knuckle sandwich to anyone that dared bother them.

As my walking slowed, her voice whispered in my ear, telling me that I should read more and live life to the fullest. Tumbleweeds blew past me right down the middle of the street just as she described it to be. Visions of cowboys and covered wagons, Model T Fords, and bicycles brushed past me as if ghosts from days gone by escorted me and haunted me with more carefree times.

Missing my family, I snapped out of my thoughts from the past when I stumbled upon the only store in Taber that could meet my needs, Fields Department Store, where clothes were reasonably priced and functional.

After trying on new jeans, two sizes bigger, I was relieved that I could breathe comfortably again, and my belly was self-contained without side-splitting pain. No longer was I poured into pants that did not fit. I also bought myself a thick jade green sweater, as winter seemed to be invading the atmosphere.

After shopping, I felt elated and continued with my tour of the town. I noticed a school, a gymnasium, and an outdoor pool, eventually coming across a dry cleaner that offered cheap alterations. I thought that if I could get the broken zipper fixed on my old jeans, then one day I could wear them again after the high-calorie camp food had worn off, and I got back into teaching fitness.

When I opened the door, a jingling bell brought the person from the backroom out front to see the customer. At first, taken aback and then delighted, I realized that I had come face to face with the daughter of my mother's best friend Ruth. We had met as children and had gotten along well, and now here we were standing in a dry cleaner with the pervasive smell of cleaning solutions and clear plastic bags surrounding us.

As the story went, our mothers used to laugh at how Connie was tall and slim with long blond hair like my mother, and I was shorter with curly hair, more like Ruth, Connie's mother. My mother had named me "Karen Ruth," and Ruth had named her daughter "Connie Frances." Unbeknownst to each other, when their babies were born, they gave them their best friend's name.

Making plans to see each other again, I left my jeans with Connie and headed back to the motel.

That night, I had hoped that Dale was going to announce his time off. I thought a road trip would be a final test and allow me to get to know him better before the inevitable arrived, with me finally going home. The evening came and went with no announcement.

With little else to do and for the fun of it, I ended up going out with Connie and her friends on a few occasions. We made the trip into Lethbridge and went to a few of her best-loved watering holes, reconnecting and rekindling our childhood friendship.

But as the days turned into a week, I was restless, not working and thinking about going home. With still no word of Dale's upcoming week off, I was tired of waiting around a motel room, walking the streets of the quaint little town during the day, and meeting the crew for drinks at night. I had decided to catch a Greyhound bus back to Vancouver one afternoon on a whim.

Before doing so, I wrote Dale a letter. I was giving up on everything. I suppose I was running away from Dale. Or was my trip up north running away from John? Either way, I felt the need to flee and to run off yet again.

That afternoon I wrote a letter:

Dear Dale,

I first want to thank you so much for the opportunity to get to know you. You have shown me another side to life. Your outdoorsy nature and easy-going persona have inspired me. You are the sweetest, kindest, and most generous person I have ever had the pleasure to know. I am writing this letter to say goodbye and to thank you. I cannot wait any longer for your upcoming time off, and even though a ski trip to Banff would have been excellent, I must be on my way. I need to go back to Vancouver. Let's stay in touch.

Love Karen

P.S.

Four strong winds that blow lonely, Seven Seas that run high. All those things that don't change come what may, But our good times are all gone, And I'm bound for moving on. I'll look for you if I'm ever back this way . . .

As I was placing the letter in an envelope addressed to Dale, he burst through the door of the motel room. Breathless, he hurriedly told me that first thing the next morning, we would be taking off to enjoy a week of skiing in Banff.

I chose to say nothing as I inconspicuously slipped the letter into the bottom of my suitcase, out of sight and out of mind.

Initially with Dale's news, I felt immediate pain in the back of my throat. My chin dipped to my chest as my shoulders slumped forward. I had almost gotten on that bus. I was ready and wanting to go home, back to Vancouver and John, fitness, and my family.

Glancing up to meet Dale's smiling face, our eyes met, and I snapped out of my reluctant state and displayed only joy toward his announcement.

I chose not to hop aboard the Greyhound bus that night because of Dale's exuberance and long overdue promise of skiing. Why would I go home now, I thought?

Sleep would not come. I tossed and turned, dreaming of John mowing the lawn and me having an abortion, or marrying Dale and him teaching our baby how to smoke. Should I ski with Dale or go home to John? Stay with Dale and break up with John? Break up with Dale and stay with John? Dishonesty was not my usual nature, or so I liked to think. Life felt like a throw of the dice and a twist of fate. I did not know what was in the cards for me. For some reason, I could not think logically as my heart was in the driver's seat.

The first thing the next morning, I climbed into my new jeans and emerald green sweater, and we were off. Once again, Dale displayed a knowledge for the lay of the land that I had no idea existed. As we exited the Township of Taber and headed toward Calgary, Dale recounted some history related to how the Banff ski resort came to be.

He told me that Banff Sunshine Village, formerly named Sunshine Village, was located on the Continental Divide of the Canadian Rockies within Banff National Park in Alberta, and that the hiking was unbelievable and simply marvellous. I had no idea that Dale even liked to hike.

As he continued, thoughts of my dad came to mind as Dale spoke of the first explorer who passed through the Sunshine area in 1841. He was Governor George Simpson of the Hudson's Bay Company, seeking quicker routes into the Columbia District. The next significant exploration party was the Palliser Expedition in the 1850s; Mt. Bourgeau is named for one of its members.

Ironically, my father had often shared stories of the railway, so I knew that everything opened up with the building of the Canadian Pacific Railway and its arrival in Banff in the late 1880s. However, I could not recall the names of people, places, and things as readily as Dale could. He said that a man by the name of Bill Peyto, a trapper and prospector, was responsible for bringing the first tourists to the area in the 1890s. He became a guide, taking tourists through the Sunshine Meadows to the base of Mt. Assiniboine, the highest peak in the Southern Continental Ranges of the Canadian Rockies.

By the 1920s, Sunshine Meadows had become a popular camping site. In 1928, a horse club called Trail Riders of the Canadian Rockies was sponsored by the Canadian Pacific Railway, which built a log cabin for them. I interjected by telling Dale about my sister's horseback riding club called the Rolley Lake Trail Riders. We both had a chuckle, and Dale went on to say that the oldest building in Banff Sunshine Village, known as the Old Sunshine Lodge, was still standing.

Again, Dale's storytelling and recollection of the history books enabled me to visualize the people and places, reminding me of the many hours I travelled with my father and how he often spoke of old days. I did not want him to stop, so he went on. His identification of dates, people, and places had me listening on the edge of my seat, and with my encouragement, he told me more, stating that in March 1929, Cliff White and Cyril Paris, two local extreme sports enthusiasts, were the first to ski what is now known as Banff Sunshine.

By 1934, Jim and Pat Brewster were leasing the CPR cabin and were offering ski vacations. They eventually bought the lodge in 1936, hired the first ski instructor, Swiss guide Bruno Engler, and in 1941 a rope tow was built. The Brewster family owned the area until 1951 then sold it to George Encil.

Cliff White Jr. and his wife Bev purchased the resort in 1961, and it was their vision that shaped the resort by partnering with other developers to build accommodation on the mountain and opening the ski slopes and adding a chairlift. In 1980 they opened the first gondola, which replaced bus access to the ski area.

From Taber to Canmore, Dale talked about yesteryear; every time he paused, I applauded. Stopping for lunch along the way, Dale enjoyed a few beers with our patty melts. He was on holiday and celebrating our time together.

I also witnessed scenery I had never seen before. It started with the sublime flatness of the Prairies and turned into the rolling hills and ranch land of Calgary. Eventually we entered a whole new world, the majestic rigid Rocky Mountains; grandiose, strong and sharp; towering and powerful.

This mild-mannered man, who I thought was a quiet and laid-back hippie, was proving to be an encyclopedia. I was able to imagine how the Rocky Mountains formed possibly eighty million years ago, and how, over time, tectonic activity and erosion by glaciers had sculpted the Rockies into dramatic peaks and valleys.

I especially enjoyed how Dale concluded that the Rockies were home first to Indigenous people. I would never have known any of this if it had not been for Dale's account. I marvelled at how ignorant I was and how genuinely interested I was in everything he had to say.

As Dale finished, I could hardly wait to tell him about my dad and how he had ridden the rails from Alberta to Northern BC as a thirteen-year-old boy in 1929, with hopes of finding gold and a better life.

I kept wondering why I had not seen this part of Canada before. I felt the need to tell John everything, as if he was a friend, or a family member, a cousin, or a long-lost brother. I then wished for his wise advice, his common sense, as to whether I was making the right choices, knowing full well that he loved me as his girlfriend and would be hurt and saddened by my behaviour. I could not stop my tormenting thoughts, and I could not share or show my true feelings to Dale.

Sitting side by side, my hand was on his leg, his one hand on mine, while the other assuredly rested on the steering wheel. Dale's storytelling while he drove, was accompanied by the music from his cassette tapes that billowed out of the dashboard: ballads, narratives, and melodies serenading us as the miles slipped past.

During breaks in the conversation, my attention was on the lyrics from Bob Dylan's song "It Ain't Me Babe," asking myself if Bob was crooning me a message, a forewarning of what was to come: *"Go 'way from my window, leave at your own chosen speed. I'm not the one you want babe; I'm not the one you need."*

Kevin and Patsy were the caretakers for a resort that consisted of ten small cabins, keeping within the Rocky Mountain Alpine theme. The cottages looked like images in a children's storybook; gingerbread houses that were missing the decorations of gumdrops, candy canes, and Smarties. Dark brown miniature log homes, with scalloped white trim and matching window boxes, now void of flowers, were piled with snow to the bottom of the window ledges. These cozy rental dwellings all had chimneys puffing out smoke from the stone fireplaces within.

We would be staying with Dale's friends, Kevin and Patsy, who lived at one of the cottages. How convenient, I thought, that they both worked at the cute little holiday spot, situated just outside of Banff in a place called Canmore, Alberta.

They were a petite couple who matched the setting perfectly. Kevin was a slight man who seemed far too young to have curved shoulders and a noticeable tremor to his hands. His hair was thin, long, and blond. Full whiskers covered his face, and he wore a beautiful, gentle smile that caused his brilliant blue eyes to squint as he often shyly grinned. He was dressed in a red flannel shirt and faded baggy jeans.

Patsy, too, was of small stature with a "rough around the edges" appeal. She had straight brown hair, enormous brown eyes, and tiny teeth with spaces in between them. Her voice was raspy, and she cleared her throat each time before she spoke. Even though it was wintertime, she wore tube tops and cut-off denim shorts, throwing a man's oversized parka over top of everything when she went outside.

It was Patsy's job to keep the cabins clean and Kevin's job to maintain the grounds outside. They both enjoyed hiking and cross-country skiing. Some would say they had a perfect gig, working, living, and playing in such a place they both seemed to love.

Arriving in the afternoon, we drank Caesars with vodka, Tabasco, and salted rims on the glasses while Patsy made us crêpes for dinner, filled with seafood from a can.

Getting to know Kevin and Patsy, as one does over drinks, I was saddened when I heard Kevin's story. Even though on the outside, he appeared to have a quaint, appealing lifestyle, working at the cabins and puttering around fixing things while keeping the grounds presentable, he always had a drink in hand, and I got the feeling that there was more to his soft-spoken nature and heavy drinking than meets the eye.

He told me that he had not seen his little girl in over three years. He proudly showed me a worn photograph of his blue-eyed blonde cherub, a five-year-old pint-sized version of himself, depicting her first day of kindergarten. A tiny waif of a thing stared longingly into the camera, almost ghost-like. She had the same thin blond hair as Kevin and a mischievous grin just like her daddy.

Kevin did not go into any details of why he had not seen his daughter, and I was not about to ask, so I just listened and allowed myself to feel bad. Kevin was a sweet-tempered soul who carried his heartache on his sleeve. His voice and story eventually trailed off, and I wished I could do or say more, ask a question, or cheer him up somehow, but sensing that he did not want to share any more than he already had, we sat in silence.

My only other experience skiing had been with Dawna and Merv at Whistler, so I was looking forward to trying a new mountain and a new ski partner. Dale was looking forward to trying the newly installed gondola.

The next morning it was unseasonably cold and windy, but we bundled up in borrowed clothes, and our spirits were high. Kevin dropped us off at the ski mountain, and after the tickets were purchased, we rented equipment and got all set up for a day on the slopes. Dale paid for everything, and this brightened my mood even more. I felt loved and taken care of.

Sparkling new gondolas awaited us. Climbing aboard and nestling in, comfortable and cuddled up, we rose toward a snow paradise in the sky. Once embarking from the silver capsule that transported us, we emerged at the top, and without a moment's notice, before I could get my bearings, Dale took off down the first run with me trailing after him.

The snow was the consistency of baby powder that flew off the back of Dale's skis like particles of white dust. My eyes stayed fixed on this man whom I saw a whole other side of. Not only could he manoeuvre in and out of Volkswagen Bug–sized moguls with finesse and speed, but he managed to include a backflip just before the straight downhill at the end of the run.

Catching up to him, I was unable to speak, with my mouth unattractively agape. I noticed that in addition to Dale's remarkable flip, he had been smoking a cigarette Marlboro Man–style the whole time while careening down the mountainside. Applause from onlookers only validated how impressed I was.

I knew Dale could ski, but it was not until after our first day on the slopes that I found out about his past family ski trips and how he and his brother would fly down the mountainside together, performing flips and tricks until crowds would gather.

Dale told me story after story about him and his friends regularly skiing at Blackstrap Mountain in Saskatoon, a small human-made slope with the nickname "the pimple on the prairie." Dale chuckled with an infectious laugh and humble smile as he shared with me how he spent his winters growing up.

Dale and his friends would form teams and skate to their hearts' content on outdoor arenas—concrete slabs that the parents had turned into skating rinks—whether it was early morning before school, at recess, or after school, and even on weekends. His stories melted my heart, and I was becoming infatuated. He was no longer a stranger from the Prairies and a mysterious guy I had met at a work camp, but preferably someone I could spend the rest of my life being married to.

The rest of the week carried on much the same way. We ate dinners and had drinks with Kevin and Patsy at night, with me in awe of Dale the whole next day on the ski hill.

Eventually, our time together came to an end, and the inevitable had arrived. It was time for me to go home, back to

Vancouver. I was scheduled to catch the train in Banff, heading west to Vancouver, first thing in the morning, and directly following my departure, Dale would be travelling east in the truck he had purchased from Ray, the vehicle called Sluggo, back to Taber.

Our goodbyes at the train station in Banff were lacking something, but I could not pinpoint what it was. Whether I was tired from a week of skiing, combined with cocktails every night, or was worrying about what lay ahead, either way, all we did was embrace, and in unison said, "It's been nice and let's try to keep in touch."

Emotion escaped me as I climbed aboard the train, but not for long. As I sat down, a rush of excitement washed over me. I loved trains and was looking forward to settling into my seat to enjoy the scenery and ten hours of reflection, followed by preparation for what was to come. The last five months had undoubtedly changed my life forever.

CHAPTER 8

"Always on my Mind"

1983–1986

THE TRIP HOME ON THE TRAIN WAS NOT AS ENJOYABLE AS I HAD expected. Between napping and pondering my reunion with John, I realized that this homecoming would be different from the time I had returned from Palm Springs. So much had happened, and so much had changed. Gone was the anticipated delight and high spirits of a reunion, being replaced with a different version of my old self, new life experiences, new friends, and a secret that plagued me with deep guilt.

I listened to Willie Nelson on my Walkman, from a tape that Dale loaned me, and I could not decide if the lyrics were meant for John or for me. "Maybe I didn't love you quite as often as I could have. And maybe I didn't treat you quite as good as I should have. If I made you feel second best, girl, I'm sorry, I was blind. You were always on my mind. You were always on my mind."

As the train rolled into the Vancouver train station, I emerged from the platform to see John waiting for me, holding two dozen long-stemmed red roses. Immediately my heart broke.

After embracing, we climbed into my car that I had left behind for John to use and drove to English Bay in Vancouver. John wanted to show me a new restaurant that he thought I would like, a romantic spot that overlooked the beach. Coincidently on this night, there was a gorgeous, romantic Vancouver sunset.

As the bright yellow sun lowered itself into the ocean, my spirits began to sink along with it. Our conversation was full of lightness and pleasantries, like two old friends reuniting to talk about the weather and what the latest statistics were on the sports teams we followed.

I had difficulty participating in any in-depth discussion, as if responding to John's many questions took a great effort. I sat, staring into the blue eyes of the man I was supposed to spend the rest of my life with, and I couldn't help but think of the last five months with Dale. How ironic that during my time up north, John ended up thinking more of me than I of him. It had always been the other way around.

Sitting across the table from John, with a multitude of fragrant roses interrupting my thoughts, I now felt like I was being unfaithful to Dale. Unable to bring myself to the truth of the matter, I explained to John that I had gone through some changes, and instead of going back to our apartment, I needed to go home to my parents' house to think. John understood and agreed.

After John paid the bill, also an anomaly because we always split everything, we went back to our place in Kits, which I had hardly lived in, the surroundings now strange, foreign, and eerily forbidden. Everything felt wrong. Dropping off my suitcase and leaving it unpacked beside the bed that I was supposed to share with John, I said a half-hearted goodbye and jumped into my car straight away, heading out to Stave Falls to see my parents and ultimately be alone.

On the drive home, I intended to think and regroup and decide if I should confess the truth, my sins, and infidelity to John.

Pulling up to the log home, before getting out of my car, I leaned my head on the steering wheel and prayed. I asked for divine intervention, a voice from God, a message from the galaxies above telling me what to do.

Some of the weight of decision-making lifted from my shoulders once I saw my old bedroom. My old PNE stuffed animals brought me comfort. The ballerina bedding, gold-flecked shag carpeting, and purple bedside lava lamp made me wish for the carefree days of my youth that, now looking back, seemed like trivial teenage angst.

I plopped down on my bed, sighed, and began to cry. Not demure, gentle sobs but loud, hoarse groans, like someone or something had just died. My throat and heart ached; the deep heavy pressure on my chest was close to unbearable. It never crossed my mind to share how complicated my life had become with my parents. Instead, I curled up into a tiny ball and fell fast asleep.

The next morning I made my way downstairs wearily, breathing in the warm smell of burning firewood and sizzling bacon. Grabbing my Walkman from my purse, I told my mom that I was going to take the dog for a walk.

My dog, Toby, a black Lab that John's friend had given me from the SPCA a few years back, rushed to my side and tried to offer me his undying companionship. Together outside, we walked the familiar horse-riding trails that I knew like the back of my hand.

Popping in an Elvis Costello tape (another loan from Dale), we entered the forest. Now in amongst old-growth cedar trees, I got the feeling that they had seen it all before.

I called out to God and prayed again, hoping that my simple childhood faith could offer me direction and a semblance of peace. It started to rain, so I asked for the water to wash away my sins.

Fresh, moist air magnified the scent of evergreen trees and damp earth. With Mother Nature beneath my feet, she encouraged me to keep propelling forward. Every step inspired the muscles in my legs to work like they had not done in months since teaching my fitness classes. Climbing over logs and trailblazing through the woods, my dog never looked happier.

Stopping periodically to take in the surroundings on a full scale helped me to appreciate where I was. My soul drank up the sight of moss-covered trees and huckleberry bushes now void of berries. I couldn't help but smile at the memory of riding my horse Cricket through these same trails and reaching down to pluck the sweet, delicious fruit from their thin, frail branches.

It was early November, the month of my birth. Soon it would be my 23rd birthday. How old and weary I felt, like my life was slipping through my hands.

Gone were the dry clear skies of Northern BC and Alberta, both starting to fade, as if blown away by the prairie wind. They were replaced by moist air and the damp, soggy ground. As I continued to tromp through the backwoods of my youth, one thing that I could identify was that the West Coast of BC was where I belonged.

Like a virus, fits of anger erupted within me as I stomped down branches, forging forward and lashing out at the earth every step of the way. Breathless, I stopped. With my hands on my waist, I realized that I wanted both men, but that was against all the rules.

Eventually, the salt from my tear-stained face began to dry on my cheeks, indicating that my weeping had ceased, making it evident that I was empty.

Abruptly turning around, I whistled for my dog and headed back. Straightening up ever so slightly, I knew what I had to do.

Relishing in the lay of the land and my music with its sympathetic vocals, I returned to my family home. I greeted my cats, curled up into tight little balls on the worn couch covered in its familiar wagon-wheel fabric. How I wished I could be one of them. I put my face to theirs and nestled into their coziness, breathing in their furry dusty scent and cold-shouldered silence.

My father was outside puttering around the property, and my mother was inside preparing food when the telephone rang. Startled, I felt my jaw tighten, and apprehension come over me. I hesitated to answer the now shrilling and obtrusive sound. As the phone kept ringing, my mother looked at me to do something. Hurriedly, I picked up the phone, and what came next was inaudible. I strained to hear the caller and finally made out that it was John, and he was crying.

Never had I heard such a sound of distress coming from him. I took the phone and cradled the receiver under my chin. With its long extension cord, I tucked it under the bathroom door. Sitting on the edge of the bathtub, I locked the door, as I could not bear for my mother to hear what was going to come next.

It occurred to me that maybe someone had died, and I wished that had been the case when I finally made out what John was saying. He told me that he decided to do something helpful, so he began to unpack my suitcase. When he got to the bottom, he found the letter that I had written to Dale.

I froze, straining to hear without breathing, blinking, or swallowing. John yelled at me through the receiver how heartbroken he was and how I had ruined everything. And lastly, that he was moving out that day and taking his belongings with him.

My goodbye letter, the one I had intended to give to Dale, betrayed me and spilled the beans. I cringed, remembering my heartfelt words to another man and realizing how devastated I would have been if the situation were reversed and I had found a letter that John had written to another woman.

John hung up on me, as my apologetic "sorry" sounded flat and meaningless to both of us.

How stupid it was for me not to throw the letter away, asking myself with regret, why I had kept it? What a horrible, irrational mistake. Everything was out.

The next day, without explaining anything to my parents, I left. I went back to the apartment in Kitsilano, a place that had once been my love nest with the one I thought to be my knight in shining armour.

Upon entering, there was an unusual silence. The door echoed when I closed it due to the emptiness I found within. John had moved out. His belongings were gone. Hesitantly going into our bedroom, my shoulders dropped, and I could not breathe. John had turned my modelling photos on the dresser around to face the wall, so all I could see was the back of the frame. Instantaneous shame and remorse came over me. Everything felt dramatic and wrong, like a terrible mistake had occurred, one that I could not fix or change and dared not try.

I did not speak to John or Dale for a few weeks. I went to the Hudson's Bay sporting goods department and bought new skis with some of my "up north money." Winter was coming, and so was my birthday.

My parents offered to help me with rent. Having told them of the breakup between John and me, they did not provide any advice or words of wisdom, but I was sure they were disappointed in me. My mother so wanted me to marry an educated, well-to-do man. But to make up for it, she told me later that my father had felt intimidated by John because of his academic status, which made me think that he might like Dale.

I could no longer afford to live alone in the Kits apartment, so I gave a one-month notice and stayed in the apartment alone until the end of November.

The last melodramatic tragedy to occur for quite some time was spending my 23rd birthday alone. November 17th was a dark rainy night in Vancouver; my apartment was cold and empty. I was lonely and sad. I called my parents, sobbing into the telephone, and they offered to come and get me. I refused their offer and decided to spend the evening rotting in my guilt and retribution. I called Dale long distance to tell him that it was my birthday. He answered the phone, slurring from a night out with the crew, and I realized I disliked the sound of his drunken voice. Not feeling any better, I ended the call and went to bed.

At the end of November, I moved back home.

January 1983 was the start of a fresh new year. John and I were finished, five years down the drain. I was guilt-ridden and bitter, choosing to stuff down all my feelings as I did not have any time to grieve. I was getting ready because Dale was coming out from Calgary to visit me.

I had not seen him since we said goodbye at the train in Banff. I had come clean with John in the most horrible of ways, and I was ready to commit with Dale. We planned to meet in Vancouver and together go up to Whistler to ski. Dale had never been there before, and I smiled at the thought of him displaying his skills to all the Whistler hotshots; my humble prairie boy could handle himself on their world-class slopes, of that I was sure.

Dale became my entire focus. While I was introducing him to Whistler, my friends, my family, and my lifestyle, I was looking forward to eventually meeting his family and friends, too. I made a conscious effort to love the one I was with.

For the rest of the winter and spring, Dale continued to work three weeks out up north and enjoy one week in Vancouver with me. He was still with his same co-workers, Ray and Clay, working in Alberta or Northern BC and travelling to Whistler and me for his one week off a month.

Using the Whistler boys' living conditions as a model, Dale and I thought that it would be fun to rent a house in Burnaby with some friends, and also more affordable for everyone involved. We found a four-bedroom home. I invited two of my friends, and Dale asked one of his to share the space and the rent.

The plan was to dwell together, entertain, have dinners, and play lots of Trivial Pursuit and charades.

One of my girlfriends was a nurse. We had gone to high school together, reconnected, and now we were roommates, just like the hit TV show *Three's Company*. Her name was Kelly, and she was a petite brunette, almost as cute as Joyce Dewitt, who played Janet on the well-loved comedy.

Kelly was single, dated periodically, and was a lot of fun. She introduced me to Grace, who moved in as another roommate. Grace was a music therapy student. She played the flute and was in a symphony of some sort on the side, as a hobby. Grace had wild, short blond hair and laughed more than anyone I had ever met before, even if things were not funny. She reminded me of Goldie Hawn from the old variety TV show called *Laugh-In* but in appearance only, because she was much smarter than the ditsy blonde portrayed on the program.

It worked, and we all got along well.

Dale invited his friend Edwin from Edmonton to move in, as well. That made five of us renting, which brought down the cost considerably.

Edwin moved to Vancouver to meet chicks, and he worked in an office nine to five. The girls and I used my EGR acronym for Edwin—Extra Grace Required—because he annoyed us. He liked to eat cold mushroom soup directly from the can and often stayed out all night (we wondered where he would go and what on earth he was doing, but dared not ask). Edwin had a permanently red runny nose, sniffling all over the house.

Dale was only home one week per month, so the girls and I endured Edwin. We were kind because being nice meant that you never let people know what you were really thinking. Edwin reciprocated; he was pleasant but refused to do the dishes.

We cooked, cleaned, and maintained the home together. Barbecuing was our standard form of cooking, and Dale was the king of salad making—the "best in the land" was the running joke. Having seen his artwork on his cassette tapes, I was not surprised by his tedious style of chopping vegetables and assembling them in a stylish, aesthetically pleasing format. Cucumbers were the exact diameter across, tomatoes diced perfectly, and each lettuce leaf was washed and gently pulled apart so as not to bruise. Salads soon became his claim to fame.

A proper proposal and marriage still rattled around in my mind, and aside from all the perks of living together, I always longed for the ceremony, white gown, and all the trimmings; traditional nuptials that only a wedding can bring—the whole kit and caboodle. For now, all dreams were placed directly on the back burner.

Summer turned into fall. I taught fitness and collected unemployment insurance, enjoying my days and weekends attending fitness workshops, and volunteering at various fitness events throughout the city. My roommates and I would have cookie-baking parties and enjoyed watching shows such as *Family Ties*, *The Cosby Show*, and *Hill Street Blues*. We went for walks around Stanley Park Seawall and talked endlessly about our relationships and bright futures.

I thoroughly enjoyed my freedom with Dale's work schedule. I liked missing him, enjoyed our one week a month together, and looked forward to him leaving again.

It was on an evening when Dale was home that the telephone rang, and it was Dale's mother calling from Saskatoon, not wanting to speak to Dale, but rather to be introduced to me and have a chat.

I was immediately thrown for a loop but was able to recover quite quickly, taking the phone into the bathroom out of habit but also for better sound and privacy. Our conversation went something like this:

Dale's mother, Marlene, spoke in a very kind motherly tone. "Hello dear, I am Dale's mother, and I thought I should call to introduce myself since you are living with my son."

Responding sweetly, enthusiastically, and rambling nervously, I said, "Oh hi! I am so glad that you called me. My name is Karen, and yes, we are living together, but it's not really how I would like to do things. It is mostly for convenience purposes, and I'm not sure if you know this, but Jeff (Dale's older brother) is thinking of moving to Vancouver. The boys are thinking of getting a roommate, and then I would try living alone."

"That sounds very nice. We would love to meet you. When do you think that could be made possible?"

Pleased and much calmer, I replied, "I would be very interested in meeting you, too. Dale and I talked about driving out there this Christmas. Jeff will be here by then, and perhaps we can all drive out there together. Would that work for you?"

"Yes, that sounds good. I am concerned about the roads, though. The driving conditions can be very treacherous that time of year

"Okay, I will talk to Dale and see what he says."

"Okay then, it was nice talking to you. Goodbye."

"Yes, I am glad that you called. Bye for now." With relief, I hung up the phone.

By November, we had made all the arrangements for Dale, myself, and Jeff to drive 3,300 kilometres round-trip from

Vancouver to Saskatoon and home again to meet Dale's twin sisters, mom and dad, grandparents, aunts, uncles, cousins, and friends for Christmas. Dale's truck, Sluggo, would transport us.

I was over-the-top excited, but simultaneously worried about spending my first Christmas away from home.

I worried about my family, wondering how they would make out without me. My two older brothers had lives, jobs, and girlfriends, and my sister had her horses. They all took up much of the space when we were together. My dad told stories that we had all heard a million times before, and the unpredictability of my mother's moods required us all to dance around her.

I was also the one who decorated the tree, hung the Christmas stockings, and made everything festive. My Christmas spirit and enthusiasm filled the room, and I instinctively knew how to make everyone happy, a role that I treasured and did not mind having.

My parents handled the news well when I told them about my trip to Saskatoon and missing Christmas at home. They did not seem sad or out of sorts, and their only concern was us driving in the winter on the highways. I, on the other hand, could care less about the road conditions and was just delighted to be embarking on another adventure. Especially if this was going to be the man that I was to spend the rest of my life with, it only made sense to be meeting his family.

We entered the city limits of Saskatoon, Saskatchewan, late in the afternoon on December 23, 1983. It had been a long touch-and-go drive from Vancouver. The roads on the Hope Princeton Highway were icy, and the visibility was poor. Mountainous roads and switchback curves with steep drop-offs into the gullies below forced me to shut my eyes tight, especially during the BC portion of the trip.

I now understood why both sets of parents were worried about us.

Dale was a careful, steady driver, always keeping to the speed limit. I was relieved when his brother asked him to put the open bottle of whisky (securely nestled between his legs) into the back of the truck. He swore up and down that an occasional swig here and there would not affect him in the least. But he followed his brother's wishes nonetheless, as I sat silently by saying nothing. Shortly after that, I was able to relax into his body, sitting next to him while he drove.

We stopped in Calgary for the night and continued on the whole next day on flat, desolate roads across the snowy, windswept prairie, finally arriving at the outskirts of our destination by dusk.

Saskatoon in the winter was unexpected. As I sat in awe, I made sure to take in everything. The snow-covered streets replicated dense icing sugar as the vehicles quietly crunched along while the tires only made a slight squeaking sound when the wheels turned. The entire city seemed to be wearing a protective white blanket, a cold shield that was secretive and calming.

I asked to sit next to the door, trading seats with Jeff so I could open the window to get the full effect of the winter wonderland that passed before us. Sticking my head halfway out of the truck like a little girl, I breathed in the exhilarating crisp freshness and watched the pretty puffs of air as I exhaled. The tingly sensation in my throat astounded me, combined with my nostril hairs instantly freezing from the below zero temperatures.

Bing Crosby songs trumpeted in my ears, sleigh bells rang, and if imagined, one could see Frosty the Snowman rolling through the streets. I wanted to yell and rejoice to let it snow, let it snow, let it snow! I felt the sprinkling of romance on the picturesque streets in the city of Saskatoon, of that I was sure.

Before driving up to Dale's family home, he pulled the truck over, and with a twinkle in his eye and a silly grin, he sheepishly explained the story of how he grew up on the street named Brown

Crescent. It was his father's idea to decorate their yard like a Charlie Brown Christmas because of the street name.

He continued to regale the history of how the many neighbours eventually followed suit and decorated their yards, too.

Dale's sweet preamble and account for what I was about to see had me listening to his every word and anticipating the spectacular surprise that lay ahead. As we turned the corner onto the infamous "Charlie" Brown Crescent, all my childhood wonderment and the magical spirit in me reawakened.

Practically every second or third house in the neighbourhood displayed the heartwarming Christmas cartoon classic of *A Charlie Brown Christmas*. Lucy, Sally, Linus, and Schroeder, Snoopy, and of course, Charlie Brown himself. Even Peppermint Patty made the cut.

Standing, sitting, playing, singing carols in deep snow, large wooden and hand-painted cut-outs of the well-loved characters adorned the themed yards. As we made our way past the character scenes and twinkling Christmas lights, we followed behind a progression of slow meandering cars, onlookers who had made the Charlie Brown Christmas on Brown Crescent a family tradition.

How exciting that I was to be a part of this popular, enchanted neighbourhood tradition, one that people from all over Saskatoon flocked to see and experience year after year.

We finally pulled up to 59 Brown Crescent, Dale's family home, in the early evening and were greeted by Dale's younger twin sisters, whose faces lit up at the very sight of me. They hugged me even before they embraced Dale, their brother. I was utterly flattered and felt welcomed with their enthusiasm. Squealing and giggling, they exclaimed that they could hardly wait to get to know me better.

Dale's father was engaging and interested in my family and me, and he, too, made me feel like I belonged, asking me questions about my family and listening intently with warm, kind eyes. Dale's mom came out of the kitchen wearing an apron and a cheerful, accepting smile, immediately welcoming us in and offering us homemade cabbage rolls and ham dinner.

Inside their quaint, cozy home, the living room was a combination of a Norman Rockwell painting and the Christmas village of Whoville from the classic cartoon *How the Grinch Stole Christmas*.

Hanging from the white brick fireplace were ten homemade Christmas stockings, each with names on them, mine included, and filled with individually wrapped gifts. Presents of all shapes and sizes nestled under the tree, decorated with bows, ribbons, and Christmas cards. The massive Christmas tree was trimmed and bulging with tinsel, lights, and all things that shimmered.

In amongst sparkling glass ornaments, stuffed jolly Santas, and candy dishes filled to the brim, there was a display of the Three Wise Men bringing gifts to a baby nestled in straw. Gazing down from the mantle were elves and fairies complete with toques and bejewelled wings.

I had entered Santa's Workshop and Baby Jesus's Manger all in one fell swoop, in my eyes, a perfect combination of religion combined with a fantastical holiday spirit. To take it all in at first glance was next to impossible.

I eagerly settled in among the laughter, festivities, and joy that this entire family unit brought forth. My heart told me that I had arrived, and this was the Susie Homemaker life that I had always wanted.

After the gifts were opened and our bellies were full, we nestled into comfy living room furniture. Sipping rum and eggnog, in the glow of the Christmas lights, I enjoyed the families reminiscing, and stories of Dale as a towheaded little boy.

The ongoing question that plagued me seemed to be getting answered: "Where is my happy ending?" was falling nicely into place.

After meeting the rest of Dale's family in Saskatoon, I hung on to the fantasy of being a part of it through holy matrimony, and at the same time, I was excited to be living on my own again.

My new apartment was an older home that had been renovated and split up into suites, located on 16ᵗʰ Avenue and Heather Street in Vancouver. I had rented the top floor with a huge veranda, and the layout was haphazard in the design but unique and stylish nonetheless.

Since I called my first apartment the "Mole Hole," then I could certainly call this one the "Hodgepodge." It consisted of a front entranceway, living room, bedroom, second bedroom, and bathroom, and each room led to another without a semblance of order. There were no hallways, just adjoining rooms. The ceilings were high, and the rooms were spacious.

The kitchen had pink-and-black-tiled countertops with a window over the sink that looked directly into the neighbouring home's bathroom. It was often hard not to be a peeping Tom—not that I was looking for anything indecent, but rather that it was unavoidable while I did the dishes. My own bathroom was small, with an old clawfoot bathtub.

The bedroom window looked out onto a large concrete wall as another older home on the next lot had just been demolished, with an oversized apartment complex replacing it. Hoping that my home would not be next in line as a tear-down in society's form of progress, I relished my authentic heritage-type home and could not have been happier.

Dale and I were a full-fledged couple. After meeting everyone in Saskatoon and feeling a part of his family, the deal was sealed for who I wanted to spend the rest of my life with.

Dale was living with his brother and another good friend, which meant we were no longer living in sin, and I could still be independent to figure out what I wanted to do with the rest of my life, at least until I could get married and have children.

I was continuing to teach fitness and was now working at the Denman Racquetball Club and another racquetball club on Albernie Street near Thurlow, both in downtown Vancouver.

Because of my experience with the European Health Spa and my two certifications, one with the YWCA, and the other with Bogie's Fitness, I found it quite easy to get fitness teaching jobs. The only challenging part was that one had to audition before getting hired.

A well-choreographed routine in front of judges allowed the potential employee to strut their stuff with an audience. I always arrived prepared, dressed in the latest trendy outfit, with freshly applied lipstick, a dazzling smile, and fun, upbeat music, all acquired from my instruction and guidance from Suzi.

Teaching aerobics classes had very readily become my passion. I liked connecting with the participants, helping people to feel good about themselves by changing their body and outlook on their health.

On a personal level, the physical benefits that I would achieve from my exercise classes were a sensation that I had never experienced in school, with the team sports I abhorred. After each class, an almost indescribable state of mind came over me, enabling my own mental, emotional, and physical health to greatly benefit from my job. Teaching fitness gave me a reason to get out of bed in the morning. I often told Dale, "What a concept, getting paid to exercise and therefore feel great."

Aside from getting paid to stay healthy, occasionally there would be obstacles and mishaps on the aerobic floor that were, at times, unavoidable.

Sports bras were rare and only just coming into fashion; most fitness instructors would still wear a regular bra. I wore whatever I had in my dresser drawer, whether it was lacy, or plain and practical. On one occasion, while twisting and turning, the clasp on my bra came undone. Mortified, with the bra tangled up around my neck, I ran to the bathroom during the cardiovascular component, leaving the participants wondering where I had gone. Sweaty and befuddled, I ran back out with a "the show must go on" mentality.

It took me months to get over my first wardrobe malfunction.

It was not the last of my exercise class and attire setbacks. I learned quickly to get over it with a grain of salt. Making a joke about any given situation with self-deprecating humour usually did the trick. Wearing my outfit inside out, a leg warmer not staying up, a cassette tape breaking, the stereo not working, and power outages were just some of the things that could go wrong.

Participants had become fitness fanatics, often becoming demanding. Whether it had become an addiction or an obsession, people were flocking to fitness studios and gyms all over the Lower Mainland. Fistfights and shoving matches broke out over preferred spots on the floor, body odour complaints, music volume, adequate cooling systems, and membership fees—all awkward moments for every instructor.

Twisted ankles, heart murmurs, flinging and flailing arms with a diamond ring going in someone's eye, all were common occurrences. One of my front-row fitness participants got her period while wearing a white spandex bodysuit. Eventually, the gal ran off of the aerobics floor, returning five minutes later in a different outfit, ready to continue.

I still drove my 1978 Chevette but preferred riding my mountain bike throughout the streets of Vancouver and to all my classes. I was once again thin, fit, and strong.

Making new friends and acquaintances was a big part of being an instructor.

Following one of my classes, a great big fellow, standing six feet five inches, a regular attendee by the name of Bill, approached me and said that he was in Vancouver on a one-year work visa from New Zealand. He stated that he loved my classes and went on to explain that he was finding it difficult to meet people. He expressed that people from Vancouver were snobby and hard to get to know.

I was taken aback by his comment and responded by saying that all my friends were not snobby, and I did not agree with his opinion. He then challenged me by saying, "Well, if your friends are all so great, why don't you let me be the judge of that?" Bill worked as a butler for a well-to-do couple who lived in a mansion in Shaughnessy, and he offered to cook my friends and me a gourmet meal while the family he worked for was out of town.

We set a date, and I rallied my troops. Dale, myself, and four of our friends got dressed up and went for dinner at Bill the butler's house. He was also the head chef, bottle washer, and nanny at the beautiful mansion where he was employed.

Upon our arrival, we were ushered into the parlour, served wine, and shortly after escorted to the dining hall. Each table setting had gold emblazoned place cards, where we all diligently took our seats.

Silence or awkward chitchat filled the room until Bill came out in a full tuxedo uniform and began the table service. We all finally erupted into fits of laughter, breaking the awkwardness, followed by lots of oohs and aahs at the splendid display that made up an exceptional dining experience unlike any other.

The elegant dinner consisted of an appetizer lasagna made with homemade pasta, fresh garden greens that Bill grew and harvested, rack of lamb with all the trimmings, sweet peas, caramelized carrots, and new baby potatoes, with butter and parsley sprigs. Chocolate mousse was our dessert. All of these were paired with just the right wines and after-dinner liqueurs to complete a spectacular dinner prepared for us by our new friend Bill.

Not only did Bill become our fast and furious friend, but he sincerely liked us and us him. Professing that I was right, we were not snobby or hard to get to know at all, he requested to become our social director, which we all enthusiastically accepted.

First on Bill's list was white-water rafting. He had always wanted to go, and now he had friends to join him. He booked the expedition with a rafting company that would take us down the historical Thompson River, which converges with the Fraser River. The brochure promised powerful rapids, big waves, deep canyons, and a beautifully warm climate.

I was excited to see a body of water that some of the first explorers to British Columbia travelled on. My father briefly came to my mind with his stories regarding these events in Canadian history. The Gold Rush and the railway had both made their claim to fame on these rivers.

Our rafting trip was to include five hours of rafting, lunch, dinner at the end, and all the necessary gear.

It was mid-July, and the weather was hot and steamy for Vancouver's standards. Taking two vehicles, we left the constraints of the city and headed out on our road trip.

Upon arrival, a mandatory lesson and safety talk ensued. As our group stood listening, adorned in wetsuits and helmets, reality set in as our guide spoke of the dangers and various obstacles involved, explaining things that could go wrong and how the right protocol would keep us safe throughout our rafting expedition.

Our guide spoke with confidence and knowledge, stating, "If you fall out of the raft, stay calm, sit upright, position your legs, and paddle out in front," all while careening down the river without the raft.

Specific terms like "hit the deck" indicated if there was a whirlpool. If our raft were to rise on one end, we would need to throw ourselves onto the floor of our raft, therefore weighing it down, balancing out the vessel, and keeping us from popping out like a New Year's champagne cork. The term "hit the deck" made sense.

After the briefing, we were all hypersensitive and alert as we boarded the bus that would take us to our raft and day of white-water adventure. Thirty minutes later, we arrived at our destination. Each of us got a paddle, a life jacket, and another briefing. Lastly, we were assigned a seat in the raft.

None of us spoke, obviously feeling slightly anxious but still up for the adventure. I, on the other hand, felt an element of terror but did not want to pull back. Instead, looking around at my friends, the guides, and my boyfriend, I could hardly contain the love I felt for them all.

The waters were flowing calmly on the first part of the journey. Everyone, myself included, wanted to go faster. As we picked up speed and the rapids began to take shape, I paddled my heart out to the coaching of our fearless leader. My legs worked to stabilize me, gripping with my feet and thighs. My arms, chest, and back began to burn with the intensity and pull from the water, while at the same time, it felt great to be working in unison with others.

Almost as if a switch turned on, the water instantaneously changed. Unexpectedly, our friend Mark quietly slipped off the side, and without a moment's notice, he disappeared, pulled into the furiously fast-running water. All I could think to do was yell, "Mark's gone!" Soon we all began to yell and scream, "Man overboard! Man overboard!" Jeff, Dale's brother, effortlessly and with inhuman strength, was able to reach down and miraculously loop his finger through Mark's belt loop just as he was about to bounce past us in the now turbulent water.

Before being rescued, I noticed Mark was following protocol. He had both paddle and legs in front, just like we had been instructed to do, in the unlikelihood that something like this were to occur.

As he scrambled to get on board with Jeff's assistance, aside from missing a shoe, he seemed fine. Mark resumed his position.

Before anyone could catch their breath, we were suddenly ordered by our guide to "hit the deck!" The front end of our raft had lifted, and we would have ended up in the drink if it had not been for the quick thinking of our seemingly confident commander. In an instant, we were spread out on our bellies on the bottom of the raft, keenly following the orders.

Our raft and all of its contents were in the swirling dervish of a whirlpool. People appeared on the shoreline from out of nowhere, shouting, tossing ropes, and running up and down the banks of the mighty Thompson River. In amongst the mayhem, as I lay face down in our hit-the-deck position, I looked up into the face of our leader. As if time was standing still, I saw a young man, younger than myself, taking charge. When I looked a little deeper, our eyes met. I saw fear in his face, and then I instinctively knew we were in trouble.

Our raft was caught between two huge boulders, with the contents, meaning us, still up on one end as we all willed it to come down. My eyes gravitated to the churning water; I could see the vibration and feel the pressure of the whirlpool sucking us under, gnawing at the raft like a hungry animal feverish to swallow its prey.

Seismic waves spilled into the raft, when all at once, like a hand grenade exploding, our raft was dislodged and out we came. As if there had never been a situation at all, effortlessly, the raft was set free. Our guide grabbed the rope, and we were hauled to safety.

Rescuers on the banks plucked each of us out one by one, but my friend Adrianna, somehow in the blink of an eye, slipped through their fingertips. She was a tiny gal, and without warning, had lost her footing only two feet from the water's edge. Like a slippery minnow whisked away from its school of fish, she was pulled back by the tumultuous undertow.

Stunned and unaware of what was happening, Adrianna's face was blank as she began to float away aimlessly. The farther from shore she was swept, the more the current and choppy water began to toss her about, and she no longer appeared to be a tiny fish but rather a child's toy rubber ducky, bobbing along, sometimes going out of sight in the swell.

I had gone to high school with Adrianna, and we rode the school bus together for four years. She was one of the prettiest girls in our school, and she never acted as if she knew it, always being ordinary and unpretentious. She reminded me of Olivia Newton-John, and she had a personality to match.

I thought of this as I looked at her from the shore. In all her distress, she still appeared sweet and serene as the water was engulfing her. I recalled how she once told me never to settle, hold out for Mr. Right to come along, as I deserved the best.

The force of the water had positioned Adrianna parallel to the raft and only arm's length from Dale. He was the last one still on board and ten feet from shore. He leaned out as far as he could and managed to swoop Adrianna up into his outstretched arm. She clung to Dale as her life depended on it.

Pulling her to safety and back up into the raft, they were both dragged into shore as Dale held the rope with one hand and Adrianna with the other. Struggling to climb up the embankment, cold and soggy, they were no worse for the wear. Jeff and Dale were both heroes that day. All gave praise or acknowledgement. Humble, they did not expect it, but both went up a level on my proudness scale.

On the bus ride back to our cars, we anticipated our upcoming dinner.

The river rafting guide whom I had made eye contact with during the harried raft trip ended up sitting beside me on the old rickety bus. From his knowing glances my way, I could tell that he knew that I was aware he had panicked. Rightly so, and in no way did I judge him or expect anything less. I was grateful for his leadership skills and how he brought us all back to the safety of the shore.

Bouncing along while seated on the bus, he reached down and grabbed my cold, soggy running shoe. Bringing it up to his lap, he took it upon himself to unlace and remove it, sock and all, to rub my foot. I was taken aback by his forward gesture and relieved and pleased with his actions. Neither of us spoke for the rest of the drive back.

Immersed in silence and exhausted, I looked across the aisle at Dale, and while reliving the day's events, I felt a small tug in my heart for him to be the one rubbing my feet, yet concluding that he had done his fair share of helping a damsel in distress for one day.

We had a lot to talk about sitting around the campfire that night. The war stories after a battle are undoubtedly better and more intriguing than the actual fight itself. Included in the white-water package deal, we were offered two beers per person with dinner; even the non-drinkers in the bunch partook and consumed a beverage or two that night.

Bill went on to plan many more dinners and outings for our group, right up until his work visa ran out. And then he was gone, never to be seen or heard from again, a kind, beautiful Māori man from New Zealand another continent far away, giving out generosity in exchange for friends, connections, and adventure.

Always in the back of my mind was the thought of a real job, a career, or something other than one or two exercise classes per day. A source of income that I could be proud of that could sustain me financially, and a job that I could easily quit or take a leave from to eventually be a full-fledged stay-at-home mom one day.

Riding my bicycle past a construction site near the racquetball club on Albernie Street, where I taught classes, I could not help but notice signs posted on a chain-link fence surrounding an empty lot, an area that was under construction. The posters said:

JOBS AVAILABLE
Unique employment opportunities
High-end restaurant
Many positions available. If interested complete the following questions and mail to the address provided

1) **Describe yourself in 500 words or less.**
2) **Where do you see yourself in five years?**
3) **Where do you see yourself in ten years?**

Applicants were to answer in essay form and then mail their application to a post office box for the upcoming restaurant, Joe Fortes Seafood and Chop House. Each was holding one of my essays before them. Once again, I was telephoned for an interview and spent hours getting ready. When I arrived I was instructed to sit at a table directly across from my three potential male bosses. I was auditioning for a job. As the interview process began, I mustered up a dynamic personality, and we were off.

According to the instructions, the first essay asked me to describe my personality. I spoke about myself as bubbly and friendly, patient and kind; going on to say that I enjoyed people, I was a team player, and taught aerobics classes.

The second essay asking where I saw myself in five years was simple to answer. I went into detail about my lifelong dream to be married, own a home, and become a stay-at-home mom.

The third and final essay asking where I saw myself in ten years was an elaboration on my previous theme.

I completed all three essays in full sentences, descriptive words, and following the instructions of five hundred words for each topic.

As it turned out, I passed, won them all over, and got the job. The three managers felt it refreshing that I was a simple girl with common goals of becoming a wife and mother.

The interior of Joe Fortes was fashioned in beautiful 1920s decor, with a winding staircase complete with a wooden handrail. Floral dark green carpets were laid throughout the establishment, and brass lamps were burning at each table. A piano bar, oyster bar, impressive wine room for meal pairings, and a daily Fresh Menu were part of the appeal.

All the waiters and waitresses were attractive, thin, and well-groomed twenty- to thirty-year-old men and women. Every one of them could have been a runway model. They wore authentic white serving uniforms, black pants, and waist aprons.

My job as the hostess was perfect. I loved working the front entranceway and thoroughly enjoyed greeting people, escorting them to their tables, and being the first person they saw when entering the restaurant.

What would become the bane of my existence were the fifty Joe Fortes shareholders.

Memorizing the names and faces of the shareholders was far more daunting than it appeared. At any given time, one or more of the shareholders could show up unannounced. They were to be given precedence over any of the regular customers waiting for a table.

The worst-case scenarios were times when a select few would be dining with their mistresses, and their wives would arrive separately looking for their husbands. The hostesses were told by all three managers to stall the spouses, not to let them in, and to notify the cheating husbands immediately—all onus of the shareholder's infidelity became the hostess's responsibility to smooth over and make right.

Under our breath, we would refer to the rotten cheating men as male chauvinists.

I had started to notice a pattern with a lot of men in general. The term Male Chauvinist Pig was used frequently among my friends and colleagues, not outwardly in a sentence for all to hear, but usually behind backs and closed doors.

A significant accomplishment came when my sister hostesses and I protested against the "no less than three-inch-high heel" requirement for our footwear. It was mandatory and part of our uniform at the restaurant to wear high-heeled stiletto shoes until all the hostesses banded together and revolted. Flat shoes were in style, and the early onset of bunions and back problems were not. Besides, it was the mid-1980s and not the oppressive 1950s, we all chanted. I explained to my co-workers that only a few short years ago, we had to fight for running shoes in the gym instead of high heels to take people through workouts.

Our request was eventually approved, and we all dashed out to purchase the latest trends in flat dress shoes from Le Chateau at the Pacific Centre Mall in downtown Vancouver.

Working up north, meeting Dale, and the introduction to his music was life-changing for me, and yet meeting his friends opened a whole other world for me.

Dale's friends were all modern-day hippies: anti-establishment, intelligent, artistic, laid-back, and undoubtedly recreational pot smokers—a common practice and activity, therefore a regular occurrence and by-product of hanging out with his friends.

As an ex-disco queen, fitness instructor, and wannabe wife and mother, I was a fish out of water among Dale's pals, who were, by association, my new friends. I never felt like I fit in among the carefree manatees that lolled languidly about, while I, a frantic goldfish, was swimming in circles.

Music festivals, art shows, farmers' markets, hiking, and many days spent on local beaches just hanging out was how we passed our free time. Someone always pulled out a hacky-sack, forming a circle with three or four others to try and keep it in the air. Also known as "shuttlecock" or "keepie uppie," the game dated back to the 1930s. It once again became common in the 1970s and gained national popularity in the 1980s within the hippie, stoner, and grunge crowd.

I often opted out of this activity, as kind as everyone was to include me. My theory was that if I could not hit a volleyball over a net with two hands, how on earth was I going to be able to keep a tiny sack filled with rice in the air with one foot?

Dale's ability, on the other hand, was remarkable, and he became well known for his coordination and ability to keep a crocheted footbag weighing a mere fifty grams in the air.

We spent hours on weekends making freestyle art, one project in particular being ceramic masks. We applied wet plaster to our faces, and after it dried, the expressionless creations were removed, painted, and decorated. Beads, feathers, and jewels were glued and formulated and then worn throughout the party.

With all that we did, marijuana accompanied us and became a staple, like water or salt and pepper. Someone always had a joint, best smoked before, during, or after an activity, or so it seemed.

In the pot-smoking department, I taught myself to fake it. Or rather, pretending came naturally to me.

I could not get the hang of it, and with each attempt to inhale the putrid smoke, I would break out into a fit of coughing; my throat burned, my eyes watered, and on one of my numerous attempts, ash wandered upward to singe my already frizzy hair. In no uncertain terms, getting high was a complete and utter disaster, a calamity, and exceptionally embarrassing in front of these non-judgmental, kind-hearted souls.

The worst part was when the seasoned pot smokers snickered at me while giving each other knowing glances regarding what a cute novice I was.

Never getting the hang of it and repeatedly inhaling incorrectly, I kiboshed the activity entirely, which therefore ensured my ability to fake it. All in all, I concluded that the others benefited from my abstinence, saving them money and their precious product in the process. All the more for them.

Since smoking pot did not work out for me and wanting to fit in was a forever goal, I once partook with Dale and his counterparts in magic mushroom tea. I figured, what could go wrong by sipping a hot cup of a seemingly natural beverage? The taste was bitter, and the flavour was that of dirt and tree roots. The effect was frightening and not social at all. Compared to a psychological thriller, I could see the skeleton of my hand right through my skin when placed before my eyes. During the whole unforgettable experience, I somehow stepped on a slug. Its body oozed beneath my bare foot as it cried out to me, "Please help me! Save me!"

The whole undertaking did not bring me any joy, peace, or tranquility whatsoever. I was sick the next day, which proved to be enough of a deterrent to stay away from the hallucinogenic liquid if the opportunity ever arose again. Later it was explained to me that I did not step on a slug but hallucinated the whole incident.

After the fact, I realized that in reality, I was ingesting poison, which brought me back to tales of Sleeping Beauty, Alice in Wonderland, and Snow White's evil stepmother, apples and potions that brought death or violent events. In other words, anything could happen when one drank an unknown poisonous beverage.

Apart from the excessive drinking, pot-smoking, and hallucinogens, my relationship was perfect. I therefore concluded that I was right where I should be. I loved Dale and his all-encompassing heartwarming family.

The Grateful Dead and Bob Dylan in Eugene, Oregon, and Neil Young at the Vancouver Coliseum were highlights and musically historical, memorable events for us both, but more so for Dale. Both concerts were lifelong dreams of his and on his bucket list. Peter Gabriel and Leonard Cohen at the Queen Elizabeth Theatre were concerts I attended with some of my friends, without Dale, but monumental nevertheless. I felt worldly and on point, up to speed with the culture of being in my twenties in Vancouver.

Living paycheque to paycheque at minimum wage jobs and traipsing about, unknowingly floundering, skiing in the winter, barbecues in the summer seemed to be a package deal that came with the man I loved. Signed, sealed, and delivered, he was mine. So, I decided to fix my boyfriend, change him, or rather bring us closer together with some of my grand ideas and schemes.

Dale was not an exercise buff, but he did like to hike and said that he enjoyed bike riding. So, I took it upon myself to purchase Dale a bicycle from the Hudson's Bay store in the sporting goods department. My mother offered to help me with the purchase. We both thought that $196 for a mountain bike was a bargain.

The day I presented Dale with the bike, he was happier than I expected, grinning from ear to ear like a little kid on Christmas morning, and I was Santa Claus. Better yet was the knowledge that we were going to start riding bikes together. Having some outdoor exercise with my boyfriend was going to be just what we needed to bring our relationship to a whole new level. I was determined to bridge the gap between my being a fitness instructor and he, a Grateful Dead "deadhead."

The day after I gave him the bike, Dale's first time out, he rode his new bike to the store to purchase cigarettes and left it outside, leaning up against the store. When he returned with smokes tucked up into his T-shirt shoulder, the bike was no longer there. Stolen in the blink of an eye, it was gone, the bike and my dreams along with it.

Feeling bad, Dale decided that he wanted to make it up to me. He came up with an idea and suggested that we go on an overnight hike, just the two of us. All I had to do was show up, and he would take care of everything.

The day arrived, and we were all set to hike the Golden Ears Mountains in Maple Ridge. Named for the ear-like shape of the double summit, when the sun shines at a specific time of day, the mountain range glows golden. The hike was to take us five hours up to the summit, where we would camp for the night and then head back down the next morning. We set out at noon, hoping to reach our destination by 5:00 p.m.

I wore shorts, running shoes, and a pullover hoodie. Dale had prepared the pack with the necessities we needed for the overnight hike.

We made our way along lush trails, up rope ladders, and around moss-covered boulders. The blackflies were bothersome, but we forged ahead, swatting and cheerfully following the well-worn path.

At 5:00 p.m., our estimated time of arrival came and went, and the sweat on our backs and foreheads started to dry as the sun slowly began to drop down behind the mountains.

With only minutes to spare before dusk, we arrived at the summit area, which momentarily captivated us. Stopping short from our eye gazing, Dale suggested we gather some fronds and set up our tent before it got dark. We were both famished and getting cold.

As Dale removed everything from his small backpack, I was expecting a Mary Poppins unpacking experience: a bottomless carpetbag with an assortment of useful items to ensure that our overnight camping would be safe and comfortable.

After he had removed every item, scanning what he had brought, I wondered how we were going to manage. On the ground, he laid out a pup tent with a broken zipper, one blanket, six smokies (a fancy term for hotdogs), matches, and a bottle of Southern Comfort liquor.

I saw my life pass before my eyes as anger and fear rose inside of me.

Speechless while annoyance engulfed me, I wondered how I could allow myself to be in the complete care of someone else, once again allowing my fantastical storybook romance naïveté to take over. In reality, I could have had a say in the matter. I also could have carried another backpack and perhaps made suggestions of what to bring; another blanket, water, buns for our smokies, and warmer clothes.

We both slept very little that night, and as soon as dawn broke, we packed what little we had and proceeded back down the mountainside. Not speaking to each other the entire way back, we drove to the nearest Ricky's Restaurant and ordered the biggest breakfasts on the menu. Still not talking, we drove back to our own places in complete silence, and went to sleep in our own beds.

My perpetual optimism carried me through the little mishaps and disappointments that I assumed every relationship had. I always felt appreciated by Dale, who loved my optimistic approach to life—when life gave us lemons, I was often capable and willing to turn them into lemonade, squeezing the lemons by hand, adding sweetener, and stirring until the feeling in my arm was gone.

Unbeknownst to Dale or anyone else for that matter, I still prayed nightly, dating back to when I was nine years old, and every night when I went to sleep, my prayers went like this:

Dear God, please bless my mom and dad, Ken, Doug, and Linda, all the animals of the world, children, and poor people. I pray for safety and that tomorrow will be a better day.

Amen

P.S. please do not let the devil get me while I am sleeping.

P.P.S. thank you for sending me Dale and his family.

I hoped that my prayers would come true, and like a magic trick, my life would be sunshine and rainbows for all of eternity. Unfortunately, life does not work that way.

There came a time when I thought that God had left me. Perhaps he was watching and protecting someone else for a short time because I could not quite understand how the next turn of events happened. I gathered that God must have a lot of responsibilities, so I never blamed him for what came next. For a time, my prayers ceased, and when I would go back, it would be to ask for forgiveness. Because what was about to happen would change my life forever.

I was still obsessing about my lifelong fantasy of marriage, a baby, and a dream home, so after reading a story in *Cosmopolitan* magazine about relationships, I decided to break up with Dale. The article stated that sometimes people need a wake-up call, an opportunity to realize that they did not know what they had until it was gone. As *Cosmo* said, a momentary breakup gave every relationship the chance to assess what they had and where they could make some changes. Most times, couples would get back together, ready to make the necessary adjustments.

When I explained my thoughts about us going our separate ways, much to my surprise and dismay, Dale accepted the breakup. He did not beg me to stay, seem sad, or torn up in the least. His reaction was unpredicted, and I assumed that time would tell, and eventually, he would miss me terribly. I speculated that before long, in his sadness and loneliness, he would plead to get back together with me. There would inevitably be flowers, a love letter, and the proposal that I had anticipated. *Cosmopolitan* promised successful results, and it was my experience that the magazine was rarely wrong.

In the meantime, it was summer, and I was just about to embark on a two-week stint at my PNE job that occurred in the last two weeks of August every year. Going back to work was similar to a family reunion or a return to summer camp.

I was looking forward to reuniting with co-workers and the exhibitors who frequented the lounge where I was a cocktail waitress.

On my first shift in the lounge, I greeted co-workers, and we all gave out hugs. Shortly afterward, exhibitors began filing in to purchase drinks before they set up their stands to sell their wares. It was great to see everyone.

One man in particular was Eric, an older handsome cowboy from Alberta. He had a cattle ranch, horses, and lots of money, about which he often boasted. His gig at the PNE was in addition to his cowboy lifestyle, a hobby, a cash cow, and only part-time. He travelled to Vancouver to set up his junk food stands and sell his products. Come Labour Day weekend, when the PNE closed its doors for another season, Eric and all the other vendors returned to their regular lives.

Everything about the tall, dark, and handsome cowboy reminded me of the actor James Brolin—piercing brown eyes, dark hair, a deep voice, and a flirtatious yet subtle and mysterious demeanour. He could be aloof at times, which only made him more intriguing.

For years Eric had come into the Exhibitors' Lounge at random times throughout the afternoon or evening to order a few rounds of drinks. He was always a big tipper and full of compliments, never staying long before going back to the midway to manage his staff and booths. I was impressed that he was not a big drinker.

It was common to get together with my co-workers after work, and this night was like any other. A group was heading over to Diamond Lil's, a bar that was a few blocks east on Hastings Street near the PNE. It was a tad seedy but had live music, cheap drinks and was an excellent place for everyone to meet up and talk about their day after all the concessions had closed down for the night.

When I arrived, I immediately saw Eric. Our eyes met at the same time, and he approached me with a broad smile and a big bear hug to match. Lifting me off the ground and twirling me around, we both laughed and were happy to see each other. I was genuinely delighted. He looked good and smelled great. About twelve years my senior, he always seemed worldly, suave, and debonair. I was thrilled that he had made it out to join in the festivities at Diamond Lil's.

Having not seen Eric at the Exhibitors' Lounge yet, I feared that he had thrown in the towel and was not coming back this year, no longer in the concession stand business. I was glad that my fears were all for naught. I had gotten to know Eric over the years, and he often chose me, specifically, over the other waitresses to serve him, sitting in my section and tipping big.

Engrossed in the attention he was lavishing upon me, it helped me to momentarily forget about my sudden breakup with Dale.

At one point, Eric winked at me, and in his low husky voice, asked if I wanted to sit in his truck parked out in the alley; with how noisy it was in the bar, he just wanted to talk with me alone, to catch up. Without thinking or batting an eye, I said sure.

Everything happened so fast. Before I could say anything like "no" or "stop," like a wild animal ravaging its prey, Eric was having sex with me, the man I had once admired and had been anticipating to see. It was fast, over quickly, alarming, and unpleasant. I had a short skirt on which made everything seem much easier for him.

Afterward, he smiled and said, "Wow, that was great. I haven't felt like that since I was a teenager. Do you want to do it again?" Stunned, all I could murmur was, "No, we better go back inside." To this, he agreed, and once inside, another exhibitor came over to him and said, "Hey Eric, congratulations on your marriage and new baby. I just saw them both this afternoon walking the midway." Eric smiled and walked away.

I stood in one place for the longest time, frozen. I was stunned at what had just occurred. How could I have been so stupid and naïve?

Everything around me became dim, like a blurred film over the camera lens. The room grew darker as I stood there alone, unable to speak. The music still played, but it had picked up speed and sounded faster, like a mad demented carnival.

I could see people leaving, packing up, and going home, but it still felt overwhelmingly crowded. The smell of sour liquor and stale cigarettes brought bile to my throat. All I wanted to do was go home. I needed to sleep, and my legs were shaking. I sat down.

Instantly getting back up, I left Diamond Lil's alone without saying goodbye and walked to my car. The minute I got home, my gut told me that I was pregnant. How had it all gone so wrong? I ran a hot shower and cried out loud to the shower curtain, "Why did I do such a horrible, vile thing?" not blaming my perpetrator, but instead, blaming myself.

Eric had always been such a nice man. I could not figure out what went wrong; nothing made sense.

Waking up the next morning, I was sick to my stomach. I briefly pretended the scene in Eric's truck had never occurred and turned on the television to watch re-runs of *Beverly Hillbillies*. I loved Granny and Elly May the best.

With a puffy salt-stained face, I went over to Dale's house at the end of his workday and asked him if we could get back together. He said yes. Not able to look him in the eye, I curled up into the fetal position and fell asleep on his bed.

From that day forward, I was physically ill every day. I did not tell Dale what happened, and I was devastated knowing I had made a terrible mistake, telling no one, not even God, as all my prayers had no meaning anymore. Often able to turn a mountain into a molehill, this time, I failed miserably to look on the bright side because there wasn't one. All I could see was a mountain. I did not have a roadmap, and there were steep drop-offs, gnarly bushes, and no manoeuvrable path to find my way.

A week later, I went to the Planned Parenthood clinic at Vancouver General hospital to have a pregnancy test. When it came back positive, I was grief-stricken. An unwanted pregnancy was not in my plans or at all what a fairy-tale romance professed to be. Where was the happy ending?

From that moment on, nothing felt clear, right, or real. I could not gather my thoughts, and I was cold all the time. In 1986, if the term "post-traumatic stress disorder" existed, I would have had it. That would have been me, the girl with PTSD.

I went in for an abortion consultation alone. I asked the doctor if the baby was going to suffer. He stared blankly at me and said nothing. On the day of the procedure, they told me that someone needed to pick me up afterward, and I would not be allowed to go home unless a person was there to collect me. I was not myself; I had become the image of myself, but Karen, the fun-loving, baby-wanting girl with the Cinderella complex, had vanished, and she was nowhere.

A friend of Dale's from his hippie entourage went with me. He offered no words of wisdom or condolences; he just held my hand and promised to keep my little secret, our little secret. I believed him.

Instead of going through with the appointment, I wanted to run away with him to a deserted island to set up a Swiss Family Robinson jungle home. We would drink from coconuts and swing from vines, raising the baby together, teaching him to swim in the ocean, and forage for food. My hippie caregiver would be my knight in shining armour, and we would live happily ever after.

I got word months later that Eric had died of a cocaine-induced heart attack while driving on the new Coquihalla Highway. I was not sad at this news, but I did wonder about his wife, baby, and cattle.

CHAPTER 9

"Heart of Gold"

1986–1988

"I gave in to the weight around me. I'd become the Lady of the Lake without Excalibur, the damsel in distress without the prince to save her, Dorothy without her slippers or Alice without her "drink me" potion. Fantastic dreams weaved into amazing tales of triumph over obstacles. I was not triumphant over anything. I was a coward"
—Brynn Myers, Falling Out of Focus

AFTER MY FATHER WAS DIAGNOSED WITH TERMINAL BRAIN cancer and given less than a year to live, I panicked, and at the age of twenty-six, I proposed marriage to Dale, who had now been my boyfriend for the last three years.

I was not getting any younger. Thinking that I was old and not wanting to end up a spinster, I had to get going on my future and the children I so desperately wanted. There would be no more mistakes, wrongdoings, or false moves on my part, I vowed to God and the universe. My deep dark secret about the abortion would stay just that, a secret, the darkest of its kind.

It was two days after Christmas, and Dale's family was visiting from Saskatoon. I had been hoping for a proposal on Christmas morning from Dale, and I think his mom was, too. When that did not happen, I took the bull by the horns, and on December 27th, 1986, I went out, purchased a ring, and on bended knee, I proposed. I set the ambiance in my apartment with candles burning and soft music playing.

The look of pleasant surprise on Dale's face when I popped the question gave me relief. I could tell that he was struggling to speak and find the right words. Drawing a deep breath in through his nose and slightly laughing as he exhaled, he responded with, "Well, I guess I have to say yes since you've gone to all this trouble."

We hugged and immediately set out to tell our families, driving over to the house where everyone was staying. Entering the home, Dale let me make the announcement. The whole family cheered in unison. There were hugs all around and well wishes from everyone.

With my father's days numbered, there was no time to think about his eventual demise. I adored my dad and did not want to lose him, yet I knew that getting married and having a traditional celebration would make him happy, which meant that I needed to walk down the aisle sooner rather than later.

We set a date for April 10th, 1987.

At last I could stop the broken record from spinning round and round in my head. The unchanging storyboard of my childhood dreams involved a perfect house complete with white picket fence, three children within, and me as a stay-at-home mom. I envisioned spending time in our kitchen, baking or preparing to host elaborate dinner parties. My children would take swimming lessons, and we would spend a lot of time at our summer cottage, swimming and water skiing behind the boat my husband would drive. This to me was a picture-perfect life.

My mother often joked that I was born wearing a wedding dress, which only served to strengthen my old-fashioned view of who I wanted to be.

Many times, I had envisioned my arm linked around my dad's as we slowly strolled down the centre aisle of the sanctuary. My father and I were looking dignified and glamorous, he in his tuxedo and I in my white wedding gown, complete with veil and flowing train. Onlookers seated in the pews would speak in hushed tones of what a beautiful bride I was and how my family must be so proud.

I vividly imagined my bridesmaids and groomsmen diligently undertaking the tasks of hosting an engagement party, bridal shower, stag, and stagette months before the big day. After the wedding, we would open copious amounts of gifts with lots of oohing and aahing, and then off we would go on our idyllic honeymoon to some exotic location, a faraway land with palm trees swaying in the warm ocean breeze. My dreams were finally coming true. Together at last, we had found true love, and soon enough, a wedding, a house, and a baby would follow.

April 10, 1987, was a beautiful spring day in New Westminster. While standing in the arched doorway, right arm linked with my dad's, I was ready to make my way down the aisle in the church-like setting of Robson Manor (formally known as the Rose Garth), the most picturesque place to be married.

Robson Manor was a romantic turn-of-the-century mansion converted into a venue with a catered service, wedding planner, banquet area, dance hall, and makeshift sanctuary. The antique surroundings had seen many weddings, dating back to the 1950s. The curving staircase and wooden banister boasted photographs of others who had gone before me: blushing brides, rigid grooms, and their attendants.

My bouquet was fashioned from the most fragrant flowers I could find, a unique arrangement that I had carefully chosen:

white orchids and white freesia, two of my favourite flowers, beautiful to the eye, and sweet to the senses. Holding them tighter than necessary, they shook in my freshly manicured hands.

My dress was from a bridal shop on West Broadway in Vancouver. It came directly off the sale rack that was routinely wheeled out in front of the store every morning so drivers and passersby would slow down and take notice, either stopping in to take a closer look, or picking up speed and continuing on their way.

My mother did not go with me to try on wedding gowns, but she paid for my dress nonetheless, a moderate $150, which in my opinion, was an incredible deal in the grand scheme of things.

Usually, the bride-to-be has an entourage going with her to pick out a gown, offering opinions, advice, and giving suggestions—perhaps including a lunch for the whole shopping experience to be considered a festive, memorable occasion.

In my case, the whole shopping expedition seemed rushed, not planned or thought-out, as I fumbled through the sale rack by myself, with sounds of horns honking, buses emitting fumes, and cars whizzing by.

With my father's imminent death on the horizon and my mother's manic state at an all-time high, I did not have it in me to shop around. Even though my dress was not perfect, the price was right, and the salesgirls thought it looked great. Fitting like a glove the first time, when I tried it on the day before my wedding, it unexpectedly needed alterations.

The shopkeeper was annoyed with me because I had lost so much weight, and she refused to do the alterations. Twenty-four hours before the wedding, with a baggy, loose-fitting gown, an emergency phone call to a tailor ensued. The first one I could find in the phone book was Ace Apparel and Tailoring. After a short conversation, they said to bring my dress in as soon as possible.

Within the hour, my dress fit like a glove once more—saved on the eve before my wedding day!

I blamed the stress of a wedding, combined with my father's cancer illness, to be the big-C culprits when it came to my weight loss and changed eating habits. Food can be unappealing and repulsive to people when the world is caving in on them.

My world was shattering, foundations were crumbling, and I was getting married amid the mayhem of death and mental illness.

Waking up the day of my wedding, I was at peace; it was happening, and there was nothing I could do about it.

After getting my hair and nails done, I drove myself to Robson Manor in New Westminster in my little yellow car. The facility had a Bride's Room where I, my bridesmaids Dawna and Sarah, and my flower girl and niece Jeanette were to get ready. Underweight, not from exercise and dieting, but from worry and loss of appetite, my last glance in the mirror caught me off guard. I had grown proud of my slimness, but on this day, I noticed a thin, frail person starring back at me in the mirror. My eyes looked enormous and sunken, and my collarbone sharp. Allowing my gaze to travel over the rest of my body, I wondered who the unfamiliar tiny woman was who was standing before me.

Minutes before I was to make my entrance, Dawna, my maid of honour, cleverly and strategically put a pair of rolled-up socks in my depleted bosom, and she loaned me her previously used veil.

Descending the winding staircase, I met my father at the bottom. We embraced and then waited for the signal to indicate that it was our turn. Only twenty feet before me stood my soon-to-be husband, eyes gazing sweetly and lovingly in my direction, waiting for me to take those first steps into wedded bliss.

Standing five feet seven inches tall, with wavy blond hair, striking blue eyes, and a kind, warm smile, Dale's outdoorsy complexion and beautiful, straight white teeth were a reminder of how we met, what I saw, and what first attracted me to him. It felt like only yesterday since we both were working on the Alaska Highway, he a surveyor, and me a surveyor's helper.

As the minutes stood still with my eyes fixed on Dale's face, I couldn't help but scrutinize his smile; it amazed me how he had never had one cavity in his entire life. He barely brushed his teeth while I scoured the life out of mine and ended up with a mouthful of cavities, braces, a retainer, and that horrible gum surgery.

For a split second, thoughts of the camping trip that John and I took came to mind. I wondered where he was and what had happened to him, his career, and who might be the lucky woman that would spend the rest of her life with him—my previous boyfriend, who was my original knight in shining armour.

Dale's best man and older brother stood next to him, equally handsome, but taller and less outdoorsy. Slim in his tuxedo, he proudly faced his brother. Next to Jeff stood Dale's good friend Mark. His warm smile gazed in my direction—all three young men filling in the space adjacent to the justice of the peace.

On the other side were my two best friends, Sarah from high school, my Palm Springs disco buddy, and Dawna, my friend from our first meeting at the European Health Spa to our Alaska Highway escapades. Maid of Honour and bridesmaid, traditional and equally supportive.

Their bridesmaids' outfits were fitted black pencil skirts with flouncy lace blouses pulled in at the waist, and flattering peplum jackets that flared just below the waistline. Dawna and Sarah had sewn their ensembles, and both were thrilled to be able to wear their clothing again. We all decided that the blouse could be paired with skinny jeans and high heels for a night on the town.

As I stood next to my dad in the doorway, waiting to proceed, I felt my whole life flash before my eyes, as it would when a near-death experience occurs.

I missed him already. My daddy. The one who had played with me and made me laugh. Driving by his side in his pickup truck, stopping for Cokes and Cracker Jacks; camping trips, charades, and backyard barbecues; building snowmen in the winter and learning to ride my bike in the summer. The first person who told me I was beautiful.

Seconds before we were to make our final walk together, I turned my eyes up toward his face one last time, noticing his handsome, chiselled features had turned puffy, as if he was an imposter and not my father. His beautiful black curly hair was now left in patches on his head from months of chemotherapy.

Dale's father had the nickname the "Rug Doctor," as he had made a career as a unisex hairstylist who also dabbled in toupees. He had kindly made an individually handcrafted wig for my father. As generous and thoughtful as it was, we all decided that it just did not suit my dad, and he chose to go with his natural yet chemically created balding head. He was still attractive and debonair, but with a slight twist—he was dying.

The wedding march began, and we were off. Walking at a snail's pace, a sense of foreboding suggested that I might be making a mistake. Rationalizations responded with positive thoughts of Dale and how I adored his family, and soon they would be my family, too.

These reflections were marked by the ever-present elephant that chased us into every room, representing the dark side of alcohol.

I was forever thinking how perfect everything would be if Dale did not drink so much, then acknowledging the fact that we both drank, everyone drank and partied, we were all guilty of indulging too frequently. Thoughts raced through my head and came crashing to the forefront of my mind. With my final steps to the altar, I only had time to ask myself if I was going stark-raving mad.

Shaking my head as if to jostle the thoughts away, I wanted to stop and sit down for a moment. I needed a chance to catch my breath so that I could find some order in my thinking. As if my legs had a mind of their own, they insisted on moving me toward the next stage of my life.

Once reaching the end of the aisle, united with my groom and husband-to-be, my father left my side and took his seat. I felt alone beside Dale. With the justice of the peace in front of us, our friends beside us, and an audience of well-wishers behind us, the ceremony began.

My last reflections were that I could fix my husband, and after all, a family was just what I needed. A home filled with love, and a baby to make three—all this would squelch Dale's desire to overindulge and drink to excess. 'Til death do us part!

We were both Christian but not practising; he was Lutheran from birth, and I became born-again at summer camp when I was nine years old. We both wanted a spiritual realm in our union, so we decided to write our vows. Or rather, I researched and wrote the vows, and he liked and approved of them.

Excerpts were taken from the Bible, Corinthians 13:4-8, New International Version.

Love is patient, love is kind. It does not envy, it does not boast, it is not proud. It does not dishonour others, it is not self-seeking, it is not easily angered, it keeps no record of wrongs. Love does not delight in evil but rejoices with the truth. It always protects, always trusts, always hopes, always perseveres.

We added the five rules of Buddhism, some Unitarian teachings, and famous quotes from the Greek Philosopher Pluto. We felt creative, poetic, and artistic. The guests were entertained and delighted with our hippy-dippy, bohemian, unconventional ceremony.

I was excited to eventually hear what was coming, "I now pronounce you husband and wife," followed by photos, a receiving line, a buffet dinner with speeches and toasts, and then dancing. The first dance was with my father. I was happy.

There was no beginning, middle, or end to my mother's mood swings. During and after her manic outbursts, she conducted herself unnaturally to how people knew her to be: unexpectedly extroverted when she was usually an introvert or unconventional when she had always been conventional.

Even taking into consideration that her husband and lifelong partner was dying, becoming unhinged and out of control was not an everyday occurrence for most people.

I overheard my mother say more than once, "Karen's wedding is doubling as a wake for Vince, one that he can be a part of." Her words were harsh and mean. I was embarrassed by her, and I pretended not to notice. I felt sorry for her because maybe she was thinking out loud like people sometimes do.

When ranting about my father, during an outburst, she brought up how people had taken advantage of him all these years, to the people who had taken advantage of him. Maybe she was finding her voice, perhaps she had been oppressed all these years, and it was her time to be heard. I secretly longed for the quiet, shy mother of my childhood to return and the fake, offensive adaptation of herself to disappear.

We hired an expensive professional photographer for the wedding because another by-product of my mother's mental health issues was her desire to spend money. She suggested we get an expert, saying out loud (yet again) in front of my dad, "This will be our last chance with your father alive to document his life, and therefore the last photos of our family with him."

I had a vision of a fake, cancer-ridden dad recorded in a keepsake album of the history of our family.

My mother and father smiled dutifully for the camera, but underneath I could see their pain. Everyone else in my family looked like wooden puppets except my new in-laws and family members, who glowed with joy.

Months before the nuptials, the wedding planner for Robson Manor had a catalogue of suggestions, kind gestures to make the wedding special and top-notch. I chose Package B, which included a buffet dinner with salmon, a justice of the peace, a complimentary guest book, and one hundred white long-stemmed roses in a basket to be handed out by the bride to all the women.

I enjoyed this activity, as it gave me a moment to connect with each woman in attendance. Handing them each a rose, I thanked them for attending, and yet what I wanted to say was, "Could you please help me? Can I look deep into your soul to find out what the meaning of life is?"

Immediately I relished in calling myself "Mrs. Burgess," and referring to Dale as my husband. "My husband did this" and "My husband did that." It was romantic and reassuring that I now had a husband I could call my own.

Our wedding night was at the Renaissance Hotel in Vancouver, and then first thing in the morning, a taxi whisked us out to Vancouver International Airport to await our flight to Mazatlán, Mexico. Our honeymoon was a last-minute decision. My mother insisted and paid for the whole shebang.

Mexico turned out to be a completely alcohol-induced holiday. Assuring myself that excessive drinking was okay because it was festive, expected, and cheap, I convinced myself that we would start fresh when we returned. It would all be okay, as I willed myself to believe that it would be—Manifest Destiny.

Dale looked ruggedly handsome and tanned in a straw hat and white rolled-up trousers with a loose-fitting shirt. We walked the beaches, rented mopeds, swam, and ate. He introduced me to the marinated seafood dish called ceviche, which was a common dish he had enjoyed while travelling in South America, before he met me.

Our hotel was decorated entirely within the Mexican theme of tiled floors in blues, whites, and rust colours. The open-air lobby was inviting, but we ended up bypassing it by sneaking around the outside because many patrons at the bar had fallen in love with Dale and insisted on buying him drinks whenever they saw him. Neither of us wanted lengthy conversations from sunburned, chatty tourists who loved to talk about themselves. So we were happy sneaking.

At night around the pool bar, there were festivities and games. Dale won a bottle of tequila by walking across the hotel swimming pool on a small pole; everyone cheered just before he fell in.

Seven days later, we returned home from our honeymoon, making a point to stop in at the duty-free shop on the way because that is what one does when leaving Mexico. Booze galore, reasonably prized, and tax-free—vodka, Kahlúa, and tequila, all bought as gifts for specific friends and family.

Once home, we started a life together. We lived in a basement suite near 33rd and Fraser Street in Vancouver. It was a one-bedroom, with a small kitchen, a living room, and a bathroom. It was dark, but cozy and our first love nest. All was decidedly good, and we settled in officially married, working, living, and being a couple.

Dale worked for a surveying company making ten dollars an hour. I thought he was far more intelligent than he was given credit for.

Unfortunately, it was the certified surveyors who made the big bucks. Dale did all the work out in the field, and then his boss would sign the plans—all the work with none of the credit. He was like my dad that way, both men kind and gentle, non-confrontational, and often taken advantage of. If it was true that history repeated itself because Dale was so much like my father, I wondered if one day I would be off-balance like my mother.

In the beginning, I tried to ignore Dale's habit of procrastinating. It took him forever to get ready to go somewhere, and decision-making was not his strong point. He felt that a few sips of alcohol or a beer or two would help him be on time. Sometimes we would laugh about it and carry on making the best of it. On the other hand, if we needed to be somewhere at a specific time, I would change the clocks, setting them back thirty minutes, so if there was any dilly-dallying, we would only arrive fashionably late and not miss the event entirely. The idea eventually wore off and did not work anymore because we became used to the wrong time.

After the wedding and honeymoon, the time felt right to start planning for a family, so I ate properly and continued exercising to prepare myself physically. Therefore, in keeping with a health regime, my desire to have a cocktail or two was non-existent. Correspondingly, I was ready for Dale's alcohol consumption to naturally even itself out or wane off entirely, still convinced that our kinship and being tied up together was all that he needed to find balance or abstain from the mood-altering substance.

Settling into the day-to-day life of being a married couple, I was unprepared for what happened next. Unequivocally and unexpectedly, my white picket fence dreams were about to be altered. I found out that I had a bigger problem on my hands than I had bargained for.

As part of being a fitness instructor, I regularly needed to take workshops and seminars for the purposes of upgrading and learning exercise trends and physiology. So I decided to take an all-day fitness workshop at the Bayshore Hotel in downtown Vancouver. It was a Sunday, and the seminar went from 8:00 a.m. until 5:00 p.m.

When I returned home from a fitness-filled day, our little apartment was in darkness. Finding my way to the light switch and allowing my eyes to adjust to the now-bright living room, I was able to see Dale sleeping on our little IKEA sofa. It was only 5:00 p.m. on a Sunday, so I was taken aback that Dale would be sleeping.

When I went over to him, he was snoring loudly, and I could not awaken him. He was still breathing, so that was good, but something was just not right. Walking into the kitchen, I noticed that all of our souvenir bottles of alcohol from Mexico were sitting on the kitchen counter. Something in me told me to unscrew the lids, and when I dipped my finger in the bottle to taste, the bitter syrup of the Kahlúa was not there, the vodka was tasteless, and the usual bite from the tequila was absent. Three twenty-six-ounce bottles had been consumed and substituted with water.

Not able to stir Dale, I was mortified, furious, and heartbroken. Acting in haste, I took one of the water-filled alcohol bottles and dumped it on his sleeping head. He murmured slightly and then rolled over. I then grabbed the yellow pages and looked up "Al-Anon" to find out where the nearest Al-Anon meeting was.

I knew that Alcoholics Anonymous had an equivalent support group for spouses and family members of alcoholics, called Al-Anon. I also knew that if I wanted my marriage to survive, I would need to try and understand the substance that was hindering our happiness. I wanted to get to the bottom of why my husband was dependent on alcohol and how on earth I was going to make him stop.

Aside from my mother's mood swings, she was still an intelligent, level-headed woman. She had many times professed that the Alcoholics Anonymous program was a lifesaver. She had a friend who went to Al-Anon, and eventually, her husband went to AA. My mom admired this couple and explained both programs to me. The friends had teenagers who also sought help and support with a group called Alateen.

She said that Al-Anon/Alateen were non-profit organizations that offered a program of recovery for the families and friends of alcoholics, whether or not the alcoholic recognized the existence of a drinking problem. The primary purpose of an Al-Anon group was to help families and friends of alcoholics if they felt their lives have been affected by someone else's drinking.

The Al-Anon program states that alcoholism is a family illness and that when attitudes are changed, then recovery for the spouse or family member can begin.

Al-Anon and Alcoholics Anonymous both practise the Twelve Steps program. The meetings are welcoming and give comfort to families of alcoholics by giving understanding and encouragement to the alcoholic.

I was often surprised and even disenchanted that my mom could know so much about certain things such as a recovery program or a support group but was not willing, nor did she find it necessary, to get help for herself in regard to her mental health issues.

At one point in my mother's marriage, she thought that my dad might have a drinking problem. Upon my mother's wishes, my father went to an AA meeting to check it out. Afterward, he stopped drinking cold turkey and never went to another meeting again.

Sometimes my parents would take an empty vodka bottle and fill it up with water to take to their parties, like a game that only the two of them were playing. My dad would make drinks with the pretend vodka, and other partygoers would be none the wiser. He told me that he was able to have just as much fun sober, while many assumed that he was drunker than a skunk.

From my dad's experience, he told me that Alcoholics Anonymous helped its members to stay sober and achieve sobriety.

He said, "Each AA meeting has the same purpose—to carry its message to the alcoholic who still suffers. Alcohol is one thing all AA members have in common. Each meeting begins with the chairperson reading the AA preamble. Then they lead a group prayer called the Serenity Prayer. Afterward, different members of the meeting read briefly from AA literature, *How it Works*, *The Twelve Traditions*, and *The Promises*. During the meeting, people take turns sharing. Their stories can offer hope, strength, and wisdom. Then the next person can speak. The meeting ends with some AA-related announcements, and then everyone stands up, holds hands, and recites a prayer. Once the prayer is over, the meeting ends."

Recalling what my dad had once said to me, although it had never applied to me before, now I knew that I needed an Al-Anon meeting, and I was slightly relieved at the prospect.

Finding the nearest meeting to my home in the telephone book, I walked out the door, leaving Dale to sleep it off on our couch.

I chose to walk there, as I felt the need to debrief and wrap my head around my decision and acknowledgement that my husband might have a drinking problem.

Once there, I followed a sign that directed me around the back to the alleyway. There I found a basement door to the building that was ajar. Tentatively pushing the door open, it loudly creaked as I made my way into a dimly lit, smoke-filled room.

A friendly older gentleman greeted me and reached out to shake my hand. The cigarette dangling out of the corner of his mouth brought attention to his ravaged, pockmarked face. But he had a kind demeanour as I allowed for his exuberant, firm grip to shake my hand. It was then that he said, "Hi, I'm Chester, and I am an alcoholic." Bewildered, I responded with, "Hi, I'm Karen, but I am not an alcoholic." Chester replied, "It's okay, dear, none of us believed we were alcoholics at first, either." Before I could explain my situation, someone pounded a gavel on a podium at the front of the room and exclaimed that the meeting was about to begin, and could everyone please sit down.

Finding a seat and looking around at the weary, peaceful faces, I soon realized that I had entered an Alcoholics Anonymous meeting and not an Al-Anon support group as I had intended. Initially taken aback, and before I could escape, we were all instructed to stand for a prayer or a mantra of some sort. Everyone spoke together, and what was happening was a tad unclear to me. It felt like I had infringed on a secret brotherhood or sisterhood meeting.

I took a deep breath and listened to the words spoken. I liked what I heard. The ill-lit, faded room blossomed before me; it had a good vibe, and I was instantly intrigued and engaged.

The speaker then looked at me, and almost as if she knew that I had something to say, she said, "I see we have someone new here tonight and I'm wondering (while looking straight at me) if she would like to get up and say a few things." I felt completely drawn to stand up and speak, if only to defend myself and the little bit of a mix-up I had gotten myself into.

I spoke enthusiastically and breathlessly, "Hi everyone. I think that I might be here by mistake. I thought that I was going to an Al-Anon meeting. I just got back from my honeymoon, and I think my husband is an alcoholic because he drank all day today, polishing off three twenty-sixers of alcohol that we got cheap on our honeymoon in Mexico." I went on to say, "I suspected that he might have a drinking problem just before I walked down the aisle, and now I'm sure of it. I don't want to leave him. I want my marriage to work, and I am really happy to be here to see what goes on at these meetings. I hope my husband will one day come here himself."

I abruptly sat down, and after a short-lived pause, the room broke into a standing ovation. I found out later that folks were impressed by what I said, especially the part about me standing by my man. Many people approached me and said that they wished their spouses had done the same.

The meeting was both inspirational and sad. The individual stories of pain and sorrow, heartache and healing were remarkable. It filled me with the hope that Dale may one day be telling his own story, in addition to getting help or offering his support to others.

As I was leaving, someone handed me a piece of paper and said, "Here, take this and give it to your husband. Maybe it will help him." Bewildered, I took the folded paper, feeling like a spy or secret service agent who had just received special documents. With head down, the unknown stranger scurried off, and when the door closed behind me, I opened up the paper, and this is what it said:

The 12 steps are as follows:

1. We admitted we were powerless over alcohol—that our lives had become unmanageable.
2. Came to believe that a Power greater than ourselves could restore us to sanity.
3. Made a decision to turn our will and our lives over to the care of God as we understood him.
4. Made a searching and fearless moral inventory of ourselves.
5. Admitted to God, ourselves, and to another human being the exact nature of our wrongs.
6. Were entirely ready to have God remove all these defects of character.
7. Humbly asked Him to remove our shortcomings.
8. Made a list of all persons we had harmed and became willing to make amends to them all.
9. Made direct amends to such people wherever possible, except when to do so would injure them or others.
10. Continued to take personal inventory, and when we were wrong, promptly admitted it.
11. Sought through prayer and meditation to improve our conscious contact with God, as we understood Him, praying only for knowledge of His will for us and the power to carry that out.

12. Having had a spiritual awakening as the results of these Steps, we tried to carry this message to alcoholics, and to practise these principles in all our affairs.

Folding the pamphlet and placing this new information neatly in my purse for safekeeping, I briskly walked back home. I was excited to tell Dale everything.

Despite it being quite late, Dale was awake and watching television, still slightly inebriated but pleased to see me just the same. As I explained how angry I initially was finding him that way, I went on to tell him about the meeting and how wonderful it would be if he could try going to one sometime.

I could not help but cry at his response. He said that he did not have a drinking problem, but yes, he had been overdoing it lately, and he would cut down on his alcohol consumption. He then added that perhaps he could be a social drinker on the weekends. After my disappointment settled, and through my naïveté, for lack of a better response, I half-heartedly said, "Okay, but could you please really try?" We then kissed and made up.

For most of my life, I had worn rose-coloured glasses, and at this point, I had only been married for two weeks. I knew that everything was going to be just fine. Dale had so much potential as a father and a husband. Plus, he was very well-liked at his job and was a hard-working, diligent employee. People loved him wherever he went, and I was proud of that.

Tender Loving Care, or TLC, was the name of an organization where I was employed just after my proposal to Dale. The nature of the business was to call in on various people who needed in-home care. Still in search of a career, I consistently seemed to end up in service or caregiving roles, and my job at TLC was no exception.

Even though I did not have any medical training in disabilities or mental health, I was given a caseload of three or four people who all had varying needs with a large spectrum of difficulties and disabilities. Climbing into my little yellow car Monday to Friday, off I would go to call in on shut-ins who required a friend, a cleaning person, a cook, or a helper to sort through their heaps of personal belongings and treasured household items.

My first client was an elderly woman who lived in an enormous mansion in Shaughnessy, an area in Vancouver with which I was familiar, having ridden my bike through many times to view the majestic vintage homes on tree-lined streets known for their beautiful cherry blossoms and enormous oak trees.

I did not have any information other than my client had dementia, and I was not to go upstairs or even mention the upstairs, as it was unavailable. She also should not go upstairs because just the mention of it caused her great distress due to a very upsetting incident that had occurred a few months back.

When I first arrived, knocking on the beautifully carved wooden door, the elderly lady would not let me in. After much cajoling, eventually I was able to make her understand I was with the TLC organization. After a short pause, I then heard deadbolts sliding across, and furniture being moved. Moments later, she opened the door with a warm, welcoming smile.

Her name was Ida, and she was a small woman with a curved spine hunching forward. With a sweet face and a twinkle in her cornflower blue eyes, wisps of silver hair surrounded her face, and she was dressed immaculately in a mauve chiffon floral dress, pearl necklace, and practical black lace-up shoes.

Like a scene from a Stephen King novel, the house was dark and filled to the brim with antique furniture, ancient paintings, mahogany wainscoting, and thick brocade draperies. The only light came streaming out of a bright yellow kitchen with Melmac countertops.

As our ghost-like faces conversed, Ida suggested we sit down in the kitchen so she could explain my duties.

She asked me to wash out her silk stockings, hang them in the bathroom, make dinner, and wash the dishes. Her meal consisted of one Shake 'n Bake chicken leg, peas, and a boiled potato. I sat across from her while she ate, and we visited.

I enjoyed listening to her recount the stories of her youth, growing up in Vancouver during the early 1900s, becoming a teacher, and never marrying. What struck me as odd was that she referred to her sister repeatedly as if she was right there with us, telling the non-existent person various things about the conversation we were having. I did not question the absence of her sibling, and after my shift, I left.

The scenario repeated itself every week each time I arrived. Knocking on the door, no one answering, deadbolts, the moving of furniture, into the kitchen for instructions, and then Ida's storytelling.

Months into my job, I had to write a report about each of my clients. In particular, how Ida was coping with the death of her sister. Ida and her sister Florence had lived together. Both were retired teachers in their early nineties. Ida did the cleaning, and Florence did the cooking. Florence became ill and was bedridden. Ida failed to feed her, so the cause of death was starvation. The authorities did not find Florence until months later.

After that, my visits took on a horror movie creepiness. I still went but felt on edge the whole time.

Another person on my list was also an older woman named Santaclara. She had thick jet black hair, assumingly dyed, and bristly whiskers on her chin. Santaclara's disposition was curmudgeonly, and she was often verbally abusive and physically aggressive toward me. Her false teeth were loose and made a clucking sound, and spit often formed in the corners of her mouth.

The only duty that I had was to push her in a wheelchair three blocks to the grocery store, assist her in picking out a half dozen items, help with payment, then bring her and the groceries to her home.

The three blocks to the store were a nightmare. The old lady yelled at me for not pushing her wheelchair in a straight line or yelled at me because I was going too fast. Once at the store, she tugged, grabbed, and poked me, often blaming me for picking up the wrong items. While in the checkout line, it was pointed out to anyone within earshot that I was a thief and a known criminal. Santaclara could be heard all over the store with her chattering false teeth clicking while she screamed, "Help, help, this woman is abducting me" or "Thief, thief, grab her, call the police, she's robbing me."

The embarrassment and stress for me were unbearable. Sideways glances from strangers were empathetic or filled with disgust, and it surprised me that no one ever called the police or at least offered to help.

I found out later that she had grown up in an abusive home and had been married to an extremely insulting man. They never had children, and after her husband died, she took care of her own sharp-tongued and reviling elderly mother and father. With all three of them now gone, she relied on TLC for all of her basic needs. I asked to change clients.

A male client named Henry, who struggled with emphysema, saddened me after learning of his story. I had never heard of this debilitating illness, and he later told me that his daily habit of three packs of cigarettes for most of his life caused him to have tiny little holes in his lungs, which is called emphysema. Because of this, he needed to be hooked up to an oxygen tank 24/7 to be able to breathe. Henry was in his early eighties and small of stature. He wore denim overalls, a red flannel shirt, and old worn moccasins for slippers. Aside from the damage caused by smoking, he seemed happy enough and was a kind man. I enjoyed talking with him while I cleaned.

Unfortunately, the cleaning part of my job was difficult and discouraging because of the sticky yellow buildup of tar and nicotine on the walls, floors, countertops, and cupboards. The more I scrubbed, the more noticeable the scummy streaks were. I couldn't get a handle on the enormity of the job. After a few weeks of washing all surfaces, I had to give up.

He became quite comfortable with me not cleaning, so he made tea and soon shared his life story while I caringly sat and listened.

His saga began by marrying his high school sweetheart and ended when he left his wife with their five small children, leaving her to raise them alone. He never contributed financially or emotionally to their upbringing and experienced immense regret since he was never able to rekindle a relationship with any of his offspring. He also depended on the caregivers at TLC for cleaning and companionship.

On one occasion, I was covering a shift for a co-worker, and the woman who needed assistance was a whirling dervish who instantly reminded me of my mother because she had stacks of papers strewn all over the floor and tabletops, clean laundry hung from the lamps, and dirty dishes heaped up in the sink. Yards of fabric and dress patterns lay among pincushions. I was at a loss as to where to begin.

Early in my visit, while she was opening her mail, she had a meltdown about her hydro bill. She threw the mail up in the air and sent me away before I could tackle any of the chaos that lay before me. I noticed that all the windows in her apartment were wide open, and yet it was stifling hot inside.

My last drop-in client lived in an old rundown apartment on Main Street near Kingsway in Vancouver. I could see that the building had seen better days as it showed evidence of impressive architecture from the turn of the century.

Upon entering, I immediately noticed that the apartment was filthy, with caked-on dust and grime that had accumulated on very sad, dilapidated furniture. My client, a frail older woman, not weighing more than ninety pounds, appeared to be just as sad as her home. I thought if I could clean her suite, it might cheer her up.

After preparing hot soapy water in a bucket, her daughter stopped by and lambasted me for not cooking lunch, stating that cleaning was not part of the job description. The years of household neglect were more than I could attack in the time that I had anyway, so I left the cleaning and, as instructed, made my way to the kitchen to prepare lunch.

Opening a cabinet to retrieve a dish, I screamed bloody murder when I was jumped by a giant cockroach, which attached itself to my clothing and would not let go. I called my supervisor, who suggested I leave, cockroach, and all. I finally got it off of me, finished making lunch, and was able to leave before finding any other critters lurking around.

I felt sorry for anyone I tended to, and my empathy was almost unbearable. I often wept on the drive home.

One day after work, my mother phoned me, and out of the blue, she informed me that she had purchased a house in North Vancouver. It was intended for her and my father, but she asked if Dale and I wanted to move in.

I jumped at the chance and handed in my resignation. I had very little TLC left in me anyways.

We all knew that my father's cancer was inoperable.

With my mother's decision to move, I wondered if she was hoping to get back all that she had once known, everything that was ever happy and good. As it turned out, my mother's memories and finding a more convenient place for my father's death was the catalyst for the move.

My mother bought a house in North Vancouver on Jones Avenue and 23rd, only a three-minute drive from Lions Gate Hospital. She felt like she had finally come home to the community where she and my father had experienced a marvellous life together.

North Vancouver was where my mom and dad built our family home; where they raised four children, started my father's bulldozing business, curled, bowled, and played bridge. They were always busy with block parties, bridge parties, the PTA, and entertaining. All of us kids took swimming lessons, skating lessons and my brothers played sports. Memories of hide-and-go-seek and cops and robbers played throughout our neighbourhood will be with me always. It was an outstanding childhood that, together, my parents had caringly formed.

I was pleased when my mother suggested that Dale and I move in with her and my dad. She offered to take the basement suite with my dad, and we could have the upstairs—a seemingly win-win situation, a perfect home and scenario for two couples.

Over and above the idyllic living conditions, my mother's manic depression came in waves. I had it figured out that like clockwork, she would have two up days and one down day. This pattern helped me to predict the unpredictable.

Her up days were wild. Her energy was insurmountable, with frantic letter writing to the Pope and the president, ideas of trips to far-off lands, and outlandish purchases. Telephone calls in the middle of the night to old friends or unsuspecting enemies were not uncommon. She would start writing a book on old ripped-open envelopes and scraps of paper, always leaving the illegible sentences scattered about the house. Sometimes I would come home to the entire contents of our kitchen cupboards strewn about on the countertops as her attempt at cleaning and sorting.

After she had exhausted herself and her up day had run out, it was guaranteed that a down day would shortly follow. She would then be quiet, reserved, and sad. Therefore the term "down day" seemed appropriate, although she liked to refer to it as her "thinking day."

During my whole life, my mother's moods had always been present. They came and went with varying amounts of severity. I was used to it and danced around them. Sometimes a tango, the jitterbug, the shimmy, or the twist. I could have won an award from my skill at manoeuvring and skirting my mother's life-altering moods.

The worst was not knowing if she was hanging by a thread, running hot or cold, or in a dark blue funk. The terminology we used in our family to describe my mother, to warn each other or indicate that something was amiss was cordial and polite, such as, "Mom is being a little down or acting a little moody today," but in reality, she would be extremely, uncontrollably mad, ridiculously happy, or devastatingly depressed. She could also be exceptionally kind and generous, walking up and down Lonsdale Street writing checks to perfect strangers. Just small amounts, but my oldest brother was able to get involved and asked her to stop, which she did.

Spending money and buying up products on the Shopping Channel when my mother was not profoundly wealthy was detrimental. However, it made her so happy, unless they arrived in the wake of a down day. Then the deliveries would sit idly by, unopened and taking up space, until her mood changed, or the tides shifted, and then each box would be eagerly ripped open.

For the first Shopping Channel shipment, the delivery guy excitedly and breathlessly proclaimed that this was his largest order to the same residence that he had ever had, with fourteen boxes in total, of varying sizes.

I was often embarrassed and mortified when the Shopping Channel truck pulled up. Box after box was trekked into our small living room while my mother delightedly unpacked her treasures, oohing and aahing with excitement.

Getting caught up in her exuberance, one could not help but enjoy seeing what oddities the channel had to dish out—even though at times I wondered if the show was intended for people like my mother, who had manic outbursts and spending sprees.

Just by dialing the phone, my mother became the proud owner of an electric wok, even though she rarely cooked anymore, a three-foot-tall glass bird figurine, hummingbird feeders and brooms of every description, a chessboard with marble pieces, durable pantyhose that never ran, a child's magic kit and numerous Tupperware storing containers, jewellery boxes, cream and sugar dispensers, a marble rolling pin, clocks of every description, shape, and size, and even a clothesline with the latest and greatest clothes pegs known to man or woman.

One of my mother's revered household duties was doing laundry, but she was so impatient for it to dry that she often pulled it out of the dryer too soon and then proceeded to hang damp laundry all over the house. On many occasions, upon entering our home, one would spot bras and various other clothing items draped over lampshades, the fireplace mantel, kitchen chairs, and ceiling fans.

The panel of telephone operators at the Shopping Channel knew her on a first-name basis and often greeted her by saying, "Hello Frances, how are you today?" Or to the viewers in TV land, "Hey everybody, Frances is calling again."

Styrofoam packing chips permanently lined the floor in every room of our house and managed to get into every nook and cranny. They statically clung to all things in their wake. We would find them sticking to our clothes, furniture, bathroom mat, or scattered on the walkway, making their way mysteriously into our car, as if Hansel and Gretel had been there secretly trying to remember their way home, placing white puffy popcorn fragments leading out of the madhouse they were trapped in.

Nothing was said or done about my mother's manic states. We carried on as if that was our normal. Tomorrow was always another day and another mood.

While trying to keep tabs and control over my mother's mayhem, I also needed to work, so I applied and was easily able to get a job at Lions Gate Hospital in North Vancouver on 13ᵗʰ and St. Georges, in the food services department.

The position was not new to me, but it was different from when I worked at VGH. There was no Stacey or John. And I was not particularly fond of the job.

Nevertheless, I managed, and I thought if one tried, one could always find humour in most things; at least that was a theory that helped me get through some of the time.

North Vancouver General was the primary hospital on the North Shore from 1929 until April 1961, and it was where I was born in 1960. Shortly after my birth, the building was repurposed, and a new Lions Gate Hospital opened on the surrounding grounds. I often thought how ironic it was in this case, that my mother gave birth to me in the old hospital, and soon my father would die in the new one.

Both my brother and father had spent time recuperating at Lions Gate Hospital, where I was now working. I remembered both situations clearly.

My brother quit school in grade nine. He was highly intelligent but also fell victim to the party scene. Both our parents insisted he get a job, so he started learning the ropes in our father's bulldozing company. While clearing a lot, they were felling trees, and a terrible thing happened. A tree that was coming down took an unexpected turn and landed on my brother's foot. It crushed his heel, and the doctors did not think they would be able to salvage it. He was only fifteen years old at the time, and they said with him being so young, they were surely going to make a good attempt at trying. As they speculated, he had many more years of walking ahead of him. He ended up in the hospital for what seemed like a very long time.

I was ten years old when the accident occurred, and when I visited him, I never knew what to say or do, so I would sit by his bed watching all the goings-on around us.

There were four beds in his room, and he got the one by the window. Our parents were thrilled about this, assuming that a window position was the best place to be if one could not walk.

I could not tell what ailments the other patients had, but I did enjoy observing the nurses whizzing in and out. They were like flight attendants and waitresses all rolled into one. I could tell they were smart with their little cups of pills and clipboards. Some were friendlier than others, but they all appeared to like what they were doing even if they were in a rush. I thought I might like to be a nurse someday, if only the job did not entail being around sick people.

When I was even younger, my dad had a heart attack, and he, too, spent time at Lions Gate Hospital. They blamed the heart attack on stress, working too hard, and eating too much bacon. I was not allowed to see him when he first went in, but after a while, they let me go. He was jovial and did not seem sick at all.

I marvelled at the beeping machines in and around his bed, and he thoroughly enjoyed telling me how the monitors worked.

It appeared that the nurses all loved him. It was like a party every time I went in; people were laughing and joking, and all the nurses were so pretty. My dad was very handsome, kind of like a movie star, and the nurses were his groupies.

My mother worried that I would be frightened of visiting my dad. I was not, but I realized she might be the one who was frightened because she rarely went.

He made a full recovery, changed his diet, and started walking daily. He always took an umbrella with him in case a stray dog was to come after him. There were no leash laws, so attacking dogs and stepping in poop were common occurrences in the 1960s.

Here I was years later and now married, and once again at the Lions Gate Hospital, but this time not as a visitor. In the kitchen, my duties included working in the dishwashing station, sending dish racks through that were loaded with pots and pans, dishes, plastic cups, glasses, and cutlery, onto a conveyor belt. The work was heavy-duty, hot, and steamy. While scraping uneaten food into the garbage, it was not easy to find humour like I always tried to do.

We had to wear oversized, heavy-duty rubber aprons over our hospital uniforms. On our feet, it was protocol to wear authentic Dutch wooden shoes for safety and to prevent slipping. The strong aroma of bleach smelled clean, but was intoxicating and not in a good way.

Another aspect of the job was setting up food trays for the various patients (as I had once done at VGH) by following specific guidelines in regards to food restrictions and special dietary nutritional needs. After the incident of mistaking mashed meat for pureed meat years prior, I was extra careful this time to decipher the difference between the greying masses of gravy-clad meat products.

The best aspect of my job was delivering food trays. I enjoyed entering the hospital rooms as a friendly face. My goal was to be like a breath of fresh air, floating in on the breeze, with a few gentle, kind words. However, after setting down the patient's breakfast, lunch, or dinner tray, and taking off the lid for their examination and approval, I immediately felt bad, as if I had prepared the meal myself and it had not turned out as I planned. The dismal selection of stringy chicken or ground round accompanied by flat wilted peas and bland mashed potatoes was often disappointing, more so to me than it was to the patient.

Smiling nevertheless, as if to say "Oops, sorry about that," I would scoot off to the next room and delivery.

I worked on all the floors and occasionally was assigned to the psychiatric ward. It reminded me of the time my mother's doctor (with my father's approval) admitted my mother, simply because no one knew what else to do with her.

When I was a teenager, her depression had reached an all-time high. There were no up days, just an extended period of down days, so she had been taken into the psychiatric ward at Lions Gate Hospital. As one would expect, she suffered a great deal while there, mostly because back in my mother's day, psychiatric wards were called mental institutions, and rarely did someone get out.

In the 1940s and '50s the dull painted walls, prison-like wards, serious-faced nurses, and clinical feel was comparable to a movie set, and not a nice one—a horror movie, or maybe a psychological thriller. *One Flew Over the Cuckoo's Nest,* with actor Jack Nicholson, comes to mind, a movie that my mother forbade me to see, as she thought it would be too upsetting because of its fearsome psychological nature.

In regards to mental institutions, my mother only knew about the barbaric stories she had read in the newspaper or movie magazines. One case, in particular, was when Frances Farmer, the Hollywood movie star, had been admitted by relatives and given a lobotomy. My mother also recalled hearing about patients who were simultaneously placed in a straightjacket or a rubber room, never to see the light of day again.

During my mother's hospital stay in the 1970s, she begged to be released, so my father, always adoring my mother no matter what her state of mind was, brought her home, with no recommendations for an after-care program, just a bottle of lithium pills prescribed in such large doses that she lost control of her bladder and one side of her body went numb. The doctor told her that everyone required a different dose and that she should monitor how her body was reacting to her prescription, and then it could be altered if side effects were to occur, which they did.

Alarmed by her body's extreme physical reaction, she threw the pills in the garbage and went back to mood swings and episodes of depression, refusing to take another pill, ever again.

Despite everything, her hospital scare was enough to set her straight for a time. She mindfully tried to keep her thoughts and emotions under wraps for fear that she would be locked away in the looney bin again. Her words, not mine.

Now here I was, working in such a place.

The first time in the psychiatric ward, I delivered a tray to a girl that I used to know from years ago when I worked at the bank. When I knew her, she was shy, quiet, and kept to herself. I distinctly remembered her wardrobe, as she always wore long dresses buttoned up to the neck, and brown well-worn flat sandals with pantyhose that perpetually bunched up at the toe, spilling out the end of her sandal. She was tall, at least five feet ten inches, and carried herself with slightly curved shoulders, which gave her a look of insecurity. Thick hair surrounded her face, and she wore oval wire-rimmed glasses. I instantly liked her.

Her name was Laura-Bell. We used to have our coffee breaks together, and it was at the diner that she confided in me that she was very religious and not allowed to dance, date, go to movies, or even drink coffee. I had never heard of such a thing, and I could only think how boring her life sounded, especially since I had attended movies regularly since I was a child, coupled with my years of disco dancing, my two most treasured activities and pastimes. I was in awe of her strict, cult-like upbringing.

Many years since that conversation, I now found myself delivering a tray to Laura-Bell as she sat upright in a hospital bed. When our eyes met, I was just about to give her a huge welcoming hello when I noticed that she had a tiny baby in her arms. The visual brought to my mind that she once said in her religion, sex before marriage would cause shame and, therefore, banishment from her family.

After noticing the baby, I looked at her hands, only to see the absence of a wedding ring. Frozen, I paused and waited to see how or if she would react to seeing me. When she looked up at me, her facial expression was flat. She slowly turned away to gaze out the window. I still waited, hanging in the balance with her tray in my hands, hesitant of what to do next. She eventually turned back in my direction, her face showing no sign of recognition.

Not wanting to upset her more, I quietly set down her dinner tray and scurried out the door. Afterward, I regretted my actions and wished that I would have acknowledged her. I went back to her room the next day, but she was gone.

Like every job that I had ever had, coffee breaks were looked forward to and diligently taken. When I was still the new girl at the hospital, on one of my breaks I spilled hot chocolate from the vending machine down the front of my uniform. My co-worker cheerfully said, "There are some clean uniforms over there; grab one," proceeding to point to a rack in the staff room. I was so thrilled by this girl's advice that I immediately changed into a fresh, clean uniform just when it was time to get back to work. It was near the end of my shift, so I wore the uniform home, thinking that I could get another wear out of it, as I had to work the next morning bright and early.

When I got to work, a dietary aide worker at least thirty years my senior, approached me head-on and unexpectedly yelled, "So you are the one that has been stealing my uniforms!" I was so taken aback by her anger and tone that I quickly went and changed to give her back what I did not know was her uniform.

Ordered into the head dietician's office, she wrote me up for theft. Strangely enough, not once did I try to defend myself. I never uttered a word about the night before or how the other dietary aide worker nonchalantly instructed me just to grab any available uniform from the rack. It was the clean laundry rack, and all the uniforms belonged to other employees. This part was left out of her suggestion.

When I returned home, my mother, in her downtrodden monotone voice, told me that the ambulance had come and taken my dad away—admitted to the palliative care ward at Lions Gate Hospital, the top floor where people go to die. They never leave and do not get better. This bit of news made me want to develop mood swings like my mother.

My shoulders felt weighted, and even though I tried to push it off, the pressure was getting heavier by the day. My dad's debilitating illness, my mother's psychological problems, and my concern over Dale's drinking were all becoming more than I could bear. I dared not think about anything from my past, as those mistakes were unfathomable.

As soon as we moved into the North Vancouver house, I had applied, auditioned, and was hired to teach aerobics classes at the North Shore Winter Club, the same place where I had learned how to figure skate and swim when I was a little girl. It felt familiar and comfortable.

As expected when teaching fitness, I was forced to be cheerful even when I was not. I soon came to realize that plastering a smile on my face, no matter if I was in the depths of despair, had a magical way of chasing the blues away or at least dissipating them for a time. But more so was the science and physical side effects of the increased oxygen to my brain and the overall sense of well-being that came from moving my body, a release of stress from exerting myself with each grapevine, squat, and jumping jack.

Aside from feeling better when I exercised, it also reminded me that physical side-effects vary for those caring for a loved one when they are dying. Some people gain weight, while others lose it. In my case, food became completely unappealing, and the pounds melted off like a secret weight loss remedy. The first indication was the oversized wedding dress. Who would have thought that I could get any thinner? But I did.

The downside, unfortunately, was that I was a fitness and health professional, proclaiming a healthy lifestyle to my clients, but not practising what I preached. How could I? My words, instructions, and advice were real and true but were lip service, nonetheless.

Covertly, I had always wanted to be small and petite. I could not help but think that maybe this was a wonderful by-product of death, sickness, and loss—a perk, a bonus, the upside to being down and faced with tragedy.

When my face broke out into a million tiny bumps, it was then that I knew something was wrong with me.

I had been after my mother to go to a naturopath for her down days (she refused to use the word depressed, manic, or bipolar), to which she finally agreed, and we went together. I went for the tiny bumps on my face, and my mother went for her down days.

We were both prescribed a tincture, little drops made up of a plant-based formula. However, once my mother's mood became elevated on her up day, her depression magically disappeared, and everything became fine and dandy. Therefore, the drops she was to take never had the chance to get off the ground or be effective. When feeling elated, she concluded that she no longer needed the drops, and therefore the naturopathic medicine sat on the window ledge, drying up and forgotten.

My skin problems did not clear up, even though I faithfully placed the drops, as instructed, underneath my tongue daily.

Simultaneously, Dale's drinking became an issue of insignificance and the least of my worries. Putting all concern for my husband and my marriage on the back burner, instead, I focused on my dying father and off-balanced mother.

When at work, I spent my breaks in the palliative care ward sitting with my dad. It proved to be convenient, working in the same building where my father was at death's door. Kind of a win-win situation, I thought. He eventually became comatose, hanging on by a thread, so I tried to be at his side as often as I could.

He was giving up the ghost. Sometimes I wanted to die right along with him. I said to Dale once, "Maybe you, me, my mom, and Toby should join him."

When I was delivering meal trays one afternoon, I ran into one of my dad's nurses. Giving her a smile and a nod in passing, she pulled me aside to inform me that my dad had eaten some Jell-O. I was elated at the news, thanking the nurse for telling me and thinking how great it was that he was getting some nutrients. Consequently then, like being smacked in the face, reality said, "Hey, wait a minute. He'll die anyway, so what's the point? Nutrients don't matter anymore."

He had so loved life. He was far too exuberant and young to die. Seventy-two years old, and it was less than a year ago when he was jumping over fences, pickling beets, and tending to his garden. His laughter was notoriously and boisterously loud, such a contagious laugh that everyone within earshot had loved it. Now he no longer spoke or laughed, but thankfully I could still hear both in my memories.

My mother's unpredictable mental state had taken a tremendous toll on my dad, but somehow he managed. They had tiptoed around both their brain issues. My father was on his way out and she was staying. It felt unfair.

One of my mother's sayings around this time was that "Only the good die young, so I guess I'm going to be around a long time." At this, she would laugh, despite the truth of the matter. Her laugh sounded mad and eerie, which always left an awkward silence in the air around us.

As a young girl, she was an adventurous tomboy. She had spirit and a lust for life, and later on as a young woman, when she left home, she was up for any challenge that the world could throw at her, marrying my father at twenty-five because she, like me, thought that she had better "hurry up," because the life of a spinster was not in her grand scheme of things.

She had always been lovely and kind, smart and beautiful. I often speculated that her rocky childhood never got sorted out, and she carried with her fragments, sharp pieces that tore away at her. They mostly just stuck in her mind as her heart managed to stay intact. For that, I was always grateful.

I learned through these times that tragedy and trauma made people say ridiculous, if not mean things. They never intended to hurt others, but somehow, their words came out in an unintentionally hurtful way.

The day my father left this world, I had worked the morning shift at the hospital, and before going home on September 25th, 1987, I stopped upstairs to visit my dad, as was my custom. His eyes were completely glazed over since he had gone blind. His lips were dry and peeling, and he was only a shell of the handsome, strong, capable father I had once known.

His speech was long gone many months earlier, forcing him to write things down until he was too tired to hold a pen anymore. He never liked his penmanship, which he blamed on his grade seven education. He was sharp, witty, and intelligent nevertheless, and who knew that charades, his preferred go-to game from years earlier, would one day come in handy when he could no longer speak.

As his illness progressed, he used hand signals and gestures to get his point across. I was the only one in the family who could decipher them. My mother often said that the day my father lost the ability to talk was the day they nailed his coffin shut, a statement that seemed insensitive at the time but was undoubtedly true.

I felt so sorry for him, for myself, my mother, my siblings, and my children that I did not yet have—another unfair circumstance that had occurred, a terrible misfortune that my dad would be dead, and my babies would not get bounced on their grandpa's knee.

On this last day, I leaned into my father's hospital bed and held his hand. His grip was still surprisingly strong, and I knew that I needed to tell him—it was inevitable that I had to authorize him to leave. I could feel that he wanted to go. He was slipping and holding on by a thread.

I could hear his shallow breathing if I listened carefully.

It was still morning when I talked my dying dad into dying. I spoke softly, but loud enough that he could hear me. Confidently and almost sternly, I said, "Dad, you have always been the best dad ever. I was the envy of my friends, and I could not have loved you any more than I did. You took care of us. Your love was evident. You came from hard beginnings, but you broke the patterns and gave us all an amazing childhood and a wonderful upbringing. You taught us that laughter is the best medicine, and we should love our neighbour, and treat others how we would want to be treated, no matter what their religion is or the colour of their skin. That goodness and kindness always prevail. Please go, Dad, I give you my permission, and you have my word that we will all be okay. I will watch over mom, and together, we will all be okay. I will be happy for you to be free."

I went home after my one-sided conversation. The minute I walked in the door, the telephone was ringing. It was my mother calling from the hospital. All she said was, "He's gone." Gathering up my purse, I ran out the door to go back to the hospital, forgetting that my older sister was downstairs napping.

I neglected to get her to tell her that our dad had died. Instead, in a fog, I drove to the hospital to see him one last time by myself.

My mom said that she was at his side when he took his last breath. She shook him and yelled at him to keep breathing. He just couldn't anymore.

Linda, my sister, had woken abruptly from a deep sleep. Later she told me that our father came to her in a dream. He was standing at the foot of her bed, calling out to her. She was naturally upset with me that I did not go downstairs to get her, and she would have liked for us to go to the hospital together. I don't know how or why, but my sister forgave me later, saying that shock and grief can affect one's thinking. It was exceedingly gracious of her. I felt bad and was speechless about my actions in leaving her behind. All I could say was sorry.

When Dale came home from work that day, I met him at the front door, and he immediately knew. He adored my dad, too. Dale was kind and comforting toward me. He let me cry and held me in his arms.

I did not know what to call it—a funeral, a memorial service, or a celebration of life. We picked a date and a location to wish my dad a fond farewell, to say *bon voyage*, *arrivederci*, cheerio, *sayonara*, and bye-bye. We were sending him off to a better place, but it was unclear to me where that better place was. I so wanted it to be Heaven.

For a reason unknown to me, someone had ordered a white stretch limousine to pick up my grieving family. Clamouring out the door from our house on Jones Avenue were my two brothers, their partners, my sister, mother, myself, and my husband. Silently the chauffer nodded as he opened the gleaming white door, and one by one, like dutiful robots, we climbed in. I could not remember the last time we had all been together like this. Perhaps it had been at my wedding, but never in a confined space such as a vehicle, where we all sat silently facing one another.

It felt glamorous, but wrong, to be enjoying the luxury of black leather seats set in in a U-shape formation, with a minibar lined up behind the driver. The sunroof was open, allowing a warm September breeze to ruffle my hair. At one point, my brother's girlfriend suggested we stand up through the sunroof above us. The driver said that was completely out of the question for safety reasons. None of us wanted to do it, anyway, except her.

As we exited Lonsdale Street and turned onto the Upper Levels Highway, the route reminded me of all the times I had ridden with my father as a little girl in his work truck. My treasured childhood memory, combined with the new experience of being in a limo, brought a lightness to the event, and for a brief moment, I was absurdly happy. Catching myself, I struggled to find balance and teetered between pain and euphoria. For once, my mother's illness seemed to be making sense.

The Capilano Crematorium had standing room only. Aside from myself, a great number of people in the community had adored my dad, and it seemed like all of North Vancouver had come out to pay their respects. Not everyone could fit inside the room, and many had to wait outside until it was over. It was the end of a long warm summer, so thankfully, the doors were kept open.

I sat next to my mother, and she held my hand. I first thought she laced her fingers in mine because she was reaching out to calm me, to let me know that she was there for me, but when I felt the soft wadded-up Kleenex balled up in her palm, I realized she was holding my hand for her own sake. I did not mind, as the last time she held my hand was when I was a little girl at the grocery store.

My oldest brother had prepared music, a mixed tape of my father's most loved songs—"The Tennessee Waltz," sung by Patti Page, and "Put Your Sweet Lips a Little Closer to the Phone," by Jim Reeves. We had an open microphone, so people were able to come up and share their memories, thoughts, or heartfelt feelings. Our long-time friend and neighbour, Michael Hocevar, summed up my dad beautifully. He said, "You could hear his laugh all over the neighbourhood, and he was a friend to all." Michael grew up next door to us, and he loved my dad. Our family was grateful for his kind, heartfelt words.

I later regretted not getting up to speak. Fear gripped me. But later I thought what a wonderful speech and tribute I could have given.

Stepping outside into the glaring sunshine, several people stood around laughing at the telling of old stories or perhaps funny memories they had shared with my dad, while others timidly glanced over at me with downcast eyes, not knowing how to act, what to say or do.

I wanted everyone to be weeping, to holler out how unfair it was, to shake their fist at the sky, and to demand answers. Their laughter felt wrong and unnerving. I yearned for someone to gallantly take my father's place, climb into the oven, and become reduced to ashes, professing that they should be taken from this world instead.

In the days and weeks afterward, grief consumed me. I felt unbelievable heartache and melancholy that I carried everywhere with me. My skin was still breaking out, and I decidedly wanted a baby more than ever. I thought for sure that a baby could fix everything, take away my guilt for the abortion, heal Dale's desire to drink, and fill the gaping hole in my heart, which in turn would mend my gut-wrenching sadness.

Days after the funeral, I took to going outside late at night to sit on the curb in our cul-de-sac. Here I would stare up into the darkened sky, begging the universe to give me answers, pleading with God to tell me where my dad had gone, how he was doing, and if he was okay. Unsure of what to make of it or how to fathom the finality of death, I spoke to no one, and no one spoke to me;

for coping purposes, grasping at straws, I made an appointment with a fortune teller.

On one of my nights alone meditating with the universe, I recalled the first time, months prior, that I had reached out to a soothsayer seeking information from another realm and how her advice had been alarmingly accurate and right on.

It was only a month after Dale and I married. My sister-in-law and I thought that it would be fun to go to a luncheon that advertised a ham sandwich and cheesecake, followed by a reading from a specialist who would predict our futures by looking deep into the coffee grounds at the bottom of our cups at the end of the meal.

Since I had a whole compilation of past hurts and pain, I thought that a look into my future might give me some hope and calm my fears about being newly married, with burning speculation that my husband had a drinking problem. Either way, I was disturbingly apprehensive and hopeful that my secret incident with the Cowboy would go unnoticed, and the guilt I carried of the baby's death would not be written all over my face.

I had become an expert in sweeping my thoughts and feelings under the table, and exceptionally good at placing the unthinkable into the far corners of my mind. I could fool most people. But unhealed wounds turned into scars that silently sat dormant, festering, unfortunately ripping open without a moment's notice. A trigger could bring on tears or anger, benign things such as a happy couple, a new baby, or a father and daughter enjoying lunch together.

But most times, I had an uncanny knack of letting life go merrily along. I could switch gears quite freely from that of pain and sadness to a charming smile and outward joy.

The grounds left at the bottom of my coffee cup said this: "You are newly married, and your new husband is an alcoholic. He will remain that way for a very long time, and then he will go far away, maybe on a sailboat, and get better. You will have four children."

I was not sure if I should cry, scream, or demand my money back. Disappointed and embarrassed, I left the restaurant and went home, trying to forget about the whole caffeine-induced sorcerer and her look into my future, assuming the trickster was wrong and yet asking myself how she could sound so right.

A year later, the disaster of my father's death besieged me, and I was seeking the unknown, the underworld, and wanting answers as to my father's whereabouts. Maybe another clairvoyant could tell me that my dad was happily living in another universe or floating above my head with invisible wings, protecting me and watching my every move. Hoping that digging into the afterlife, the underworld, would not cause more trouble than it was worth, I was desperate. I needed answers.

The night before the arranged appointment, I had a dream. *My telephone was ringing so I answered it. The connection was bad, and I could faintly hear my dad on the other end. He was speaking in his usual exuberant, enthusiastic voice as I had remembered it. Even though the call was faint, I positively knew that it was my father. I asked him where he was, what he was doing, and if he was okay. He responded with, "All I can tell you is that I am very far away, but I am working and doing well. I just wanted to ask about your mother to see how she is doing." Before I could respond, the line went dead.*

In the morning, groggy and nervous from an unsettling sleep, I drove across town to the west side of Vancouver to meet with the psychic. I was looking for answers, a message, closure, peace, something—anything that could help me get through the earth-shattering mournfulness that was all-encompassing. I could not shake my father's passing.

Arriving and uneasy, knocking on the door and being let in, I could see straight away that her home was not filled with signs of witchery but was quaint and average. No incense was burning or crystal ball beckoning to come into the light. Void of tarot cards and heaven forbid, a Ouija board, I felt safe from the lurking of demons and evil spirits.

Seeing the normality of my surroundings, I let out a sigh of relief, signalling to my guide and the universe that I was ready, willing, and open to get started.

The woman in question specialized in reading people's auras and was about to read mine. She instructed me that after her reading, she would meditate more on any deep-rooted questions I might have that were plaguing me.

Diligently having done my research beforehand, I found out that auras can reveal information about your thoughts, feelings, and dreams. All living things radiate an aura from the energy they emit. These special vibrations and colours can be seen by gifted people and those trained in the healing arts who can manipulate energy fields for effective healing. By paying attention to how you feel in someone's presence, you can get a gut feeling about the essence of the person or object that it surrounds.

Before we began, my guide explained to me that there are seven levels to a person's aura, and each level has its unique frequency. If one level is unbalanced, it can lead to an imbalance in the other levels as well. She went on to say that learning to see someone's aura can tell you a great deal about the person and his or her character. I was pleased with this, and was all ready with my question for when she was ready, as I had only one—where was my father now? Seated five feet in front of me, closing her eyes and taking a deep breath, she began.

The reading went like this: "Your life was on track, and you were headed down the right path, which had already been mapped out for you. Something happened, there was a shift, a turn of events, and you took an immediate sharp turn in the opposite direction, and now you are embarking on the wrong path. You will be okay, but this new route will be much harder than the way you were supposed to be going."

I thought of John and my decision to choose Dale. I inwardly rolled my eyes. Letting out a sigh, I allowed her to continue. Her message from the other side—or wherever she was getting her information about my aura from—went on to say that I was a kind, generous person, always looking for the good in people and wanting to make people feel comfortable, and that I would live to be very old and wise. In fact, people would seek me out wanting my advice and words of wisdom.

When the reading was over, as she had previously mentioned, she asked me if I had any specific questions. I went on to tell her that my father had just died, and I wanted to know where he had gone, what he was doing, how he was doing, and if he was okay.

The psychic closed her eyes and bowed her head. She breathed in slower deep breaths and calmly exhaled. After about five minutes of meditating, she opened her eyes and said to me, "All I can tell you is that your dad is very far away, but he is working and doing well."

She appeared bewildered by what she had said to me. I told her about my dream that I had the night before, and we both smiled in unison. Her words were verbatim to what had transpired in my dream and the phone call from my dad.

From that moment on, I was given some relief but eventually gave in to new thoughts that plagued me. Had I chosen the wrong man?

I still dreamt vividly and often. Some nights I would be enveloped in dreams and visions of my dad, which felt smooth, like riding on angels' wings. The voices were liquid and gentle, calling out to me, wistfully painted memories of my childhood. He would be in the garden tending to his vegetables, laughing at a TV program, throwing me up in the air as a little girl, holding my mother's hand, and laughing his loud, claim-to-fame, boisterous laugh. Captivated, I never wanted to wake up and was disappointed when I did.

On other nights, intermittent nightmares came forth, of twisted images, my sick father wrapped up in thin hospital sheets, alone in his sickbed. His thin, gaunt face and weary eyes looking up at me, pleading for his life back. Death, like a thief in the night, would rob him while holding me captive, away from the dad I adored.

I had promised him at the end, while he disappeared, that I would be okay. So, with every ounce of strength I could muster, okay is what I set out be. I created a new term for myself. I called it "desolate hope." I knew from that day forward I would forever miss the only man I had known who had a heart of gold.

CHAPTER 10

"Faith"

1987–1992

THE LOG HOME WHERE I SPENT MY TEENAGE YEARS WAS NOW vacant, and my oldest brother Doug lived next door to it in another log home with his wife and baby daughter. Parts of my dad were everywhere on both properties, instilling in me a desire and urgency to be near what was left and salvageable of him.

Dale and I were still residing with my mother in North Vancouver on Jones Avenue. We decided to ask her if we could move out to the family home in Mission. We were ready to branch out, have a life, and raise children out in the country, leaving the city behind. Pregnancy was once again at the forefront of my mind.

Our thoughts were that we would renovate the now older log home, fix it up, and pay my mother rent. Dale was very handy, and he either knew what to do, or he would certainly learn. I admired how once he put his mind to a project, it would get done. Slowly, nevertheless, but surely.

Karen Harmon

Months earlier, I had lost a baby with a tubal pregnancy. I had experienced a twisting cramping sensation, knowing that I was pregnant because it was not the first time, and for some reason, I just knew that something was wrong. My doctor scheduled me for an ultrasound to make sure everything was okay. Showing up for my appointment, I was distracted, as my dad was dying, and Dale's usually calm and pleasant nature seemed off. He had become introverted, quiet, and grumpy.

After drinking copious amounts of water, I sat in the waiting room, trying to blank out fleeting thoughts of despair. All alone, my expectations were mixed, and it was not until I was called for my turn, changed into the provided hospital gown, and was lying down on the makeshift gurney bed that I started to relax. When the ultrasound technician rubbed jelly all over my stomach, I felt a sense of relief, the darkened room gave me peace, and the instruments they used to check what was growing or not growing inside of me felt cool, which calmed my nerves considerably.

With the repeated swipes over my still-flat tummy, alarm bells started slowly to go off, becoming louder, shrill-like, and then almost deafening. Foreboding crept in that something might be wrong, and when I looked up into the face of the technician, I could see that she was concerned, as well.

Eventually, a doctor appeared, and then he took a turn at moving the medical magic wand all over my abdomen. They murmured to each other in hushed tones that sounded like another language entirely, and then they both fell silent. Neither one of them was allowed to tell me what was happening because it was protocol for my doctor to do the telling. I did not ask, and they could not tell.

I continued to lie there silently, biting the inside of my cheek while conjuring up thoughts of the unwanted abortion I had just over a year earlier, a procedure inflicted upon me, by me, with the help of health care professionals who at the time, also fell silent. Knowing now that I had done terrible damage to myself physically and emotionally, I never once thought to blame the dead perpetrator who forced himself on me.

They telephoned my doctor and brought me the phone. She gave me the bad news.

I stayed in the hospital that night, so emergency surgery could be performed to remove the fetus (my baby) from my fallopian tube, as I was having a tubal pregnancy. If it were to rupture, I could die, so time was of the essence.

Another baby was about to die, and I could only wonder if it was all my fault yet again.

They operated on me at 4:00 a.m., and that same day Dale came to visit me. I cried about everything. He found a wheelchair and scooted me all over the hospital to take my mind off my troubles—out to the gardens, in the elevator downstairs to the cafeteria, and before going back to my room, we went outside so he could have a cigarette.

I momentarily felt happy, like I was in one of those movies where the handsome boyfriend did not want his sick girlfriend to die, so he treated her to some fun, making mischief in and around the hospital before her inevitable death was to take her away.

The next day I was to be released at noon. It was a Saturday. Dale was not working, but he did not come and get me at the scheduled time. He showed up late, not arriving until after 6:00 p.m. His breath smelled strongly of alcohol. I cried when I saw him and was upset that he was six hours late to pick me up. I could tell that the nurses felt sorry for me.

The consolation prize for my loss was thinking of my dad, who was now far, far away, bouncing my unborn earthly babies on his heavenly, angelic knee. He had two knees, and now he had two grandchildren up there with him.

"Perhaps they are not stars in the sky, but rather openings where our loved ones shine down to let us know they are happy."
—Ancient Inuit Proverb

By January 1988, I was pregnant and willing to do anything it took to keep the baby safe, healthy, happy, and alive. My weight was still incredibly low, weighing in at 105 pounds at five feet six inches. Food still did not appeal to me. But for the sake of my precious cargo, I started to eat.

I was in fear of slipping on the wet floors at the hospital, which led me to hand in my resignation. With no concern about income, lost wages, or building a nest egg, my pregnancy was all I thought about.

My optimism crept up, as did my weight.

I loved the changes to my body and how the baby growing inside of me was going to change everything even more. I began to feel hopeful again and not just on the outside.

I kept teaching fitness and started swimming. I was famished all the time and craved salami and mustard on crackers. I enjoyed not working at the hospital and took the time to care for myself— swimming, prenatal stretch classes, and getting massages. I felt like I was healing emotionally and physically. I loved being pregnant, even though the first three months brought intense nausea.

Every day I sent positive vibes and admiration down into the soul of my unborn baby, anything that I could muster to ensure that my child would feel wanted and cherished. Intuition told me that I was having a girl.

My mother took me on an all-day shopping spree in Bellingham for a whole new wardrobe of maternity clothes. When we were coming back across the border, she was experiencing an up day, so she appeared to be unhinged, and the customs agent made us go inside for three hours of interrogation. Even though we claimed all of our purchases, they assumed that we were a drug-smuggling twosome. A mother-daughter team. A crazy lady and prego. I sometimes felt like we belonged on *The Jerry Springer Show*.

After my mother's agreement to us moving to the property, Dale worked tirelessly every weekend in the log house. He drywalled the entire inside, as the 1970s-style wood panelling was outdated, dark, and dingy. We planned to paint the interior a light pastel blue to freshen and brighten it up. The cabin had burned down once when I was a child, leaving the outer shell intact but badly damaging the inside log walls. My father built it back up again, sandblasted the burned log walls, and then covered them in wood panelling. Now we would be covering the panelling with drywall.

To help Dale, we arranged work parties with friends and family, accomplishing all the necessary taping, mudding of the drywall, painting the interior, and decorating the baby's room, which was my old bedroom. It looked out onto a lush, green backyard surrounded by the forest—a bright and airy room with remnants of teenage dreams.

The working bees we created were fun, and the potlucks consisted of great food, crowd-pleasers such as potato salad, baked sesame chicken, lasagna, salads, and desserts. In attendance was Dale's brother, and his best man Mark, a few family members, and some of Dale's kind-hearted, relaxed hippie friends. Everyone worked together.

The strains of Neil Young and the Grateful Dead played in the background, the beer flowed, and we all had a good time renovating the log home that would soon be our dream home. At the end of each evening, we built a fire in the firepit my father had created years prior. Dale brought out his pride and joy, an Ovation guitar that he was continuously teaching himself how to play.

The baby's due date was October 31st, a Halloween baby. Instead, she arrived early on October 19th, 1988, anxious to get out and greet her parents who longed for her. Dale let me choose the baby's name, so I decided on Jessica after the Hollywood movie star Jessica Lange.

Jessica was everything I had ever dreamed about in a baby. My heart ached for the miracle of birth. I cried tears of joy for her and the loss of the others.

My mother sent twelve long-stemmed roses to the delivery room, and she told me later that she also smoked an entire pack of cigarettes, one after the other while waiting to hear. She was not the kind of mother to race to the delivery room and had always professed to be nervous about babies, even her own.

As comfortable as I was holding my bundle of joy, I also willed her not to cry. She dutifully listened and obeyed. She scarcely uttered a peep. Visitors came and went, and the whole time, my baby was as good as gold, quiet as a mouse, knowing full well that I would have to quiet her down in front of people, which might indicate I was not a capable mother.

Having been underweight when I got pregnant, I ended up with an extra sixty pounds on my body. My feet were so swollen that they bulged out over my shoes, and I felt like Little Lulu from the comic book series. With my heftiness not diminishing and dropping off immediately after giving birth, I was mortified and confused, expecting that it would have magically disappeared as the baby appeared through the birth canal.

Taking care of my baby, losing weight, and worrying about my husband's alcohol consumption soon became the next priority for me.

My mother sold the house that we had all lived in and rented herself a two-bedroom apartment on Third and Chesterfield in North Vancouver. Directly across the street, kitty-corner from where she was living, she got a job at the local 7-11 convenience store.

At sixty-eight years old, she had not officially had a job in the outside world since she was twenty-six. My heart broke a little bit for her because she seemed old, alone, and yet needed to find work.

My worry was all for naught, as she loved her job, her new co-workers became her friends, and all the customers her grandkids, as she told it. She felt new and improved, vivacious, and confident.

Strangely enough, she worked the graveyard shift, which seemed odd, as it meant that she had to deal with (at her age) all the late-night drinkers and partygoers who were coming in with the munchies. Again, unrequired on my part to worry, because she found the customers to be incredibly polite, cleaning up their act considerably when they saw her behind the counter, reminding all the hard-core drunks of their sweet grandmothers.

In one instance, she offered a male customer a Kleenex, as she thought he had a cold because he was sniffling. He informed her that he had just done a few lines of cocaine out in the parking lot. Being well versed in the ways of the world, she was not shocked in the least, gave him the tissue, and carried on with her various other 7-11 duties.

She was diligent in following the rules and guidelines that had been set forth for all staff. One, in particular, was that the floors needed mopping every two hours, which she loyally and willingly did. But she wondered why other staff failed to follow the instructions and take their turn. She stated that in her day, one did what the boss asked and followed the rules to a T.

Showing up on time in a crisp, freshly pressed 7-11 uniform would not give anyone the impression that she lived in a messy apartment in complete disarray. Her glass figurines, popcorn makers, and never-used electric wok from the Shopping Channel sat with a variety of unopened boxes, adding to the clutter. Her television blared 24/7, and she was perpetually happy as a clam since her moods had shifted to an upward spiral.

On the odd occasion, when she was not jubilant and flying high, she showed up for work anyway and then went home and slept, not answering her telephone, as if missing in action.

"A dog is a man's best friend," a phrase I had grown up with, meant very little to me until the untimely death of my dog Toby, a nine-year-old cocker spaniel and black Lab mix. He was a gentle and devoted family member. At the time of his demise, I realized that Toby was grieving the loss of my father, and my vivid imagination believed that he had deliberately ended his life, whereas my common sense told me this could not be possible.

It was a sunny day in late January, and I had not seen the dog all day. I called and called, but unlike his nature, Toby did not respond. Dale was at work, and dusk was falling. On a sickening hunch, I walked over to the above-ground pool, and there I found the lifeless body of my precious four-legged companion. He was lying at the bottom of the swimming pool in shallow water. There was a thin layer of ice covering him, reminding me of Sleeping Beauty's glass coffin. I was instantly horrified and devastated. Toby had been my dog, but he was my dad's best friend—a part of my dad now gone.

When Dale arrived home from work that night, he struggled to dig a grave in the half-frozen ground. We picked a spot out by the horse corral, wrapped Toby in a cozy blanket, and laid him to rest with his red leash and dog dish. We cried together over the fresh mound of icy dirt. I found myself hoping and praying there was such a thing as dog heaven.

When Jessica was eight months old, I was feeling good and began to ponder the life I wanted for my daughter. I had gone briefly to Sunday school as a child, and a Christian summer camp at a place called Anvil Island. Later on, and throughout my lifetime, I had taken it upon myself to pray quietly in the comforts of my bedroom in a wishing, begging sort of way, and then I would give up entirely when my prayers did not get immediately answered.

With no spiritual direction and not raised in a religious home, I encountered the "grass is always greener" mentality, thinking other families were better than mine and not finding out until much later that many families were far worse.

After giving birth, I was determined for Jessica, my untarnished fresh-faced baby girl, to have some spiritual teaching and moral direction. I entered the searching mode.

Beginning open-minded and optimistic every morning, I truly was a generally happy person. Whether it was a God-given talent or strictly naïveté about my daily struggles, I knew that exercise was a key component in helping me to feel good. Therefore, I found myself applying for and landing another fitness teaching job.

Starquest Fitness, a facility in Maple Ridge, was only a twenty-minute drive from our home. Packing up Jessica three mornings a week, with a diaper bag that contained every baby-orientated necessity—Cheerios, cut-up grapes, sippy cup, lotions, rattles, toys, diapers, and blankets—together we would go to my classes.

Upon arrival, she went into the daycare provided, handed over to Auntie Tracy, the beautiful, well-coiffed, stylish and doting caregiver. I then darted out onto the aerobics floor to inspire and motivate, burn calories, and tone.

When the class was over, everyone would get together for coffee over at a local McDonald's. The children would play, the babies would sit dutifully in high chairs, and the women would gab.

I visualized the whole bunch of them as "stay-at-home moms," living in four-bedroom homes with patio furniture and husbands that did not drink but rather read the newspaper and worked nine to five. I loved my time with the women and enjoyed pretending to be just like the image I made them all out to be. There, while passing the time in MacDonald's, the grass remained perpetually bright and pleasant on the other side of the fence.

Everything took a turn when one of my fitness participants invited me to her house for coffee. As much as I wanted to go, I hesitated because I was not sure if I had the capacity for a friend. I devoted most of my time and energy to my baby, mixed in with my worry and concern over Dale's drinking. He had started drinking a six-pack of beer on the way home from work, a one-hour drive from Vancouver. By the time he got home, he was bleary-eyed and slurring.

My idea that a baby would change everything had not quite kicked in yet.

While weighing the pros and cons, curiosity got the better of me, and combined with my inability to say no still being quite prevalent, I accepted her offer and went with baby in tow to my new friend's house.

She had a lovely home, and after she made tea and we exchanged pleasantries, she told me that her husband was a pastor of a Mennonite church. I was dying to learn more about what her husband did. I did not know the difference between a pastor, minister, reverend, and priest, and as she explained, I was hoping that she would invite me to church.

After a yummy lunch of macaroni and cheese, she did just that and invited me. She followed by saying that she would still love to be my friend even if I chose not to go.

I was eager to try the whole church experience. I perceived it to be something that I had been searching for all along. When I explained my new friend to Dale, I asked if we could go to her church. He hemmed and hawed, grappling with his decision, finally saying yes as long as it did not become an expected routine. I took that as a positive sign, so come Sunday morning bright and early, off we went to church, like a proper on-the-other-side-of-the-fence family.

I began to have an understanding that throughout the journey of life, we meet many people along the way. Each person has a purpose, and no one we meet is ever a coincidence; therefore, all life experiences are important, mistakes and all.

I was inexperienced at church and not prepared for the undertaking and major involvement that was required by going to this one.

Upon arrival, people mingled around chit-chatting with one another, and at precisely 9:00 a.m., the entire place broke up into smaller clusters, called adult Sunday school. Each group was studying a different topic. I went into the "Women and How to Entertain" group. The children went to Sunday school, and babies such as Jessica went to the playcare. This process lasted one hour.

Following the group sessions was a coffee break. Off to the side were big urns of coffee, tea, and platters of cookies. More mingling about took place, and shortly after that, we gathered for the actual church service, which consisted of announcements, singing, a collection plate, and a sermon, plus a call to come forward for prayer for those that were in dire straits.

Directly following the service, many volunteers cleaned up, and then the whole congregation went out for lunch.

By the end of the morning, we had spent over three hours with strangers, singing, praising, worshipping God, studying the Bible, and then eating lunch at Ricky's Diner, located in the mall. This was an activity that required money that we did not have. However, I was delighted when someone offered to treat us.

We talked, shared, got to know other people, and I quite enjoyed the whole process.

On the drive home, I speculated that a person would need to go to bed early the night before and be prepared to talk and listen for a better part of the next day. It was remarkable to me how friendly and sincere everyone was. It truly felt like the people I met were interested in me, and the whole playcare idea was such a lovely option. Overall, I came away feeling loved and inspired, aside from the fact that I did not have a clue as to what the pastor was talking about.

Unfortunately, it was all too, too much for Dale—overwhelming, perhaps. I understood, but I was still disappointed that he said he would not want to try attending church again for quite some time.

Fixing my marriage and my husband's drinking problem was turning into a daunting, seemingly impossible task. Problem-solving, setting boundaries, and tough love was not yet in my vocabulary, and I did not grow up in a home where these forms of relating were common everyday occurrences.

So, not knowing any better, I decided that we needed a vacation. A holiday away would surely bring us closer together. Fun and frolicking in the surf, sleeping, reading, and eating delicious food could be the be-all and end-all to a happy, healthy marriage, I was sure. Being free from stress, financial woes, parenting, work, and household duties for a while would certainly be the answer. I was convinced this was the solution to my quandary.

I got wind of a tremendous deal. Friends of a friend told us about a trip where airfare and a seven-night stay at a hotel in Hawaii were only $405 a person. As reasonable as it was, we still could not afford it, so for the sake of my marriage, I wanted to get a full-time job in addition to my fitness classes.

My main goal in life was to be a stay-at-home mom, so I was only planning to work long enough to afford a long overdue vacation that was bound to fix my husband, which would prove to be well worth it in the long run.

Using my waitressing experience from the Exhibitors' Lounge at the PNE, I applied and got a job at a restaurant in Maple Ridge.

I applied for the night shift, so Dale would be home from work to take care of Jessica. If there were an overlap with our schedules, my mother would come and help out, too.

On my first shift, I cried all the way to work with having to leave my baby at home with my mother. Once there, I was called into yet another backroom, bringing back memories of my Bootlegger clothing store days when I was suspected of being a thief. Except this time, ten years later, I was told that my shirt was wrinkly and asked if I owned an iron. I was most appalled.

On my next shift, my boss told me to be the bartender's assistant. Spending my entire eight-hour shift in hot steamy water with drink glasses, pots, and pans brought back memories of my food services hospital jobs.

By my third shift, I had caught a cold, and the blisters on my feet were causing me to limp. When I was pulled aside and told that I had set the tables all wrong, tears stung my eyes, and I called my mother on my break. She instructed me to quit and said that she would pay for our trip to Hawaii.

In the meantime, my mother decided to quit her 7-11 job and move out of North Vancouver. She said, "One cannot go back. People change, and North Vancouver is just not the same as I remembered." She moved into a two-bedroom high-rise apartment in Maple Ridge, called Gordon Towers.

She now had time to take care of Jessica, so Dale and I could travel to Hawaii to heal our marriage. We were both tremendously excited for sunsets, walks on the beach, warm water, and a multitude of other tourists all clamouring for a break from hectic lives and bad weather.

To get the cheap deal, we took a room that was situated on the second floor, next to the boiler room and the ice machine. The view was of a cement wall. But we did not mind or complain in the least.

The beaches were packed. Fortunately, our hotel was only a few blocks from the ocean, so we had fun traipsing around, renting mopeds, and somehow finding a daily happy hour where drinks were half price. I kept thinking how much better our trip would be if I could let loose like I did back when we were dating.

Since I quit drinking during my pregnancy with Jessica, I had grown to dislike it, which was tricky because most of the time, I was policing Dale's alcohol consumption—not a very fun or productive pastime.

Everywhere we went, I noted the many couples, and I couldn't help but wonder if they were all in Hawaii to repair their marriages, too.

One day at the beach, I reached into our backpack, looking for suntan lotion, and instead pulled out a hidden bottle of whisky. An argument ensued as to my disappointment, so Dale took off toward the water with a bright yellow air mattress that had popped. In his handiness, he tied the end of the air mattress in a big knot, which gave him half of a flotation device with a cumbersome bulging tail. Nevertheless, Dale pounced into the waves along with other sunbathers, big burly muscle men surfing and skimboarding.

Aside from my annoyance, I couldn't help but laugh at how sweet and unpretentious Dale was, my humble guy who could care less how he looked on his flimsy $1.99 makeshift air mattress with a giant, obtrusive knot at the end.

For some reason, I kept reacting to Dale's excessive drinking the same way—disappointment, complaining, crying—and yet I continued to expect a different outcome. Aside from my Nancy Drew detective work, the trip proved to be fun, and we did grow closer even though my comments about his drinking failed to have the intended outcome, with Dale once again saying that when we got home, he would cut down on his alcohol consumption considerably.

At the end of the trip, I changed gears, deciding that baby number two would be good for our marriage, and a brother or sister for Jessica was essential.

Our house was charming in a cuckoo clock sort of way, with dark stained logs, A-framed peaks and bright red begonias in the window boxes. Dale and I routinely emerged as the cute little couple from within, who happily poked our heads outside to smile and wave, while the clock chimed, "Cuckoo! Cuckoo!"

The log home still held many fond memories of my father, and Dale enjoyed keeping up the yard, which made me proud. He enjoyed reminiscing about the story he had told me when we were first getting to know each other. It had become family folklore about Dale's relationship with his grandpa Pete and how he followed him around the garden like a little shadow. Jessica was now Dale's little shadow tagging along after him, listening intently as her daddy explained the various flowers, vegetables, and plants he so lovingly tended to.

Dale had planted cherry tomatoes to grow up the side of our house, so on their walkabouts, he taught and encouraged our curly-haired little daughter to pick off the vine and pop the red delicacies into her birdlike mouth, laughing at her surprise when the tangy-sweet juice exploded and ran down her chin. Dale loved her, and in pure Grandpa Pete fashion, he enjoyed showing her the lay of the land.

Our garden was blooming, healthy, and flourishing, even though our marriage was struggling to stay alive.

Trying to stay afloat financially, I was perpetually thinking, planning, and scheming of ways to pay the bills. Dale's drinking kept getting in the way of his good qualities and my inability to put food on the table. It seemed to me that if he could quit drinking or cut down considerably, as he had many times promised, then subsequently, less of our hard-earned cash would be wasted.

Deciding that Dale needed more credentials under his belt and a degree to increase his wage so he would finally get paid what he deserved, I suggested he go back to school to get his surveyor's ticket.

When I was three months pregnant with our second baby, Dale applied for a student loan; at six months along in my pregnancy, he started the civil engineering program at BCIT in Burnaby.

I was satisfied and excited to enter the next promising stage of our life.

As a bonus, there was always the chance that going to university might curb his drinking or force him to stop. Therefore, his self-confidence would soar, we would stop arguing, and our family would rise above the poverty level, living happily ever after, once and for all.

Dale had long since sold his truck Sluggo to a shyster, a con man, and never got the money. Lord knows we tried, but in every uncertain term, a crook can easily find their next victim, who just happened to be a trusting soul like Dale.

We lived an hour's drive from BCIT, so he needed to use our only car to go to and from college, which worked out fine because I had stopped teaching fitness and was happy to stay at home, taking long walks with Jessica, tending to the house, and hanging out next door at my sister in-law's house with her and my niece and nephew.

Baby number two arrived, and what we thought was going to be a boy was a beautiful towheaded baby girl with a striking resemblance to her father. We both agreed on the name Emma. The delivery went well. It was fast, with a slight scare as the cord was wrapped around Emma's neck. I was instructed not to push, the doctor untangled the cord, and voilà! Emma came into the world in only three pushes and a two-hour time frame, which included the one-hour drive from Stave Falls. She barely cried and seemed relaxed about being born, at peace with the world.

Still struggling financially, I was disappointed that we could not afford to get equivalent professional hospital photographs taken as we had done for Jessica.

Rumour had it that the photographer pinched the toe of the babies so they would open their eyes in alarm, then he snapped the photo, and like magic, the image of your one-day-old baby, red-faced and squinting, would rest on your mantelpiece until graduation. Either way, I was temporarily brainwashed into thinking a professional photoshoot mattered.

What doubled the blow and made matters worse is that I found out on the day Dale picked me up from the hospital that he had used our last bit of money on a case of beer to celebrate, and we had only enough gas to get home.

Despite his striving and hard work at technical school, it could not take away my embarrassment and shame that we were having trouble providing for our girls. I regularly went to the food bank, cooked a lot of macaroni, and was thankful for the garden. My mother helped us out whenever she could.

Putting on a brave face and pretending that everything was okay, we made do.

Unlike the dozen red roses my mother had sent to the delivery room when Jessica was born, she had missed Emma's birth entirely because she had gone travelling to Australia and New Zealand, oddly enough with one of my single friends from high school. She had grown to dislike Christmas and the holidays, and since Emma was born December 27th, my mother was traipsing around in the utmost manic state.

When introduced to Emma, Jessica instantaneously adored her baby sister, receiving her as if she had always been there. Only twenty-six months older, she became a loving devoted caregiver, consistently checking in to make sure Emma was warm enough, well fed, and content. I encouraged her sisterly concern and empathetic love. I praised her and thanked her, often saying that this was her baby, too.

Not sure if my approach was right, wrong, or indifferent, together we manoeuvred through the newness and transition from her being the centre of my world to now being my right-hand helper and companion.

The day we drove home from the hospital, a wave of coldness came over me, and I felt extremely tired. Something felt amiss, not like the usual fatigue at bedtime or after an accomplished day. I kept my feelings and symptoms to myself. Once Emma was born, Dale had started to spend Monday through Thursday at a fellow student's house so I could use the car. I would pick him up Friday at the end of his school day and drive him back on Sunday night.

At six weeks old, Emma was diagnosed with a respiratory infection and almost died. One evening during a late-night feeding, I noticed that Emma was struggling with irregular breathing while I was nursing her. She was gasping for air and couldn't seem to feed and breathe at the same time. Living out in the wilderness, with no immediate health care services, I became distraught and took her to the local hospital, a twenty-minute drive away. Told that she might have an ear infection, I was given a prescription for amoxicillin and then sent home.

Later the next morning, I had a gut feeling that things had gotten worse. It did not appear that Emma's breathing was improving, so I called my doctor's office and was told to take her to Vancouver Children's Hospital immediately.

The minute we got in the door, Emma completely stopped breathing. The commotion was like none other I had ever seen before—an entire emergency team engulfed her tiny little six-week-old body, suctioning her and trying to clear her airways.

Dale sat panicked at her bedside. All I could think to do was run out into the hall, calling over my shoulder as I left, telling Dale not to leave Emma's side. They worked on our helpless baby to stabilize her while I walked the hospital corridors, wringing my hands. When I returned, Dale had tears streaming down his face, and Emma was weakly breathing again.

I kept thinking of what could have happened if I had not brought her in.

For the next two weeks, I slept on a mattress on the floor in Emma's hospital room. They did not have any available cribs, so they put her in a big hospital bed. She looked frail and defenseless.

Sick and listless, she lay still most of the time. Friends and family came and went, bringing me food and comfort. My friend and her husband (now my pastor) drove from Maple Ridge to visit us. We all held hands and prayed around Emma's oversized bed. I used every ounce of my strength willing the minuscule being before us to grow strong and to live.

With Children's Hospital being a teaching hospital, many groups of medical students came through to observe and be taught by their teaching doctor. One quiet afternoon while Emma lay recuperating, a doctor and his students came through and interviewed me about Emma's previous symptoms and present diagnosis.

After I answered his questions, he turned to the interns and said, "Always value everything a mother says to you about her child. No one knows her child better than she does." The doctor had the utmost respect for all mothers, and he instructed his students to do the same.

The feelings of coldness and fatigue did not leave me while at Children's Hospital and followed me all the way home. I cried easily and was tired all the time, still telling no one.

Emma recovered, Dale continued at BCIT, and my children gave me a purpose to cook, clean, read stories, and go for walks. My exercise classes three times per week forced me out of the house, and the routine became another duty and specific place that I needed to be. The physical benefits of my workouts kept me treading above water.

The exercise forced me up and out into what felt like an unreal world of normalcy. I would look at my co-workers and fitness participants, bewildered, thinking that *they* had something wrong with them because of their obvious energy and light-heartedness.

Putting on my actress hat transformed me into a fitness instructor, performing for my clients like a trained seal, dutifully offering fitness tips and a warm, inviting smile, even if it was the last thing I felt like doing. When I was finally home, alone, and not on display, I could not shake the heaviness and exhaustion that encompassed my mind and body.

A smokescreen had developed over my eyes; thankfully, I could still see my children.

I found solace in the perfect families at church. I packed up the girls every Sunday morning, and off we would go. While there, I learned about peace, forgiveness, and unconditional love that I could receive from Jesus. The people all said that there was power in prayer, and like a dry sponge, I wanted to soak up every aspect of it.

At the beginning of every sermon, we were encouraged to turn around and greet our neighbour. We all shook hands like we were making a deal of some sort. At the end of every sermon, we were encouraged to go upfront for prayer, like getting a seal of protection before going home to mayhem.

I was often the first to leap out of my seat and lunge forward. The people in the prayer ministry held my hands while I bowed my head and cried. Their spoken words over me and pleadings with God to help me as they scanned my face looking for clues, flattered me that they cared. At times I could feel the mending and stitching together of old wounds with an invisible needle and thread. And then a liberal dousing of supernatural ointment was lavishly applied to my scars. Sunday after Sunday, I relished the attention and kindness I was receiving.

With my daughters safely tucked away in the playcare or toddlers' Sunday school–program, I sat by myself, next to my friend, the pastor's wife, straining to understand the well-rehearsed message to the congregation. The scripture and teachings were confusing and hard to make sense of, like a foreign language where I could only understand every third or fourth word.

Each week I persevered, hoping that God and these spiritually-minded people were just what I needed, regardless of my inability to understand the enlightenment in the teachings. I so wanted what they had and tried to figure out how on earth I was going to achieve it, all the while failing to think or wonder what went on behind closed doors once the flock had dispersed, and everyone went their separate ways.

Faintly, I remembered that my mother had once stated that religious people were hypocrites.

Dale was fine with me going to church; he liked knowing our girls were in a safe and moral environment. He enjoyed my retelling of the message that was delivered and descriptions of the various people I was getting to know. But after a while, I started to withhold the news. It felt like I was feeding him their lives, like I was manipulating him to fall for their goodness. As the church embraced me, his opposition to going was creating a wedge.

At the end of Dale's first school year, he suggested we host a party, a barbecue for his classmates and teachers. We had a wonderful yard for entertaining, with a firepit, trampoline, and an above-ground swimming pool that were all my father's doing, remnants of his hard work and love. Dale's garden and window boxes were bursting with red begonias and made for an eye-pleasing, comfortable, and cozy setting.

On the outside, it appeared as though I had achieved my white-picket-fence lifestyle, but the contents within did not resemble my childhood perception of what should be perfect or normal. If I were in an Ann Tyler novel, I might have just packed up and walked away, leaving everything behind that I was trying with all my might to fix, gone without a trace.

Having been mailed an unrequested Canadian Tire credit card, I used it to purchase groceries for the party. I wanted to impress and ensure that everyone had a great time.

As Dale's classmates arrived, I was surprised by how young they all were, some of them directly out of high school. Dale was thirty-four, having gone back to school after many years in the field and trenches, so in comparison, he must have seemed ancient.

From the sounds of things, the other students adored him. Person after person approached me to tell me how smart they thought Dale was and how impressed they were with Dale's ability to achieve ninety-eight per cent on the exams while he regularly had a six-pack of beer in his locker. They said that he took swigs throughout the day, as if I already knew about this amazing feat, exclaiming how cool Dale was and how remarkable that he never appeared to be outwardly drunk.

Instead of being pleased with their rave reviews, I was angry and disappointed that yet another opportunity for Dale to quit drinking had only allowed him to maintain the habit and still excel at something within his addiction. On the other hand, the comments and praise from his fellow students confirmed my thinking that he was an intelligent man, which brought on an inkling of pride that warmed me. I wondered why everything seemed to be unbalanced.

A full-page article came out in the *Province* newspaper about alcohol addiction. It described the characteristics and how alcohol affected the breakdown of the family. A case study was taking place, and a group of therapists and counsellors were looking for young families to participate. The criteria were that one person in a relationship had to have an addiction to alcohol, with a spouse who did not, and there needed to be at least two or more young children in the family. If someone wanted to be a part of the program, there was a phone number to call. If accepted, the individuals would not only get free counselling, but they would also get paid to do it.

I could not believe my luck! Finally, a program that might work, I thought. But how I worded it to Dale would be crucial to his agreement to participate.

Dale was such a kind, giving person, always wanting to help others, so I strategically planned how I would word my request. I said to Dale, "I read something interesting in the paper. A research company is looking for assistance from the public, and they are paying people to come and answer questions about how alcohol has affected their life, marriage, and family. According to the article, we would be of great assistance to the project, and we sure do need the money. I was wondering if we could do this."

Without giving it too much thought, Dale said yes. We met the criteria, were accepted, and registered.

Everything started on a positive note. Our counsellor, Geoff, was soft-spoken and user-friendly toward therapy. At the beginning of our session, we engaged in light banter, and as an icebreaker, Geoff and Dale spoke about hockey, Dale's favourite sport. We filled out a few questionnaires, and then the counselling began.

In the middle of the room was a large inflated beer bottle, four feet tall. Geoff asked me to place the bottle somewhere in the room that would represent where the substance of alcohol was most prevalent in my marriage. I got up, picked up the prop, and placed it on Dale's lap. Next, it was Dale's turn to do the same thing. Except he picked up the large plastic beer bottle and placed it way off in the corner.

For the next hour, Geoff talked about health, addiction, boundaries, and compromising. Dale was mostly silent. At the end of our time, because Dale said very little, Geoff asked him if he would be more comfortable attending the sessions on his own, suggesting that maybe Dale did not feel comfortable discussing things in front of me. I was eager for Dale to do what worked best for him. So, if he felt more comfortable without me in attendance, I was happy to support that, too.

To me, our first appointment was enlightening. Dale did not think the same; for him, it was embarrassing and awkward. On the car ride home, Dale said that he thought Geoff was nice, and the session was not that bad, but he still did not think he had a drinking problem. He agreed to attend the next session by himself.

Before our next appointment, Dale did something that I had been begging him to do. It greatly pleased me but frightened him to death. He took it upon himself to not drink over the entire weekend. One of my arguments with him was that if he didn't think he had a problem, why didn't he just stop, then? He often responded that he drank because he enjoyed it, not because he had an addiction.

For the next three days, while abstaining from liquor, Dale was white-knuckling it. He didn't sleep, broke out in a continuous cold sweat, and his entire body started to shake, especially his trembling hands. It was like the grip of death was upon him. It scared the wits out of him. I wanted to say "I told you so," but I chose not to.

Because Dale was to attend the next appointment on his own, he made arrangements to go directly after school to his private session with Geoff. About thirty minutes after his scheduled time, my telephone rang. On the other end, Geoff told me that Dale didn't show up for his time slot. My first instincts were to be annoyed, followed by offering an apology, and then making up an excuse to protect Dale, or me, or everyone for that matter.

Instead, I didn't take Dale's behaviour personally. I told Geoff that even though I was sad he was a no-show, I didn't have any control over him. Geoff followed up by praising me and said I had taken the first step in not being codependent. My response felt so right, not planned or contrived and completely comfortable.

Geoff finished the telephone conversation by telling me that whether Dale chose to come back or not, I was welcome to continue the counselling sessions and finish the case study, and I would still get paid in the process. Initially feeling reluctant, and then obligated, I accepted his offer.

During the sessions, rather than discuss Dale and my marriage, we talked about my childhood. Mostly we talked about my father's death. When I questioned Geoff as to why we were not talking about my relationship with my husband and his alcohol addiction, Geoff asked me to think of an onion, with the different layers each representing a time where trauma and pain had occurred. Issues that I had not dealt with or healed from could stack up, layer upon layer. Therefore, to get to the root of the problem, I needed first to peel off the onion layers separately, one at a time. He then explained that it was a process and not an easy one.

In addition to the case study I was involved with, my children, church friends, and exercise classes kept me continuously marching along. Dale marched, too, but to the rhythm of a different drum.

I learned early on that conversation about God was not everyone's cup of tea, and some of my unchurched friends might refer to my prayer sessions as cultish, or my more optimistic friends might conclude that, through prayer, I was getting in touch with my inner self. By no means did I want to come across as a religious fanatic, Bible-thumper, or offend anyone, so I quietly did my thing, trying not to be overzealous or preachy, even if I sometimes wanted to.

The Al-Anon meetings that I periodically attended referred to God as my higher power, and they certainly did not talk about Jesus, whereas the counselling sessions with Geoff focused on me and me alone, and I felt the most freedom there.

Geoff thoughtfully listened as I talked about missing my dad terribly and how unfair death was, how hurt I was by my mother's outbursts. I shared that both my parents were smart and funny and yet seemingly absent, my father through death and my mother through bipolar disorder.

The bottom line is that I saw more clearly, blaming Dale less for my unhappiness, and weight was lifting from my shoulders. I figured out that from the time I was a little girl until now, I had been trying to please someone else—everyone else. My patterns kept me on a perpetual path of never being good enough or happy enough. After each session, I felt physically taller and emotionally lighter.

Sometimes, however, without a moment's notice, I would fall back into my old self. The regressions brought a hammer crashing down on all the work that I was accomplishing. Confusion clouded my vision, with momentary lapses that brought hopelessness, which made me wonder what the hell I was doing on all accounts.

The counselling was working, but old habits were hard to break. If Dale arrived home from work slurring or came in from the garden inebriated, disappointment would once again engulf me. When the girls called out for their daddy, his face lit up, and I would melt. My emotions went back and forth, causing my head to spin. Hidden banter in my mind turned into outward arguments with Dale. It infuriated me that he could not see the money turning to liquid as he drank it away, losing sight of his health and our marriage in the process.

Cracking the code on his addiction was proving to be next to impossible. Like a vicious circle, intermittent thoughts would come along, making me think that maybe I was the one with the problem—two steps forward, one step back.

Dale repeatedly tried to convince me that he was fine, but I was never quite sure what he meant by the word *fine*. He was not a textbook case or like an alcoholic that one sees in a movie. He did not get falling-down drunk; he was not abusive physically, and he loved the girls and me wholeheartedly.

I frequently asked God what happened to the fresh-faced man whom I had met so many years before while working on the Alaska Highway, the man whom I had chosen over another.

A woman who attended the church approached me one day after the service and said, "My father was an alcoholic, and my five siblings and I always blamed our mother for not doing something." Another lady asked me if I was okay. When I said, "Yes, why do you ask?" she said, "Everyone at church knows your situation—that you're married to an alcoholic—and they're all praying for you."

The two comments shocked me. No longer a secret, my private life was lying there like a dumped bag of groceries rotting on the side of the road—smashed tomatoes, spilled milk, and the sack that everything came in was torn and irreparable. I was mortified, angry, and embarrassed.

After that, I did not want to go back to church, to the place and people I had come to know and trust, to the ones I was trying to fit in with, thinking then that I did not belong and wondering why I ever thought I did. As I watched the unified families and saw the fathers playing with their children, it reminded me of how families should be. It became blatantly obvious that I was alone, my family of four minus one. An important spoke in the wheel was broken.

Once in a while, I would find solace in reading from the Big Book, more or less the Alcoholics Anonymous bible. A sacred text of AA groups around the world, the book was filled with stories, steps, theories, wisdom, and personal advice from a wide variety of people. My goal was always for the betterment of my husband. I circled and underlined, folded over pages and tried to memorize:

"Most people drink because they like the effect produced by alcohol. The sensation is so subtle that, while they don't admit it is harmful, they cannot, after a time, comprehend the truth from the false. To them, their alcoholic life seems the only normal one." Page 27

"The thought that somehow, someday he will control and enjoy his drinking is the hope of every abnormal drinker." Page 30

"We talked of intolerance while we were intolerant ourselves. We missed the reality and beauty of the forest because we were diverted by the ugliness of some of the trees." Page 50

The wisdom and interpretations of the Big Book are left up to the reader to use as they choose. There is comfort for the alcoholic in knowing that they are not alone, that what they feel is not unusual, and there is a solution.

I was mending, changing, finding my voice, and not completely ready to throw in the towel on my marriage or God.

My saving grace came right out of left field. It unintentionally played a huge role in the biggest decision I was ever to make. A friend of mine, Colleen, who was more of an acquaintance from high school, contacted me to ask a question.

During high school, she and I were in different social cliques; me with the shy, nerdy girls, and her with the party-hardy cool kids. We met by chance while sitting in our high school library at a study table. Simultaneously, the people we were each sitting with all got up from the table and vanished, each going their separate ways, leaving Colleen and me alone at the same table. We naturally moved to sit closer together so we could converse.

We chatted freely and laughed like two old friends shooting the breeze. Not meaning to, we spent an entire block together, an unlikely pair, which could have been socially awkward, but it was comfortable. When the bell rang at the end of the period, we stood up and said goodbye, never to speak again until another chance meeting a year later.

The scenario had drastically changed. I was a candy striper. She was a patient in the Mission Memorial Hospital, with a concussion and pins in her foot. I gathered that she was obviously drugged up on painkillers at the time and perhaps did not recognize me. To her credit, I looked completely different and out of character as I was wearing bright red and white stripes that ran perpendicular, on a starched, crisp uniform, a flattering outfit with a fitted waistline apron and matching hat. My white stockings and practical white nurse shoes pulled the whole ensemble together.

I had been enlisted to conduct twenty-four hours of community service as a punishment for shoplifting. It was a mistake, really—my friend and I were trying to put the Lee Press-On Nails that we were stealing back on the shelf when we got caught red-handed.

Even my cool, only-once-spoken-to friend who lay stretched out before me would never have guessed that I was a criminal. Perhaps I could have fit into her group of friends and counterparts if she had only known. Now she was lying in a darkened room, quietly healing and recuperating. Rumour had it that Colleen had been in a car accident after a late-night party.

As I refilled her water jug, she was no longer cackling with laughter and throwing out witty remarks that had become her claim to fame. Instead, she gazed out the window silently. I stared at her for a while. Eventually, I moved on to the next room and the next unsuspecting patient.

As fate would have it, we met up again, a third time, ten years after high school graduation at a mutual friend's wedding shower. Both of us were all grown up. I was a mom with two kids, and she was a high-powered businesswoman. Gone were the cliques and awkward elements of puberty and high school social standings.

We got along famously at the shower and decided to exchange telephone numbers. Only days later, her call came in, inviting me to go on a cycling trip with people that I did not know on a bicycle I did not own with the money I did not have. I was elated, and accepted her invitation without giving it a second thought.

Meanwhile, my daughters were two and four years old, Dale was in his second year of technical school at BCIT, and I had six months of counselling under my belt. Gone were my chills and feelings of fogginess; there was a light on the horizon, and for my sake, I was going on a bicycle trip.

I was torn to leave but excited to go. I felt a glimmer of hope, as if I was emerging, poking my head out of the obscurity.

Having always been proud of my hopeful optimistic nature in the past, I decided to look both words up in the dictionary and sure enough, right there in black and white was proof. I was starting to get my groove back.

Hope: *"the feeling that what is wanted can be had
or that events will turn out for the best."*

Optimistic: *"disposed to take a favourable view of events or conditions and to
expect the most favourable outcome."*
—Webster's Dictionary

When I was asked by Colleen to join her cycling group, I knew that I needed to go. I so wanted a break from my back-and-forth thinking, moments of strength with Geoff's help, and crashing-down weakness between appointments. I had spent a lifetime of worrying, which, I was learning was completely unproductive and useless, only making my brain whirl in chaos.

The trip was the first week of July 1991. My mother bought me a brand-new bicycle, a white mountain bike that had black flecks of paint splashed on it in a trendy way. I borrowed saddlebags, and I had just received $600 for an income tax rebate.

Dale had agreed to my trip. Aside from us growing apart, he was always generous in so many ways. My mother and my sister-in-law, who lived next door, offered to help Dale with the children in my absence. I was going, and everyone was on board.

I wondered what the women would be like, and speculated how in shape they must be. Rock-hard bodies, legs like pistons, and health food nuts came to the forefront of my mind. With images of me falling behind the beautiful Olympic athletes on my snazzy new bicycle and getting left on the side of the road, my imagination ran wild, and the usual pattern of worry was momentarily all-encompassing.

The trip would entail touring around the Gulf Islands and staying at different bed and breakfasts. But first, we arranged a meeting to discuss routes and get acquainted with each other. Aside from church socials, I had not been out with other women in years.

The restaurant was dark and loud, becoming exceedingly louder as I made way to the table. Taken aback by deafening shrieks of laughter, F-bombs, and beautiful, inviting faces, I was instantly charmed and made to feel welcome. Speeches and the clinking of glasses, ear-to-ear smiles, and snorting guffaws were contagious, and I could not help but join in. I felt honoured to be a part of the camaraderie. They swore like troopers, and I wondered if I would be able to let loose and swear like a truck driver, too. I so wanted to.

Jessica cried, and Emma stood up, trying to balance on her chubby little legs to kiss me goodbye. At the last minute, I almost chickened out, but memories of the gal pals of my early twenties and nights on the disco dance floor pushed me to get in the car. It had been years since I had felt the togetherness and support from other women, and I had a feeling that this trip would be monumental.

Dale gave me a ride to the Tsawwassen Ferry terminal, with my bike jammed in the backseat of our car. He wished me well.

After my first day on the bike trip, I quickly found out that I truly was the weakest link, trailing behind the others until my thighs were completely on fire, my bottom was numb, and my lungs felt like bursting. I could not keep up and (yet again) wondered what the hell I was doing.

After reaching our first destination, I quickly realized that a good workout is when you hate doing it, but you love finishing it.

The first order of business was to get paired up with a roommate and assigned a bedroom, or rather, to go running through the B & B giggling and staking one's claim on an available bedroom as quickly as possible. Then it was happy hour, with appetizers and drinks.

I had not had a drop of alcohol in what seemed like years. I'd become reluctant to partake in something that I loathed when watching my husband consume it. For some reason, this felt different. No longer was I keeping tabs on someone else, fretting and worrying about another person or the dangers of drinking and driving. Suddenly, it was just eight other self-sufficient women and me, equal in so many ways, and yet we couldn't be more different.

We made toasts and ate nacho chips while we relived our first day of cycling hills, in awe of gorgeous scenery, helping each other fix flat tires and taking cinnamon bun breaks every ten minutes, or so it seemed.

I was settling into the routine and decided that there was no other place that I would rather be.

After a full day of cycling on our fourth day, during an evening of dancing and barhopping, I was the one to buy the first round of shooters. Colleen and I surprised the others by bringing over a tray of none other than Kamikazes, which put me back in the saddle again.

The next day was a short day of cycling, so we took the afternoon off to mill about, nap, read, and in my case, sleep. I slept for the entire afternoon. Waking up, I was physically and emotionally exhausted. Emerging from my darkened room, I saw Colleen in the kitchen, so I meandered over to sit up on a barstool to chat. She looked over at me and asked me how I was doing and how Dale was.

From her simple question, her politeness, and interest in me, I burst into tears. I broke down and allowed for the truth to spill out. All the years of trying to keep it together, being a people-pleaser, and striving to be a perfect wife and mother, everything combined brought forth a barrage of tears and an outpouring of emotion.

The possibility to self-destruct, to explode with heartbreak and immeasurable disappointment, was not far off. My breakdown and my first time sharing with a friend caused a commotion, and the other women began to gather. With a captive audience, I shared everything: my dad's death, my mother's mental health issues, my marriage, and how hard I had been working to keep it running smoothly. As I described my inability to make Dale stop drinking and how I still loved him, I sounded weak and desperate.

With the listening ears, caring eyes, and support of the other women, I came to terms with something: I had changed. I was not that person anymore, the girl with the Cinderella complex. They validated how strong I was and what a great mom I had become, even though some of them barely knew me.

I achieved immense healing while laying the foundation for lifelong friendships, all because a friend asked me how I was doing.

On my ferry ride home, the strangest, most unexpected event transpired.

After I loaded my bike below deck with the cars, I made my way upstairs to the passenger area. I pulled out my latest novel, feeling completely and utterly at peace, fit, emotionally cleansed, and excited to embark on my plans for the future. The other women were all milling about getting snacks or rummaging through the ferry gift shop while some sat outside on the deck, admiring the BC coastline.

Just as I was settling in, out of the blue, I heard a voice call my name. Looking up from my novel, I saw John standing before me. We had not seen each other in over eight years. He was smiling from ear to ear and very happy to see me. At his side were two little boys.

Mixed in with my prayers about a normal, healthy marriage to Dale, I had also hoped that someday I would have the opportunity to see John again, if only to apologize.

My face lit up to see him, my ex, my first real true love and steady boyfriend. His face was beaming back at me. It was all I could do not to jump up to embrace him fully. Instead, my practised, well-rehearsed monologue came tumbling out.

I profusely apologized for hurting him those many years ago when I chose Dale over him and thanked him for the wonderful five years we had shared. I even went as far as to say that I still thought of him from time to time and of what we had shared, adding that I hoped he was doing well. Looking down into the faces of his cherub-faced little boys, I knew that he was.

John was happily married, so I chose not to divulge the inside scoop about my troubled marriage. I wondered if I would ever get another opportunity to share the next chapter of my life with him or if it even mattered.

Sitting polarized after our impromptu meeting, I watched John leave, carrying both of his little guys tucked securely under each of his arms. I was left with mixed emotions, thinking about the order of things and the "what ifs."

My struggles had shaped and moulded me; the path that I chose, whether it was directly or indirectly, made me. My mother's mental illness and my ability to manoeuvre around her unbalanced behaviour taught me how to adapt my needs to suit hers. It carried over into my relationships with Dale, my friends, and my co-workers. My father's optimism, sense of humour, and good character influenced me. Both my parents were comical and loved to laugh even amidst the darkest of times. What struck me as an epiphany was that I realized right then and there on the ferry boat that I was a good mother, and I could hardly wait to get back to my daughters. I could not foresee my life without them, any of them.

When the ferry docked in Tsawwassen, I emerged with my bike trip friends, feeling the freshness of new relationships, unforgettable memories, unity like peas in a pod, and now preparing to part ways. With tears in our eyes, we gave out hugs and took away a little piece of each other that day. Something big and powerful had happened, and we all knew it. "Same time next year" were the sentiments all around.

After being dropped off at my log home by Colleen and unloading in the driveway, I stopped to take in the immense beauty of the bright-green manicured lawn, framed with swaying evergreen and alder trees. The window boxes on the darkly stained log home were overflowing with their usual striking red begonias, and the lilac tree that my father had planted for my mother was in full bloom.

I heard their laughter first. Adjusting my eyes from the landscape, I zeroed in on Dale in the middle of the lawn, performing backflips for the girls while they giggled and clapped, shrieking, "Do another one, Daddy."

My heart swelled before breaking.

After returning home from my trip, strengthened by female friends and self-help books, the counselling sessions with Geoff, and coming to terms with my unanswered prayers, I asked Dale to leave.

I had read a book called *Love Must be Tough* by Dr. James Dobson, which one of the church ladies had given me. It talked about not enabling. It reminded me of the poem, "If you love something, set it free. If it comes back to you, it was meant to be; if it does not, then it never was."

I needed to live apart, to remove myself and the girls from the addiction, but also the unhealthy patterns that both Dale and I had created. We needed time and the opportunity to regroup. My stipulations were clear and concise. I expressed to Dale how much I loved him and that I did not want a divorce. I was not angry. I spoke out of love.

I wanted him to take one full year to get help, recover, and live a healthy, clean life. I had envisioned him as a sober husband and father so many times that the prerequisite I was dishing out felt right and necessary before we could rebuild. My decision was a lifeline for me.

Reading the book *The Five Stages of Grief* by Elisabeth Kubler-Ross and David Kessler, I learned that all losses are created differently, and we cannot tuck messy emotions into neat packages. We all have different responses to loss, as there is no typical loss.

I devoured the information about the five stages: denial, anger, bargaining, depression, and acceptance, and how it could be used as a framework for a process, whether it be from death or a shattered relationship that leads to divorce. I learned that there are tools that help us frame and identify what we are feeling. I felt better knowing that not everyone goes through all of the stages or in a prescribed order.

These stages gave me direction and knowledge of grief's terrain, making me better equipped to cope with life and loss. I liked how it said that our grief is as unique as we are. I wrote down each definition on recipe cards and used fridge magnets to put them on my refrigerator.

Denial: Denial and shock help us to cope and survive the loss. Life makes no sense; we go numb, and we wonder how we can go on or why we should even try to go on. There is a grace in denial as nature's way of letting us see and feel only as much as we can handle. As we accept the reality of our loss, we are unknowingly beginning the healing process.

I learned from my counselling sessions with Geoff that I had not fully grieved the loss of my father, the traumatic incident with Eric, and my mother's mental health issues. It made sense to me that working on marriage was next to impossible if I had so many other layers of grief that were blocking the way. Pain and hurt piled upon one another, like the layers of an onion and not the sweet kind, but rather the strong cooking onions that burned the eyes. I was able to bring closure and acceptance, even though I knew that I had more layers to peel off and was not finished with my healing yet.

I had no idea how angry I had become, so the next definition astonished me, especially since I was not typically an angry person.

Anger: Anger has no limits; it can extend not only to your friends, your family, yourself, and the loved one you have lost but also to God. We may ask ourselves, "Where is God in this?"

Underneath the anger is pain. It is natural to feel deserted and abandoned, and we live in a society where anger is feared. But anger is strength, and it can be an anchor, giving temporary structure to the nothingness of loss. The anger becomes a bridge over the open sea, a connection to the person you have lost. The anger is just another indication of the intensity of your love.

I was angry that I had an abortion when I had always wanted a baby. I was angry that my dad had died, and was mad at my mom because she was unpredictable and unstable. I became irate at Dale and frustrated with his inability to manage his drinking. I was upset that there never was or would be a storybook romance. I blamed others for my struggles.

Bargaining: A temporary truce; "What if I devote the rest of my life to helping others? Then I can wake up and realize this has all been a bad dream." I was lost in a maze of "what-ifs" and "if-onlys." Guilt is often bargaining's companion. I was frequently finding fault in myself and how I handled things.

I often thought that perhaps if I could not beat the addiction, then I should join the addiction and drink right alongside him. I had witnessed other wives who just went along with their husbands and drank as much as they did, conceivably to "make a go of it." At times I bargained with myself that he did not have a drinking problem, that I was overdramatizing. I spoke highly of him, telling others about his many good features and attributes, playing with denial like a friend.

Depression: The loss of a loved one is a very depressing situation, and depression is a normal and appropriate response. The depression stage feels like it can go on forever, and it is not a sign of mental illness. When reading this, I was relieved because of the times I compared my moods and feelings to those of my mother's.

I learned that not experiencing depression at some point would be unusual. If grief is a process in healing, then depression is one of the necessary steps along the way. I masked the depression stage; it was with me always like a buddy or a friend that I carried around in my pocket, undetectable to everyone but myself. I wondered when and if I would ever snap out of it. Depression is a stage. We are living in a fog, experiencing great sadness.

Acceptance: Finding acceptance may be just having more good days than bad days. We can make new connections, new meaningful relationships, but not replace who we have lost. Instead of denying our feelings, we listen to our needs; we move, we change, we grow, and we evolve. We invest in our friendships and our relationship with ourselves. We begin to live again, but we cannot do so until we have given grief its time.

My mother often quoted author and comedian Erma Bombeck that "Normal is just a setting on your dryer." But even Erma could not get through to me. I had to figure things out for myself. People often think of the stages as lasting weeks or months. The stages are responses to feelings that can last for minutes or hours as we flip in and out of one and then another. There cannot be a timeline placed on any aspect of grief.

Building relationships and friendships with my bike trip friends helped me to look outside the box that I was hiding in. The packing tape that was stretched tautly over the lid was unexpectedly ripped off by none other than me, opening up my can of worms to become vulnerable, to share my story, to cry and be heard, never before realizing that the outcome could be acceptance and love. I was not my husband nor my past hurts, nor the right, wrong, or indifferent decisions I had made along the way.

CHAPTER 11

"This Used to Be My Playground"

1992

DALE WAS RELUCTANT TO LEAVE, AND I DESPERATELY WANTED him to stay.

The summer I returned from my adventurous and enlightening bike trip, reading my new self-help book, I absorbed it page by page. It sounded like the advice I had been longing for, the golden ticket to a happy ending. *Love Must be Tough* by Doctor James Dobson had all the answers to all my problems right there in black and white. Clear explanations, steps to take, boundaries to make, all rolled into a nice, neat package of love and kindness, just like a cake mix—add the ingredients, stir and bake in a 350-degree oven. *Love Must be Tough*, a sure-fire method to save my marriage and the only way to prevent a divorce.

But what if that someone did not want to be saved? By me, Jesus, Geoff, or anyone else?

I learned that Dale's addiction to alcohol was not only hindering his health but was also stalling the growth of our marriage. His inability to quit drinking and to be clear-headed forced us to drift apart. We were unable to have a simple conversation, let alone life-changing and healing unity within our marriage.

Dale felt shame, and I felt elevated with new information from the book. It suggested tough love. Taking the author's advice, I chose to be strong, kind, and no-nonsense about Dale's reluctance to get help or even acknowledge that there was an issue. I made sure that I expressed my love for Dale when asking him to leave. I built him up instead of tearing him down. I promised to take him back if he sought help and if he could stay clean. I expressed that I was excited to see the changes in him that were yet to come.

I told him that I could not wait forever and suggested he take one year to get his act together. In the meantime, he could see the girls whenever he wanted to, provided that he was not drinking or drunk, and he had my word that I would never speak badly about him. I promised that I would wait for him.

When I had a handle on taking steps to change my life, my mother's finances were waning, and after the separation took place, she wanted me to move out. She could rent the house for far more than I could afford to pay and then possibly sell it if need be. I was not in disagreement with her request, but I had two little girls to keep in mind.

Finding a place and paying rent, with only a three-hour-a-week job in fitness, felt impossible. My mom did not give me a timeline and was very kind, although she had become a lot sadder in the process. The down days were upon her.

Having just become a single mom and in dire need of an income, I accepted another fitness teaching job at the Maple Ridge Drug and Alcohol Treatment Centre (MRTC). After I was offered the job and told who my clients would be, it was the last thing I wanted to do. I questioned being around such people when someone of the same sort had dashed all my hopes and dreams. But I reluctantly accepted the offer.

In doing so, I discovered a whole new element to the story of addiction, something that all the books in the world could not have taught me. No support group, therapist, or prayerful Christian could have ever explained to me what I came to realize in teaching fitness at such a facility.

It was at the treatment centre that I obtained breakthrough information. I learned that drug addicts and alcoholics were not their addiction, but their addiction had become them. They were good and kind human beings; they sought healing and were openly seeking help. They, too, were grieving.

It was through teaching fitness and making connections with strangers in treatment that I was able to begin the long walk toward forgiveness and a better understanding of Dale. I soon grew to love my job and all the clients who sought sobriety.

"Your best days are ahead of you. The movie starts when the guy gets sober and puts his life back together; it doesn't end there."
—Bucky Sinister, Get Up: A 12-Step Guide to
Recovery for Misfits, Freaks, and Weirdos

My mother stepped up and helped me by looking after Jessica and Emma while I taught my classes. With the extra responsibility came a purpose for her. The girls were two and four, and Jessica had a knack for caregiving and sat comfortably at the helm. She took pride in minding the store and explaining to Grandma what she and Emma needed. Grandma had a knack for being fun and funny and willingly followed her granddaughter's advice and rules.

The first month after my rise and climb to strength and coping, I cleaned, sorted, and forged through every cupboard and closet, trunk, box, and bin, under beds and behind furniture. In the second month of being on my own, I joined a music CD club. Within days my package arrived, and I was playing Tracy

Chapman, Blue Rodeo, Simon and Garfunkel, Amy Grant, and Amanda Marshall CDs.

A new pastime became dancing and singing along to my new music collection, with Jessica and Emma as my partners. Together we would twirl and laugh, jump and gyrate, as if within every movement there was healing and shedding of dusty old worn layers.

It was in the third month that I started to look for an apartment. I had prayed and prayed that something would land in my lap, but nothing did. I traipsed all over Maple Ridge, applying and hoping that I could get into low-income housing. Much to my dismay, a huge pile of applications were in line before me; mine was at the bottom. The office staff said that it could take months, if not years, for my name to come up.

Feeling discouraged but not defeated, I finally found an apartment on Laity Street near Maple Ridge Hospital. It was an older building, and the rent was to be $550 a month for a spacious two-bedroom apartment. I only had enough money for a damage deposit and had no idea where I was going to come up with the monthly rent. Acting on faith, I handed over the money and signed a one-year lease.

When I got home, the flashing light on my answering machine was blinking to indicate there was a message. Pressing the play button, I stood astounded and then elated with what I was hearing. It was the Baptist Low-Income Housing Complex telling me that a two-bedroom, two-storey townhouse unit had just come available, and if I wanted it, I must let them know as soon as possible. My rent, when calculated, came to $239 a month, based on my meagre income.

I kicked myself for signing a lease at the other place one hour before because now I had been accepted at a much more suitable place.

Summoning up the courage to beg for my deposit back, I inhaled deeply and dialled the number for my new landlord. Thankfully, my lucky stars were shining directly upon me; the landlord returned my deposit check, and I accepted the low-income housing offer. We would be moving in less than two weeks to a beautiful, relatively new townhouse complex that I could afford.

I had read somewhere that moving was categorized to be as stressful as a separation from a spouse. Now I was faced with both at the same time.

When the time came and my moving day arrived, a group from the church showed up with four vehicles and many able bodies. Hearing the cars and trucks pull up, I was startled, as I had not yet finished packing. I was not ready!

Sorting, packing, and moving were arduous and time-consuming. I mostly cried throughout the entire process and was perpetually interrupted by my daughters, who needed care and their mommy.

Where to get the boxes and containers stumped me right from the start. What to keep and what to throw away was agonizing, the memories, and shattered dreams heart-rending.

On the day of the move, I was in a state of disarray. Boxes were half-filled, some were overstuffed, and many were still empty. Cupboards had remnants of serving dishes, an unused punch bowl missing the little glass goblets, and a treasured crystal devilled egg platter, all sat waiting.

The footsteps on my doorstep, bringing the kind and willing church members, found me unorganized, with tears and mascara smeared all over my face. Panic-stricken, I frantically tried to fix everything. Grabbing a stuffed bunny with one missing eye, a pair of mismatched socks, and two-year-old Emma under my arm, I hesitantly answered the door. I was certain that the do-gooders would be annoyed with me and might turn around and leave because I was not ready and was too scattered.

On the contrary, bustling into my home with extra moving containers, sandwiches and cookies, friends and acquaintances smiled and offered up hugs. One woman took Emma from my arms while others started moving boxes and furniture out to the waiting vehicles. A few people took over the laborious job of packing. Some grabbed rags and spray bottles and dug into cleaning.

I found myself standing in the middle of a three-ring circus, surrounded by remnants of my life. People busied themselves around me, handling my belongings with care and attention, offering up expressions of "God bless you" like they were coins from a pot of gold over the rainbow. My lungs opened, my eyes cleared, and my smile returned.

Starting Over

1992

I looked around the cluttered living room, assessing the damage, until I spotted the soft curls on my four-year-old daughter's head while she sat with her little sister in an empty packing box. Both were contentedly colouring, Jessica carefully trying to stay in the lines while Emma, sitting as close to her big sister as possible, was eagerly scribbling.

Pondering their sisterhood with a full heart, I gazed at my daughters as if I was a bystander, lingering and wondering what would happen next. I felt like I was a person not wanting to leave the movie theatre, hanging on until the closing credits had scrolled off the screen, eventually emerging from the darkened cinema to face brilliant sunlight or perhaps a dreary evening rain.

For the last thirty-two years, I had watched a movie of my life unfold, unable to control the course or path; the script was written, and the actors had been cast. As the story took on twists and turns, plot changes, and various climaxes along the way, I sat idly by watching the series of events unfold.

Thankfully alive and seemingly unscathed, I decided that nothing was regrettable, everything was memorable, and I could learn from it all. Like any other moviegoer, I had sat patiently, waiting for the plot to thicken or the knight in shining armour to arrive. Comedic interludes were just as prevalent as the nail-biting cliffhangers. Perhaps the happy ending was not meant to be, or maybe this, right here and now, was the happy ending, and I could not see it yet.

I was pleased with what a beautiful little girl my oldest daughter, Jessica, had become, not just outwardly but on the inside, too. Her spirit was soft and gentle, especially toward her two-year-old little sister. I realized now that she had become more of a mother to her younger sibling than I had been.

I looked deeper at Jessica's bowed head as she filled the pages of her Cinderella colouring book, and I felt her determination. I was filled with compassion and reminded of how she worried about me, silently asking if I was okay. It was evident and showed in her constantly furrowed brow and ever-present look of concern as she stared into my eyes and pleadingly searched my face for answers. I would do my best to respond, interjecting, and interrupting her deep, brooding thoughts. My father always told me that laughter was the best medicine, so as often as I could, I would engage my girls in stories, jokes, and silliness, even if it was the farthest thing from my mind.

The first thing on my to-do list was to find some semblance of order amongst the stacked boxes, furniture, and garbage bags full of clothes. I was looking forward to my new beginning, our new beginning, and a fresh start in our unfamiliar home—subsidized housing for marginalized people.

Receiving a lucky break and chosen from a long list of applicants just as needy as me, it had only been two weeks since I had started praying, and now here we were in a two-bedroom, low-income townhouse unit, myself and two little girls. We were alone, the three musketeers, all for one and one for all.

Today I would finish unpacking, and tomorrow I would be applying for welfare. I was relieved to be free.

"Everyone has that moment, I think, the moment when something so momentous happens that it rips your very being into small pieces. And then you have to stop. For a long time, you gather your pieces. And it takes such a very long time, not necessarily a better way. More, a way you can live with until you know for certain that this piece should go there and that one there."
—*Kathleen Glasgow*, Girl in Pieces

I grappled with feelings of shame and embarrassment. A friend said, "Social services and welfare were put in place for people like you, someone who is going through a difficult time, struggling, faced with hardships, and in a state of not knowing what to do. Sometimes all people need is a helping hand, support, and a stepping stone toward a new beginning and a fresh start."

Without fail, that was me.

Tucking my girls into their brand-new bunk beds, a gift from my mom, and kissing them goodnight, I breathed in the clean, fresh scent of strawberry bubble bath. Wearing matching *Beauty and the Beast* nightgowns, they giggled, and I wondered if they would be able to fall asleep.

Walking down the hallway past the bathroom and my very own washer and dryer, I padded into my spacious bedroom. I crawled into bed exhausted, and deliberately nestled into the centre of my queen-sized bed. With arms folded across my chest, I was relieved and elated, now wondering if I would be able to sleep.

As I lay in bed, I contemplated where I was now and how I had arrived here. After I made Dale leave, by practising tough love, things had gotten worse. In the log cabin, the mice had started to come. I could hear them in the rafters at night and found their droppings in my kitchen drawers.

When my girls got scared, I told them to visualize the mice in top hats and tails, the mother wearing an apron and the little brother mouse wearing suspenders to hold up his trousers. I told them to imagine them all singing with Cinderella and whistling merry little tunes. Some were tap dancing, but the whole lot of them were very hungry and looking for crumbs. One crumb to a cute mouse could be a whole meal for his family, a wayward pasta shell, a feast. I did not dare tell them that the mice were probably rats, and they were infesting us.

My mother was now at my beck and call. Her mental state had dramatically improved, and she appeared to make me, Jessica, and Emma her main priority, along with Bingo at the Haney Bingo-Plex in Maple Ridge.

The day after we moved in, I had an important task ahead of me, so my mother arrived to look after the girls at 9 a.m. and brought them some bubbles to blow, the kind where the lid has an attached wand. She had a case of them from the Shopping Channel.

Walking into the welfare office, I sheepishly approached the front desk and explained my situation. After being given a number, I took a seat. Every chair except one had a person on it. I felt like I was in the wrong place. Tired faces looked at me, whereas I felt rested. Some people appeared unkempt, and I had just showered, displaying fresh curls from my Velcro rollers. Most were staring at the floor, and I was staring at them. I wanted to know what their circumstances were, their backstory, and what brought them to this point in their life.

Perhaps we could form a circle and share our heartfelt dreams and ambitions. Or maybe we could point fingers at those who had wronged us. Abstractly, I could tell them about my mother's famous baking powder biscuit recipe; I laughed inwardly at the thought of it.

When a woman called my number, I stood up a little too abruptly and accidentally crushed a red crayon into the floor with my heel. Walking to the available agent, I pretended not to notice the crayon that had wedged into the heel of my boot. I was nervous and was speculating that I could very well get turned down for financial assistance. If that happened, then what? I wondered.

In less than ten minutes, I was handed a check for $1200, and two seconds later, I was walking out the door. I wanted to thank the lady profusely, but I was afraid too much eye contact might encourage her to take it back.

First up, bank, next, groceries and then home to my waiting children, and my mother who was looking after them.

Emma did not know the extent of the separation or comprehend what was happening; she was only two and a half and still drank from a baby bottle. Jessica was four and a half and asked me regularly where her daddy was.

I tried to make arrangements with Dale to see the children, but because of the boundaries I had set in place, he could not abstain from drinking long enough, so he ended up being a no-show on most occasions.

Strangely, I was not mad. I was disappointed, yes, but mostly heartbroken. The alcohol was like an evil force that had invaded him, and he could not get away from it. He was stuck, trapped; the pressure from his addiction was eating him alive. He was starting to appear ravaged and not just on the outside. He was sad and remorseful. So how could I, on top of everything else, be angry?

I kept my word and never said anything bad about him. I had read in a book to be careful when talking about your children's father because your kids are a part of him, and when you criticize their dad, you are criticizing a part of them. I was unsure how accurate this information was, but I wanted to do everything right. I strived to help my daughters and Dale get through this as unscathed as possible.

I even still speculated that eventually, Dale would quit drinking, and we would all be a family again. The situation we were in was temporary. The book said so and stated that love must be tough. I had to agree, as this was the toughest love I had ever endured in my life.

Christmas was coming, and my mother had packed a bag and left. She decided last minute to take a trip to Montreal. My brother was living there, so she went to see him in the notoriously cold wintertime. She had just purchased a hot pink parka from the Shopping Channel with matching hot pink furry boots. She was seventy-two and tickled pink with her purchases.

I, on the other hand, was preparing myself and my daughters for the best Christmas I could muster. I still had the Canadian Tire Mastercard, so I was planning to buy their presents at Zellers, a local reasonably priced department store in Maple Ridge.

I was also hoping that Dale would be sober, although I had a hunch that he might be drinking. I bought him two presents from each of the girls. He had stopped taking my calls or answering the phone at his friend's house, so he was unreachable. I worried that something terrible had happened to him.

Three days before Christmas, I got a phone call from the church asking me if I would be interested in receiving a Christmas hamper. I had already decorated, baked, and shopped, but regardless, I said yes to the hamper. Two days before Christmas, I got a phone call from a nice family, one that I liked and knew from the church. They invited the three of us over for Christmas dinner. I happily accepted.

One day before Christmas, we decorated a small tree, and the Christmas hamper arrived.

I was surprised to see six bags filled to the brim with wrapped gifts, and an enormous box of food. Each bag was labelled. Two bags were for a four-year-old girl, two bags for a two-year-old girl, and two bags were for a single mother.

I cried at the sight of it all—anyone would. Then I cried at the presents that I had already purchased. Instead of being happy about the dinner invitation, I felt like a charity case, and then I cried some more.

On Christmas Eve, I took the girls to the A&W fast-food restaurant, and we all felt special to be the only ones there. We ordered onion rings with extra ketchup and root beer that came in frosted mugs.

Afterward, we went to the Christmas Eve service at the church. It was nice. The message was about baby Jesus in a manger and how the innkeeper had given the desperate mother a place to stay. People brought gifts to the King, and they followed a star to find their way to him. I glanced around at the congregation and all the families displaying togetherness, and I felt a slight pang in my heart.

Once home, we put out cookies for Santa, carrots for the reindeer, and then I announced that I heard Santa's sleigh on our roof and his footsteps. Jessica and Emma scrambled upstairs to their beds and fell fast asleep. I then thought briefly of baby Jesus and all the struggles that lay ahead for him.

Alone, I placed the abundance of presents around the tree. I turned off all the lights in the room except for the tree. Sitting down and looking around, I was pleased with my clean, well-maintained townhouse. I couldn't complain, I was making it, we were going to be okay.

Before going to bed, I cried for the very last time about my failed marriage and the man that I loved, the father of my children. I just knew that he was a good man, even if he did not think so himself.

Dale was not able to join us for Christmas. Unfortunately, his demons had once again hogtied him to the liquor bottle that I sadly accepted he could not live without.

My bike trip friends were doing it again. The winter had been long, and the spring had seemed shorter. Soon it would be summer, and I had decided to go cycling again with the women who had no idea that they were so instrumental in assisting me in finding my voice and in living without weights on my shoulders.

In the meantime, my fitness classes were going well, especially at the treatment centre. Clients had the option to attend three one-hour exercise classes per week, as part of their recovery program, along with counselling, AA meetings, and proper nutrition. I marvelled at the transformation in the people who wanted to change, to lead a clean and sober life.

It was hit and miss with Dale; the year was not up, but he was still drinking. I thought that he might have hit bottom by now. "Hitting rock bottom" is a phrase used when talking about addiction. However, rock bottom is a concept that means something different to each addict. It usually refers to a time or an event that causes an addict to reach the lowest possible point in their disease. It is a time when a person may feel that things cannot get any worse.

Most addicts need to hit bottom before they can begin the addiction recovery process. For one person, it could be the loss of a marriage; for another, it might be the loss of a job or a home. Even though Dale had lost all three, he was still drinking, and his life had become unmanageable. The AA book says that there is not a tried-and-true method to predict what your rock-bottom moment will be.

Aside from my emotional growth, faith, exercise, and trying to be the best mom I could, I still hoped and prayed that Dale would take action and get sober. A few months before I was to leave on my bike trip, he called me up and asked if he could stay with us as he was at a loss and had nowhere else to turn. I was scared to say no, but I did. I followed up with a solution. I said enthusiastically, "The treatment centre has a four-week program. That would give you a place to live temporarily, and you could get well at the same time." Surprisingly enough, he said okay.

At the time, if you were in dire straits and there was a vacancy, you could get into the Maple Ridge Drug and Alcohol Treatment Centre without too much red tape. The stipulation was that you had to detox first.

If a person drinks alcohol heavily for weeks, months, or years, they may experience mental and physical problems, especially if they abruptly stop drinking. Alcohol has a depressive effect, and it slows down brain function, changing the way nerves send messages back and forth to the brain. When the alcohol level suddenly drops, the brain stays in this keyed-up state, which in turn causes withdrawal. The biggest concern is seizures and hallucinations, meaning a person can hear, feel, and see things that are not there. Other side effects are confusion, racing heart, high blood pressure, fever, and heavy sweating.

I helped Dale find a detox centre in New Westminster, a facility that had round-the-clock nurses, twenty-four-hour monitoring, and medical treatment if necessary. I was hopeful and, at the same time, on guard. While in detox, Dale phoned me every night, and our conversations revolved around the girls—things they were doing, activities they were involved in, and how much they missed their daddy. After five days, Dale asked if I could bring the girls for a visit. He stated that he had never felt better.

I explained the hospital-like setting so Jessica and Emma could have a bit of an idea of what to expect. We bought flowers and a giant bag of sunflower seeds. When Emma asked why, I decided to tell the truth. I explained that their daddy was trying not to drink beer anymore, and sunflower seeds would help him by giving him something else to do instead.

When we arrived at the detox facility, the doors were locked, so we rang the outside buzzer, and a nurse came to the big steel doors and let us in. I told her who we were there to see, and without skipping a beat, Emma held up the bag of sunflower seeds and said, "We are bringing these to my daddy because he drinks too much beer!" The nurse smiled and took us to Dale's room.

After a ten-day stay, I was amazed at how clear his eyes had become. Dale looked healthy and well. After a two-week stay, the detox centre transferred Dale to MRTC.

Dale embarked on the four-week treatment centre program. He had the time because he was finished school and speculated that he would land a job soon.

He seemed to be making progress. He became popular and well-loved by fellow clients and all the staff. He was a kind, caring, gentle soul—what's not to love, I thought? Even the maintenance workers told me what a great guy he was. I took the girls to see him on the Sunday visitors' day.

Around week three, before his four weeks were up, Dale somehow smuggled alcohol in, got caught, and was kicked out.

I had allowed myself to become excited about his upcoming treatment centre graduation ceremony; I was falling in love with him again, and it was hard not to take his stumble personally.

Shortly after his untimely dismissal in the recovery program, Dale managed to find a tent and started living at the Golden Ears Provincial Park campsite in Maple Ridge. I was both concerned and perturbed at the same time.

I took it upon myself to drive up there on a whim, as a nagging worry was tugging at me. No one had heard from Dale since he left treatment, and it crossed my mind that he might die. When things appear to be going well in life and then suddenly they are not, the blow to the heart and soul is devastating. And for some, simply unbearable.

Driving around and around the happy, carefree campers, I eventually spotted a small tent with an array of liquor bottles neatly stacked in front of the zippered-up fly. With trepidation, I parked and walked over to the ominous setup. I called out Dale's name, with the volume of my voice increasing, but got no answer. I peeked inside the tent and found it empty all except for a nicely laid out sleeping bag.

As I climbed in my car, I felt like someone was watching me. My eyes darted in amongst the trees, tents and makeshift clotheslines but saw only families—the kind that I wanted to be a part of. Everyone was oblivious to me and affirmatively minded their own business. I had done all that I could do.

Summer was only a few weeks away, and with Jessica starting kindergarten in the fall, I was determined to make the summer enjoyable and entertaining.

First, I needed to train for the upcoming cycling trip. I was given a baby carrier for the back of my bicycle and proceeded to go out riding with Emma sitting behind me, chattering away. I tried to do all my training while Jessica was in her pottery classes.

When I had my first baby, Jessica, I thought she could save me. She was the one that I longed for and was desperate to have, after the ones before her were not given a chance to live, either by choice or by circumstance. There were a lot of expectations on a six-pound bundle of joy, from filling up space in her mother's guilty heart, to fixing her alcoholic father.

The reality was, all she had to do was show up. Then it became our job, as her mommy and daddy, to nurture, care, love, and raise her. No strings attached. But now, Jessica was showing signs of emotional distress, worrying all the time, crying unexpectedly, and pinching me. I found out that through welfare, I could take her to see a play therapist.

When we got to the appointment, Jessica was put in a playroom by herself, so the therapist could watch her play through a one-way mirror.

In doing just that, she observed that Jessica did not play with any of the toys but rather walked around the playroom, picking up each doll or plaything, examining it, and then putting it back the same way she had found it. The outcome of the play therapy session was that Jessica lacked trust from feelings of abandonment. I also learned that she was a tactile learner.

It was then recommended to me that I put her in pottery classes, that it would be therapeutic for her to use her hands to express herself artistically. Welfare would pay for the classes. As for the abandonment issues, I did not know what to do about that other than love her.

While Jessica pottered at a local community centre, Emma and I climbed up hills throughout the back roads of Maple Ridge. We sang and hummed Disney tunes, and when I was too out of breath to even whisper, Emma contentedly ate a bag of Cheezies, enjoying the wilderness while I pedalled. On more than one occasion, she would call out to me, "Can't you go any faster, Momma?"

My heart swelled having her nearby and knowing that after our bike ride, we would soon be picking up her sister. Both thoughts brought me an abundance of joy, once again reminding me that all was not lost.

Jessica's handiwork and pottery collection consisted of an ashtray for her grandma, a larger ashtray for her dad, a clay bunny for Emma, and a miniature clay basket for me to hold my trinkets.

A family from the church offered to take care of my girls while I was away on my bike trip. They lived in a large house, had children, pets, a tree fort, and both parents to ensure a complete package deal; and Jessica and Emma had each other, for which I was grateful.

Just like the previous year, my bike trip friends gathered to discuss the upcoming trip. A couple of the women took it upon themselves to book places, and by July 1st, we were off. Some of them detected my transformation, but I chose not to talk too in-depth, as I was still evolving and grieving.

The previous year had appeared to be quite intense for all of us, so I decided to take a year off and let someone else share and possibly have a meltdown. Even though I had made tremendous leaps and bounds, their lives still seemed far more intact than mine.

I desperately wanted to fit in, and more important, to appear "normal" because I valued my new friends, worldly women of the universe. By watching and listening, making mental notes with how they did things with and for their families, I tried to figure out how I could obtain a modified version of how they lived, events they made happen in between their jobs, activities, husbands, friends, and families.

Some of the women liked to camp. They shared their stories of road trips, tents, and s'mores by the fire, swimming, boating, and what a wonderful family experience it was.

Returning home after ten days of cycling and camaraderie, I decided to save up for a tent, a camp stove, air beds, and sleeping bags.

I then found out that the church I had been attending all this time had a family camping event coming up. I jumped on board, signed up, and took my girls camping with the church. One family had a boat that they generously took kids for rides on. We played games as a group, young and old alike, and everyone helped each other out in one way, shape, or form, myself included.

At night after drinking cocoa, when the fire had died down, we all brushed our teeth with a cup of water, laughing as we spit into the bushes. The girls and I cuddled up in sleeping bags in the confines of the tent, reading by flashlights and talking about the day's events until I could hear the slow, steady breathing sounds that sleep brought. I then allowed myself to languidly drift off with the slight inkling that the grass was now only slightly greener on the other side of the fence.

Waking up refreshed to brew camp coffee, make bacon and eggs, and begin another day of camping activities, I marvelled at the absence of hangovers, empty beer cans, and the grumpiness that nightly alcohol consumption brought. I relished spending time with families that could have fun without drinking or substances of any kind.

As church people, they professed to be spiritual and not religious, which also added to the charm. There was no evidence of Bible-thumping.

For the rest of the summer, my mother treated us to waterslides and the PNE fair. She also insisted the girls have swimming lessons. She still had highs and lows but maintained more of a continuous high either for the sake of the girls, or I liked to think, perhaps her moods were evening out.

She came up with a grand idea to combine my desire to visit my in-laws in Saskatoon with a trip for her to see her friends in Taber, Alberta. If I drove, she would pay for the gas, and as she suggested, we could camp and stay at hotels along the way. I had kept in contact with Dale's family. They wanted to see us, and we wanted to see them. My mother would be my driving companion, plus seeing her hometown and childhood friends might do her a world of good. I said "Yes, let's do it."

I could hear the voices of my bike trip friends influencing and motivating me every step of the way.

I learned early on that the more belongings I took with me on outings, the happier my baby was. Therefore, my life, not just hers, would be easier and breezier wherever we were.

In the event of fussiness, at my fingertips would be a rattle, a grape or Cheerio, a stuffed toy or sippy cup, to be given as a peace offering or soothing technique. Diapers or a sweater were other options, not just from a diaper bag but from a multi-purpose baby tool kit.

Along those same lines, with the planning of our Maple Ridge to Saskatoon road trip, I came up with an idea. My biggest fear was the length of time we would be spending in the car, which undoubtedly could bring on crankiness, simultaneously causing more stress for me. I came up with a remarkable plan that I would replicate time and time again, even sharing my ingenuity with other parents in the years to come.

Before leaving, I purchased an assortment of small toys, new and used, colouring books, and games. I planned to gift-wrap them individually, and every two hours along the way, I would let the girls open a present each. Consequently, they would be kept busy and always anticipating the next present. Also, we would stop every two hours to get out of the car, tidy it up, and do jumping jacks, go to the bathroom, and have a snack. They were two-and-a-half, and four-and-a-half years old, and we had approximately 1500 kilometres one way to cover.

What was not planned or anticipated was a severe case of the chickenpox each, thirty-five-degree Celsius weather, no air conditioning, as well as a smoking and sleepless grandma who talked without ceasing for the entire drive and well into the night. I, in turn, fell into the role of Girl Guide leader, summer camp director, head chef, bottle washer, maid, counsellor, entertainer, and chauffeur.

Other than that, all was well, and I managed. Creating a memorable holiday, we took our time and spent a few days to reach our final destination.

The first leg of our journey took us approximately ten hours to get to Christina Lake. There we camped for two nights. The girls loved the freedom and the nature of camping. They helped me to the best of their ability to put up the tent, and by the end of the first night, they both had fevers and full-blown itchy red bumps. We swam in the lake regardless and walked to a local ice-cream parlour for treats.

Grandma chose to sleep in the car because she was not planning on sleeping anyway and was worried that if she got down on the tent floor, she would not be able to get back up again. I looked out through the tent window flap periodically throughout the night to ensure the car was still there. In doing so, I could see the burning ember of her cigarette as she sat upright in the passenger reclining seat.

Packing up with little help from the girls and no help from my mother, as she was making new friends in and around the campsite, we drove from Christina Lake to Calgary, where we spent two nights at a hotel with a pool, room service, and cartoons, a great way for the girls to heal up from the chickenpox. My mother spent most of her time on the balcony, smoking, while I curled up with a book.

After dropping my mother off in Taber, Alberta, and continuing to Saskatoon, I was then completely on my own with my girls. In some ways, it was easier, and in a lot of other ways, it was not.

Reconnecting with Dale's family in Saskatoon was wonderful. They supported me wholeheartedly, but we never spoke about Dale and the state that he was in. Rather, an abounding number of stories were reminisced about his childhood. The girls loved hearing about their daddy when he was their age.

There was an underlying, unspoken awareness we shared, a vision and hope that he would recover. A terrible mistake had occurred, one that was unintentional and not meant to be. Dale was a family man, but it was not working out that way. His decline was gradual, like that of a leaky faucet or broken gas line. The alcohol seeped in through the cracks when no one was looking. It permeated his life.

My mother later phoned my in-laws' house to inform me that she did not need a ride home on our return. She had decided to stay for an extended period in Taber. She was reliving the stories, places, and events of her youth, and in the sharing of memories with old friends, she had become her old self again. I could hear the peacefulness and normalcy in her voice.

She was herself there, and I could only think what a relief it must have been for her.

When our visit to Saskatoon came to an end, I had a longing to stay. Dale's family—our family—took care of us, and we were enveloped with hospitality and felt loved.

On the inevitable drive home, the car fell silent, the girls slept, and I daydreamed, trying to predict our future. At the rest stops, all three of us went into one bathroom cubicle. Holding Emma in my lap, juggling her and my purse, was no easy feat. Jessica helped me as much as she could.

We stopped in Taber to see my mom, to stay the night, and then onto Calgary to stay at my cousin's. From Calgary, it was a long haul home. We were all tired and cranky for the duration of the drive.

Just outside of Kamloops, I filled up with gas, and when I went to take extra money out of the debit machine, it said I had insufficient funds. I thought for sure that I had just over one hundred dollars left, but math had never been one of my strong points, so maybe I had made a mistake with my calculations.

Regardless, I was relieved that I had a full tank of gas, and we were only a three-hour drive from Maple Ridge. I settled in behind the wheel to drive the rest of the way home.

Just after Merritt, I noticed a sign stating that we were ten kilometres away from the toll booth, which brought on instant panic when I remembered that I had no money to pay the toll. It was ten dollars, and I did not even have ten cents.

I scrutinized each hitchhiker, wondering if I should pick one up, thinking that if I did, they might have the money to get us all through. But my gut was afraid to stop, as my precious cargo was too important to me. If by chance I picked up a nut or a crazed lunatic, things could turn out badly. I just couldn't take any chances. All I could do was keep driving and then hope and pray for a miracle to occur.

My hands gripped the steering wheel tighter with each kilometre. I could feel the tension climb up my arms, into my neck, and rest squarely between my eyes. Squinting, I held back tears. Outside of the car, the rain had started to downpour.

Arriving at the toll booth, I looked around my car, and I saw it in a different light. No longer did it appear to be the car of a fun family vacation, but rather a distraught woman on the run filled to the brim with two little girls, luggage, camping equipment, blankets, pillows, bicycles, and toys. Our organized travelling fun car had turned into a discombobulated mess. I felt doomed when the toll booth agent slid open her window as blowing rain moved in on her.

Rolling down my window, and before I tried to speak, my throat tightened, and the tears that moments before filled my eyes sprang out like a sprinkler. Feeling and hearing my distress, Jessica and Emma both started to cry, too.

I explained my dilemma to the best of my ability, stating that I had no money to pay the toll and just enough gas to get home. The toll booth operator was point-blank, and without any expression on her face whatsoever, said no, I could not go through unless I had the money, and if I tried to force my way past and drive through anyway, she would send the police after me within minutes. Explaining that the fine for breaking the law would be exorbitant, she finished by telling me that I had to turn around and go back to Merritt or Kamloops.

I considered driving through, and then I visualized sirens blaring, handcuffs, and my daughters taken from me. I thought about turning around, but without money and not knowing anyone in the other towns, it just made no sense to me. I felt stuck.

Seeing my obvious distress, she softened ever so slightly and said the only other option was to phone someone and get them to put the ten dollar toll on their credit card. But I would need to pull over, park, and go inside a small building that was off to the side, where the pay telephone was.

Doing just that, I tried to sound in control and explained to the girls that we needed to get out of the car and go inside to make a phone call. The skies had darkened, and the rain was coming down in buckets. Holding Jessica's hand and carrying Emma, we ran across to the building where the phone was.

Another person, a man, was speaking on one of the phones. Standing next to him and picking up the receiver on the other available telephone, I did not know who to call. I was stumped and embarrassed. As I stood with the receiver in my hand, looking down at the floor, I noticed the man was wearing cowboy boots, and the floor was in great need of mopping. I gathered he was a cowboy headed back to Alberta. A brief image of dead Eric came into my mind; I winced.

Standing in limbo, I rocked Emma under one arm and racked my brain, trying to come up with a name, someone I could call. The seconds turned into minutes, and I was still drawing a blank.

I did not have a phone number for my mother, the obvious person for me to call.

The man finished his call and left. Alone, it was just the girls and me in the small empty room, two pay telephones, a table, and a few ashtrays. Within minutes, the door to the little shack flung open, and the cowboy walked in again. I hung up the receiver and looked up as he approached me. He said that he sensed I might be in trouble, and when he went back out to his truck, he told his wife about my two little girls and me. She instructed him to come back inside to see if we were okay. Before I could say anything, he opened up his wallet, and I saw that he had a ten-dollar bill and a twenty-dollar bill. He gave me the twenty.

Profusely thanking him, he left before I had a chance to go overboard with my appreciation. Gathering up Jessica and Emma, we fled back to the car to pay and proceed through.

After paying at the toll booth, I was overcome with annoyance directed toward the woman in the booth. I gathered that I looked suspicious, a deliberate rule-breaker, a scammer, and a con artist. I could have been a degenerate on the run. Irritation transformed into feeling like a victim and a little bit of a loser, followed by shame, in that order.

When we finally arrived home, I bathed the girls, gave them a snack, read them a story, and put them to bed. I went back downstairs to make a cup of tea. Plugging in the kettle, I noticed that sitting beside the toaster was a note with familiar neat printing.

Dear Karen, it was raining and cold, so I had to break into your home. Your kitchen window does not lock, and you should get that fixed. I saw your chequebook sitting by the telephone, so I wrote myself a cheque for $100. Sorry about that. I will pay you back. I hope that you had a nice trip.
Love, Dale

A year had come and gone since my tough love project first began with Dale, and it was not working out the way I had hoped and intended—that my husband would put the girls and me above his alcohol addiction. The substance had dug in, had its hooks in him, and was not letting go. On another level, unexpectedly and unabridged, I was doing okay. As a single parent, I was managing. There was peace and a semblance of calm in my life. I was free from the debilitating factor that alcohol brought with it.

Yet I still found myself asking the reoccurring question, "Where is my happy ending?"

Jessica was starting kindergarten, and because I wanted to have the best possible opportunities for my girls, considering my circumstances, I put Jessica in a French immersion kindergarten. School clothes, school supplies, a lunch kit, and nutritional snacks were purchased and assembled. She was a big girl and ready for the next twelve years of her life to unfold. The question: Was I?

After her first day, which was mainly an orientation for students and parents, we were sent home with a letter asking for parental volunteers. I so wanted to be a part of her education, or at least get a glimpse into where she went every morning Monday through Friday; volunteering would be ideal.

Upon signing up on the provided clipboard just outside the classroom door, I came up with an idea of how my fitness expertise could help out the teacher and her class of five-year-olds. I approached the teacher and asked her if she would be interested in me coming in to teach a child-orientated exercise class once a week. She responded with an enthusiastic yes. So, I went home and started planning out the program.

I used Jessica and Emma and some of the other children from the complex to create a class geared toward the imagination of a child, incorporating fine motor skills, gross motor skills, balance, and relaxation, and bundling it all up into a thirty-minute child-friendly exercise routine.

I went to Value Village (a thrift store in Maple Ridge) and found twenty colourful scarves and twenty assorted pairs of sunglasses.

I would create movement with the scarves to represent superhero capes, flying dragons, and twirling fairies. And later I would use them as blankets for the relaxation component. The music I chose to go with the creative play was the Gypsy Kings, Beethoven, and Mozart.

The sunglasses worked in conjunction with Beach Boys surfing music. As we twisted on the pretend sand or imagined ourselves catching some rad waves, we balanced on make-believe surfboards, eventually falling into the ocean to swim.

When I volunteered at the school, Emma came along, too. Jessica was thrilled to have us both there. She proudly watched me lead and participated in the fun and movement with her new peers.

Months into my volunteering, I had slowly become friends with Jessica's teacher. We eventually met for coffee dates, and it was during those times that I shared with her about my dilemma of being on welfare and wanting a career but afraid to leave my children. As if it was a light-bulb moment, an epiphany, or just a brilliant idea, Jessica's teacher suggested I take a one-year teaching assistant course at Douglas College in Maple Ridge. She followed up by saying that I had a gift working with children, and not only was I a natural, but if I got hired, I would have the same hours as my children, 9 a.m. to 3 p.m., and the same Christmas, Easter, and summer vacations.

My perplexity shifted to a lack of funds to pay for college. I promptly made an appointment with my welfare caseworker.

Unbeknownst to me, Social Services did not want me to be collecting money from the government for the rest of my life. Welfare is a temporary fix, perhaps longer for some depending on the situation, but temporary just the same, or at least one would hope.

After meeting with the agent, she relayed to me that there was a back-to-work program set in place for welfare recipients.

She suggested a one-year college diploma course called the SETA program, which stood for Special Education Teaching Assistant.

The only obstacle was a waiting list and fear on my part that I was not smart enough to go to college. The voice of my high school guidance counsellor came back to me: "No sense in Karen applying for university since she is in the general math program," and even further back to elementary school days when my mother would say, "Math is just not Karen's thing." In retrospect, my parents were proud that I graduated high school, as neither of them had done so.

At the age of thirty-two, as a single mother collecting welfare, I taught fitness almost every day, volunteered in my daughter's school, had supper on the table at 5:00 p.m. nightly, went to the food bank periodically if necessary, had friends, went to church, read copious Oprah Winfrey–recommended books, and felt fairly content.

Missing from the equation was a man. And the man I wanted was not well.

Gathering up my grade twelve transcripts and filling out the Douglas College application and criminal record check, I found out that I would need to write an entrance exam if I wanted to get into the SETA program.

There would be basic math questions on the test, of which I was petrified. Consequently, my friend Lori said that her husband was a math whiz, so she offered him up to tutor me. He proved to be kind and did not make me feel dumb in the least. If I were to pass and get accepted, the course would be four nights per week, as well as every Saturday. My mother offered to babysit during my hours of schooling.

I was shocked and unprepared when a telephone call came in from the RCMP, saying that I needed to report to the police station as soon as possible because something had come up on my criminal record.

Panic ensued, and all I could think about was my one-time shoplifting incident when I was seventeen and was handed down community service hours as a candy striper at the Mission Memorial Hospital for my crime.

My mother could not watch my girls this time, so I took Jessica and Emma with me to the police station. Jessica was sure that the police were going to arrest me, and her concerns were not far off, as it had crossed my mind, as well.

Entering the Maple Ridge police department, I reported to the front desk. When asked to wait, my nerves started to get the better of me. But I had to hold it together for my daughters, the education and eventual career I needed. Waiting truly is the hardest part, as it gives the imagination time to work its magic, which had already proved to hinder my thought process many times in the past.

The background check, with my maiden name Karen Bonner, brought up that I was wanted for theft, disorderly conduct, failing to show up for a court date, and perceivably on the run, which, in no uncertain terms, is the type of person ever recommended to work with children, which I completely understood.

It turned out to be a case of mistaken identity, as I had green eyes, and the other Karen Bonner and possible convict had brown eyes. I was five feet six inches tall (and could not become a runway model), and she was five feet two inches—four inches shorter than me.

When all was said and done, I was accepted into the program and could start in the New Year.

As Christmas approached, and in keeping with my mother's desire to miss the holidays entirely, she suggested a trip to Disneyland for her, myself, Jessica, and Emma. Who could refuse?

The girls were over-the-top excited, and because we would be in Disneyland for Emma's Birthday on December 27th why not celebrate the well-advertised theme-park birthday breakfast with none other than Mickey Mouse and Disney's crew of characters?

In pure debacle fashion, my mother ended up being exceedingly down for the whole trip, and it was discovered that one had to book months in advance to have the privilege of dining with the likes of Cinderella and Snow White.

Showing up on the day of Emma's birthday, with empty bellies and anticipation of hugs from a cast of Disney characters, they turned us away at the restaurant. The consolation prize was a Mickey Mouse–shaped pancake in a smaller part of the dining room, but no special guests in attendance. Emma cried heartfelt tears of disappointment. I felt like a bad mom, and I should have known to book in advance.

While I traipsed around the most magical place on earth, my mother dragged her feet, with shoulders slouched, as a worrisome look masked her face. Emma cried, hating to be in a stroller. Jessica tightly gripped my hand, in fear of Mr. Toad's Wild Ride, flying elephants, the evil queens, and poisonous apples.

My days at Disneyland had me carrying Emma, cheering up my mother, and protecting Jessica from all things evil. Wanting to get our money's worth, we attended the park every day for three full days.

Even though the days were long and arduous, I still managed to daydream of better days to come as I stared a little too long at the seemingly happy families going on rides, as we ate smoked turkey legs, and watched the parade of people all around us.

There were a few perks at the end of the day, including swimming in the hotel pool, and watching television before bed.

My education took off with a bang, an explosion of fireworks to every aspect of my being. I thoroughly enjoyed College, and my confidence soared. On my first essay assignment, I received ten out of ten for a mark. With tears in my eyes, I approached the teacher, and she naturally thought that I was upset, but was immediately elated when I told her that my letter grade was the first A I had ever received in my entire life.

The girls were proud of their mommy, and my mother stepped up to the plate and showed up diligently Monday through Thursday, from 5 p.m. to 9 p.m., to care for Jessica and Emma at the complex where we lived.

The only drawback was when my mom's behaviour was outlandish for grandmotherly standards. Her go-to bedtime snack for the girls (after they brushed their teeth) were marshmallows heated up in the microwave oven. The girls particularly loved how they expanded, sometimes blowing up and then turning into a hard, sugary candy blob. Hardened marshmallow takes quite a toll on the inside of one's microwave oven, not to mention the enamel on a child's teeth.

I arrived home one evening to find the girls sound asleep upstairs in their bunk beds, and my mother sitting in the middle of my living room with wet toilet paper wrapped around the length of her arms and legs. Emma was hoping to one day become a nurse, so Grandma was allowing her to practise her bandaging skills. For the toilet paper to adhere, it worked better if it was wet. Not wanting to ruin their handiwork, my mother read a book while the girls tended to their grandmother's pretend broken bones. Messy, but creative and fun with no real harm done, and much easier to clean up my mother than the inside of a microwave oven.

The nine-month course flew by, and I enjoyed every minute of it. I was able to continue teaching my fitness classes during the day, make dinner, and then leave the girls in the evening to attend college. Near the end of the program, I ended up doing my practicum at Jessica's school.

Being on welfare from start to finish was just less than two years. I said goodbye to the service that treated me remarkably well, a program that (once I got over the shame and embarrassment) gave me the tremendous gift of an education, and therefore a career, in addition to therapy for my daughter, dental care, a roof over our heads, and enough income to sustain us until I could figure out a suitable life and get my head on straight.

When Jessica graduated from kindergarten, and I graduated from college, I applied and got a job in my field at her school, which I concluded was almost the same as being a stay-at-home mom, my lifelong dream. I saw glimpses of Jessica throughout the day, on the playing field, in the gymnasium, the library, and during our shared lunch hour. When Jessica started grade two, Emma began kindergarten. My girls and I were living, working, and playing together.

There were still times of insecurity and loneliness, especially as a single parent. Often it was more noticeable to me in the most inconspicuous moments. One particularly tough instance was after attending a church function in the winter; we went out to the parking lot and, holding my daughters' hands, we made our way across the frozen expanse to the car. I found myself envying the women whose husbands insisted they wait on the curb while they retrieved the car, pulling up as their wife stepped gracefully into the heated vehicle, thus saving her from slipping and sliding in high heels. Watching them being whisked away brought images of Aladdin and Jasmine on the magic carpet ride while crooning the song "A Whole New World."

Kindergarten graduation, plays, and dance recitals; tooth fairies, bake sales, and birthday parties; visits to Santa, decorating the tree, and Christmas concerts; colds and fevers; learning to ride a bicycle, swimming lessons, and gymnastic competitions; science projects, scary movies, and pickups from summer camp; father-daughter dances, dating boyfriends, and high school graduation; learning to drive, part-time jobs, and college. Dale had missed most of it. His struggles continued for many years. I kept my promise and only spoke of him in a kind, loving way, careful not to ridicule the part of my daughters who assisted in their creation. It was great advice, and I do not regret taking it.

I will not deny that many times I was heartbroken, annoyed, and frustrated, crying into my pillow or sharing my thoughts with another single mom or counsellor about how unfair everything was, especially when it came to Dale's loss and missed moments in life.

Keeping the peace felt right. When the girls were teenagers, I opened up more and became realistic, validating their feelings of missing their daddy, and again, how unfair life sometimes was.

Family, friends, and acquaintances often tried to find fault with Dale, but I knew that he had a heart of gold and was worthy of my patience and of my not outwardly being angry. Although the alcohol masked his true feelings, deep down inside, he was a good man, a family man. He could not find his way out of the entrapment that plagued him. I always knew that he was much angrier at himself than I could ever be.

Dale and I eventually divorced, and his family insisted on staying in touch, which the girls and I gladly accepted with open hearts and minds. A few times, the girls travelled to Saskatoon to visit cousins, aunts, uncles, grandparents, and of course, Dale. Those memories they will always appreciate and cherish.

The finality of life is death, and unfortunately, some of us are called to our final resting place sooner than others. Our youthful selves will point out how unfair and unexpected death is when the tragedy encompasses those of us who are left behind.

It was in early fall 2013 when we received word that Dale was in the intensive care unit at Saskatoon Memorial Hospital. Jessica was twenty-five, and Emma was twenty-three. My daughters were only two and four years younger than I had been when my father died of an inoperable brain tumour.

At the time of the devastating call, Dale had been sober for five years, but the alcohol had taken its toll. His body had deteriorated, and there were many complications with his health. Therefore, the family was sending for Jessica and Emma to be at their dad's bedside.

Ironically, during a chance encounter, I met my second husband, Paul, at the drug and alcohol treatment centre where I taught fitness. It was a brief introduction and then a year later, I met him again at an AA dance. He was leaning up against a wall, his arms folded across his chest, his fingers tucked in under his armpits. Remembering that we had met one year prior, my breath caught in my throat upon seeing him again. He was incredibly handsome and my old self would have been extremely intimidated. But instead, new confident Karen strode over to him and we started chatting, like we had known each other for years.

I was careful not to introduce him to my daughters for quite some time. I needed to check off the boxes on my list to be sure he measured up. On many nights while alone in my bedroom I composed a list of what I wanted in a man.

After a one-year courtship, Paul and I got married. Emma was seven and Jessica was nine years old. Both were the flower girls at the wedding, and Paul—their stepdad-to-be—gave them each a promise ring, stating that he was not trying to replace their biological father, but rather asking for their permission to marry me and join our family of three as a package deal. He promised to take care of them to the best of his ability, hoping to be a parent they could depend on.

Our marriage began as an instantaneous family. There were growing pains, bumps along the way, and even roadblocks. There were also learning curves, lots of joy, and many heartwarming moments.

Three years after Paul joined us, we had a baby, a son who united us as a family of five. Mackenzie was a new addition, similar to a new puppy being added to the family. Everyone was thrilled at the sight of him. The girls rallied around their little brother, Jessica nurturing him, dressing him up, and holding him for hours, and Emma as a playmate, sharing her adventurous spirit and teaching him the wonders of play, crafts, and hours of backyard fun and trampoline-jumping. Paul was always careful to treat all three of them as equals.

Ten months before the fateful telephone call and message for the girls to come quickly, all five of us had travelled to Saskatoon and Charlie Brown Crescent for a good old-fashioned Christmas in a winter wonderland, with Dale and the whole Burgess clan. We all arrived at the Burgess home at separate times that Christmas; Mackenzie and I on the train, the girls flying in days before, and on Christmas Eve, Dale and I drove to the airport to pick up Paul.

I smiled inwardly at the irony of it all. There I was driving in a car with my ex-husband to pick up my current husband. Paul generously and sweetly sat in the back seat while Dale and I (ma and pa style) drove us back to the picturesque family home. The two men chatted back and forth from front seat to back seat about hockey, the weather, and road conditions.

Christmas stockings had been made in advance by Dale's mother for Paul and Mackenzie, emblazoned with their names glue-gunned in white felt and lined up with the rest of the Martha Stewart–type stockings hanging from hooks on the fireplace. Shimmering wrapped presents stretched far and wide underneath the enormous decorated Christmas tree.

Once again, I was in awe of the storybook setting while ornaments and baubles garnished the home around me. Baby Jesus had not changed, still nestled safely in the straw of the little wooden manger just like I had remembered him.

Everyone was included in the family that year as we turned a page to the "Life Goes On" chapter. Dale introduced Mackenzie to outdoor skating only blocks from the house, giving him his first hockey stick, while the new grandpa in his life bought him a beautiful pair of boy's ice skates, both men relaying stories of the past, growing up on the prairies, frostbitten winters, and skating at recess, lunchtime, and after school.

During that unforgettable Christmas, stepdad and biological father became friends, daughters benefitted from their unity, a boy fell into an instant family, and a mother's heart swelled with the blossoming beauty of new beginnings. Editing and rewriting a story can happen. Endings can be changed, and there are no rules or policies when love is at the forefront. Not overnight, perhaps, but I have learned that anything is possible for the sake of peace and unity.

When the dreadful call came, Jessica and Emma dropped everything—their jobs and life as they knew it. Both were frightened and unsure of what to expect, but they felt the urgency to go. Paul suggested I go with them. Another family member purchased an airplane ticket for me, and together the girls and I went. Paul stayed home with Mackenzie.

It was harrowing and heartbreaking to see Dale comatose, unable to speak, and lying helpless in ICU. It was at that moment that I realized the importance of my involvement. I was there to assist my daughters during this crucial time for Dale and for us.

We stayed at the grandparents' house, and every morning the three of us got up early, made lunches and left before 9:00 a.m. It was our mission to arrive at the hospital when the doctors were making their rounds so we could listen to the discussion about Dale, his condition, and possible progress. The doctors and nurses were remarkable, referring to us, asking our opinion, and offering insight and hope to Dale's prognosis.

While Dale slept and his body struggled to stay alive, the girls asked if we could pray. So we surrounded his bed, holding hands. His limp, dry hands gently grasped his daughters' hands and joined their hands to mine. I mustered up as many heartfelt prayers as I could think of: prayers of gratitude that we could be together, prayers for miraculous healing, and prayers to make up for lost time; prayers asking for strength physically and emotionally, prayers of peace and forgiveness.

While our heads were bowed, without them seeing me, I would glance up into the faces of my precious offspring and the man I had once vowed to spend the rest of my life with, searching for a sign from their expressions that they approved of what I was saying, willing my words to speak to them and bring forth a God who lived and dwelled in and around us. It was during this time that I had flashbacks and memories of how I had longed for a spiritual life with Dale when we were married. Now, here it was under different circumstances.

Dale eventually awoke, and although he still could not speak, he nodded while we continued our ritual of prayers, visiting, and recollection of happier times. He smiled, as we all did, in amongst the tears that repeatedly stained our faces.

We decorated Dale's area around his ICU bed with trinkets and photographs, Kodachrome images ripped from yellowing photo albums that had been saved and treasured—a life of snapshots and portraits, images to ponder and take note of, now displayed like an art gallery but in a sterile, disinfected place of mourning and loss.

We felt a kinship to the nurses who came and went. They were kind and gracious, and as we gathered day after day, night after night, hoping and praying for a good outcome, the head nurse eventually suggested that they move Dale to the end of the unit, still in Intensive Care but at a different section apart from the row of silent patients, who were mysteriously encapsulated with crisp, hospital green curtains, unaware, waiting for visitors who seldom came, or the next stage of their tragic tales to unfold.

We were thrilled that Dale had a window, a wall, and an empty bed next door, which gave us room to spread out and tack up even more photos. We watched back-to-back episodes of the game show *Family Feud* on the overhead television.

While Dale slept, I continuously noticed and thought about the other patients, what their backstory was, what brought them to this stage, and if they were going to recover. It was sometimes bleak and sad. It was also at this time that I remembered my dad, holding his hand at his bedside many years before. I could not help but make the connection and wonder how many times I would be assisting at the end of someone's life.

Jessica, Emma, and I would go back to the grandparents' house in the evenings for dinner and report the goings-on at the hospital. Then we would go back to Dale's bedside to say goodnight. From sunrise to sunset, we were there.

The brisk cold September had turned into a frigid Saskatchewan October.

We took lunch breaks from our hospital vigilance and wandered around the streets that encircled the blocks of the institution. Holding hands, wrapped tightly in borrowed scarves and thick winter coats, seeing our breath in the cold air, and rarely speaking, but in our hearts, we bonded, knowing that we were there for each other.

One evening, I thought the girls should have a night off, and I went to the hospital without them. From my teaching experience, I had an idea to get hold of a whiteboard and marker. Even though Dale's grip was weak, he managed to communicate better this way. Using the alphabet—ABC, and so on—we slowly spelled out words co-operatively.

He told me how sorry he was and regretful that things turned out the way they did. I agreed with his sentiments, and I, too, relayed my remorse and that it was all okay, that I forgave him as I forgave myself, and I always knew that he loved us deeply. I was able to thank him for our beautiful daughters, his family, and the many things that he taught me. I told him what a good person he was. I forgave him for his struggles, and he apologized many times over.

Dale did not leave the hospital, and we eventually had to go back home, back to our jobs and responsibilities of rent and careers. Sadly, and reluctantly, Dale passed away. Like me, with my dad, the girls were not at their father's bedside when he left this world. And like my father, I knew that Dale preferred it that way, and he was not alone. His loving parents who brought him into this world took over our spot at his bedside to say their final goodbyes as he left this world.

Many amends and healing had taken place during that trip, but grief was yet to follow.

My pain and love found a place to coexist side by side. Happiness for me now does not negate the pain of losing someone. I carry both of them.

Some may call my story a school of hard knocks; I like to say it is a journey of no regrets and that the ending makes no sense without the beginning. Life has a way of growing in and around the gnarly bits.

There are glimpses into my happy ending every day. The sun, moon, and stars are a constant reminder that every morning we can all start fresh. Happy endings do exist. We can all have a happy ending, creating our future every day, one present moment at a time.

In loving memory of
Uan Dale Burgess
April 6, 1958 – January 14, 2014

"To everything there is a season and a time to every purpose under heaven.

A time to be born, a time to die;

A time to plant, a time to reap;

A time to kill, a time to heal;

A time to laugh, a time to weep;

A time to build up, a time to break down;

A time to dance, a time to mourn;

A time to cast away stones, a time to gather stones together;

A time to gain, a time to lose;

A time to rend, a time to sew;

A time for love, a time for hate;

A time for peace. I swear it's not too late.

To everything there is a season, and a time to every purpose under heaven."

Written by Pete Seeger

Performed by The Byrds

Inspired by Ecclesiastes 3:1–8

This is my Happy Ending

AUTHOR'S NOTE

Writing about my past was an emphatically challenging process and very well could have broken up my current marriage. Thankfully, it did not.

When we look back on our lives and think about mistakes, missed opportunities, unfulfilled dreams, pain, hurt, and struggles, it is almost unavoidable not to compare who we are now with our younger self, wondering if we made the right choices and thinking how our life could be different, better, or possibly worse.

A by-product of walking down memory lane, especially to unlock our past, is to blame ourselves, our parents, or lack thereof, and even the partner we are no longer with or the person we are closest to now. They can all become the victims of our pain.

My life has been a series of unfortunate events with extraordinary moments, joy, and life lessons. The fog that engulfed me was often intermingled with strength and weakness, happiness and hurt, each working together, complementing each other, much like enemies embracing in the shadows to make amends and then go their separate way until meeting again.

My best advice that I want to make clear is to tell you that you are not your mistakes or the horrible things that may have happened to you. You are lovable, unique, and wonderful. Open the wound and cry. Let the healing begin.

Rather than blame ourselves and others, as difficult as it may be, it is extremely helpful to eventually try to forgive and think about the life lessons we have learned along the way. The process may take a while, but it is never too late to get started.

Love yourself and be yourself.

The telling of my story has been one of the most rewarding experiences I have ever had. The more I wrote, the more I healed. The more I healed, the more I could forgive.

Life was throwing me curveballs left and right, but then I picked up a bat and taught myself how to swing.

I leave you with this:

"If laughter is the best medicine, then crying is an important vitamin."

—Karen Harmon

"Gypsies, Tramps & Thieves," performed by Cher, released on September 1, 1971, by Kapp Records as the album's lead single. The song was written by Bob Stone and produced by Snuff Garrett.

"You're the One that I Want," performed by John Travolta and Olivia Newton-John, released May 17, 1978, by RSO. *The Original Soundtrack from the Motion Picture Grease*. Written and produced by John Farrar.

"We Are Family," performed by Sister Sledge, released in April 1979 by Cotillion Records. Written and produced by Bernard Edwards and Nile Rodgers.

"Time Warp," performed by Richard O'Brian, featured in the 1973 rock musical *The Rocky Horror Picture Show*. Songwriter and composer Richard O'Brian.

"Ain't No Stopping Us Now," performed by McFadden & Whitehead, released April 1979, recorded 1978 Sigma Sound Studios, Philadelphia, Pennsylvania. Written and produced by Jerry Cohen, Gene McFadden, and John Whitehead.

"Keep It Comin Love," performed by KC and the Sunshine Band, released May 16, 1977, by TK Records. Written and produced by Harry Wayne Casey and Richard Finch.

"Leather and Lace," performed by Stevie Nicks featuring Don Henley, released October 6, 1981, Released by Modern Records. Written by Stevie Nicks and Produced by Jimmy Lovine.

"Waiting for a Girl Like You," performed by Foreigner, released October 1981 by Atlantic Records. Written by Mick Jones and Lou Gramm, produced by Robert John "Mutt" Lange and Mick Jones.

"Torn Between Two Lovers," performed by Mary MacGregor, released November 1976 by Ariola America Records. Written by Peter Yarrow and Phillip Jarrell, produced by Peter Yarrow and Barry Beckett.

"Tangled up in Blue," performed by Bob Dylan, released January 1975 by Columbia Records. Written and produced by Bob Dylan.

"It Ain't Me Babe," performed by Bob Dylan, released by Columbia Records, August 8, 1964. Written by Bob Dylan, produced by Tom Wilson.

"Dust in the Wind," performed by Kansas, released January 16, 1978, by Kirshner Records. Written by Kerry Livgren and produced by Jeff Glixman, Kansas.

"Always on my Mind," performed by Willie Nelson (1982). Song by B.J. Thomas, released in 1972 by Decca Records. Written by Wayne Carson, Johnny Christopher.

"Love the One You're With," performed by Stephen Stills, released November 1970 by Atlantic Records. Written by Stephen Stills and produced by Stephen Stills and Bill Halverson.

"Heart of Gold," performed by Neil Young, released in January 1972 by Reprise Records. Written by Neil Young and produced by Elliot Mazer and Neil Young.

"This Used to Be My Playground," performed by Madonna, released June 16, 1992, by Sire and Warner Brothers. Written and produced by Madonna and Shep Pettibone.

"Turn, Turn, Turn," performed by The Byrds, released in 1962 as "To Everything, There Is a Season" by the folk music group the

Limeliters and then some months later on Pete Seeger's album, *The Bitter and Sweet*, written by Pete Seeger in the late 1950s and first recorded in 1959. The lyrics—except for the title, which is repeated throughout the song—consist of the first eight verses of the third chapter of the biblical Book of Ecclesiastes.

Made in the USA
Monee, IL
14 December 2021

85348228R00225